HOW
THERAPISTS
DIAGNOSE

HOW
THERAPISTS
DIAGNOSE

Seeing through the Psychiatric Eye

*Professional secrets
you deserve to know . . .*

*and how they affect
you and your family*

Dr. Bruce Hamstra

St. Martin's Griffin
New York

Production Editor: Suzanne Magida

Design by A Good Thing Inc.

Library of Congress Cataloging-in-Publication Data

Hamstra, Bruce.
    How therapists diagnose : seeing through the psychiatric eye /
Bruce Hamstra.
        p.   cm.
    ISBN 0-312-13087-2
    1. Mental illness—Diagnosis.   2. Mental illness.   3. Consumer
education.   I. Title.
RC469.H35   1995
616.89'075—dc20

                                                                    95-43878
                                                                    CIP

10   9   8   7   6   5   4

A WORD OF CAUTION

Written for the informed mental health consumer, this book is intended as a general guide to the typical assessment procedures and common diagnostic categories used by the majority of mental health professionals. Not all diagnostic categories or subcategories have been included. *It is not meant to be used as a source for self-diagnosis or diagnosis of others.* Mental health diagnosis is an extremely complex process requiring extensive clinical training and experience. Simply reading one or many books on the subject does not in any way provide sufficient knowledge to make diagnostic determinations. The reader is advised to seek out a qualified mental health professional if questions should arise concerning any of the diagnostic categories described.

CONTENTS

Appendices

LIST OF
TABLES

ACKNOWLEDGMENTS

First and foremost, I would like to thank my dear friends Martin and Ellen Greenberg of Greenberg Consulting, Dobbs Ferry, New York. Without their extraordinary wit, wisdom, creativity, persistence, and uncanny ability to illuminate concepts in a sparkling new light, it is highly unlikely that I would have anticipated or even accepted the need for a book like this, much less attempted to write it.

I am extremely grateful to my agent, Jane Dystel, and my editor, Bob Weil, for taking on a rather unusual, controversial subject. Their insight, support, and encouragement have been invaluable.

As always, words simply cannot express my deepest thanks to my lovely, brilliant, talented wife, Marsha. She and the ever-present lapcat, B. W. Binswanger, make it all worthwhile. And finally, I am saddened to report that Gary Meador, the young psychologist mentioned in the introduction, did not live to see the publication of this book. I hope he would have approved.

HOW
THERAPISTS
DIAGNOSE

INTRODUCTION

PROFESSIONAL SECRETS
YOU DESERVE TO KNOW

The purpose of *How Therapists Diagnose: Seeing through the Psychiatric Eye* is to give you a look inside the world of the therapist and the seemingly mysterious process of mental health diagnostics ... from diagnosing the simple "adjustment disorders," to the "sexual disorders," to the more complex "personality disorders." By learning the assessment techniques and diagnostic criteria that professionals use in sizing up their patients, you will gain access to some important tools that may help you understand yourself and others. Until now, much of this information has only been available in highly technical books written for the professional.

In addition, as a consumer, you should know the criteria that mental health professionals use in determining a diagnosis. If you see any mental health professional, privately or through a clinic, YOU WILL BE GIVEN A PSYCHIATRIC DIAGNOSIS. Furthermore, this information will be sent to your insurance or managed care company and will remain in your file forever. Granted, it can be changed. But the initial diagnostics remain a permanent part of your record.

But there are other things you should know. The "symptoms" you or a loved one may present to a therapist are extremely important in determining the diagnosis and type of therapy—but, as you soon will see, other, more practical matters also have an influence. Believe it or not, therapists sometimes "overdiagnose" in order to justify treatment to insurance companies. Other times they "underdiagnose" because they don't want the patient to be labeled by a more severe diagnosis. Some books written for the

1

mental health consumer touch on these issues, but most gloss over the bureaucratic influences that go on behind the scenes.

A PERSONAL DILEMMA

The original idea for this book was suggested by several friends outside of my profession. At the time, I completely rejected it—a knee-jerk response instilled by years of training in a profession that operates under a cloak of mystery. My concerns, at the time, centered around the release of professional information and the potential for misuse and abuse by untrained individuals. Inherent in this assumption, of course, is the questionable notion that this information is somehow "powerful" and that therapists do "powerful" things that are beyond the realm of public understanding. Although I had rejected this myth years ago, I was inadvertently supporting it by my protective stance. Like most other therapists, I justified this on the basis of "professional ethics."

Despite persistent arguments from many other people, I continued to have doubts about the idea until a young psychologist friend ended up in the hospital with a life-threatening cancerous tumor the size of a grapefruit. Since he carried a very frightening medical diagnosis, he had been more than curious about how the diagnosis was made, what the various medical tests meant, and how all aspects of his treatment were being determined along the way. Since the diagnosis was made from clinical tests and other *objective* information, his physicians had been very willing to share this information. In essence, they were willing to be held accountable for the diagnosis and treatment they were providing. And my friend, lying there in pain, subjecting himself to all sorts of invasive procedures, had a right to know the basis for them. This was no place for mysterious diagnoses "beyond his understanding" or procedures with no adequate explanations other than "this is best for you." The physicians had an ethical responsibility to share this information at the appropriate time, to be held accountable. My friend also had a right to know about the bureaucratic and financial considerations that impinged on his diagnosis and treatment.

The absurdity of my position suddenly became obvious. The mental health field stresses honesty, but, in reality, it does not practice full disclosure or accountability. For example, if a client asks about his or her diagnosis, particularly if it involves the more nebulous "personality disorders" rather than a more "concrete" diagnosis such as obsessive-compulsive disorder (OCD), therapists generally do an evasive song and dance. They become quite proficient at the song and dance, eventually losing the initial guilt they may have felt about it while in training. The guilt is turned off "for the patient's best interest." Nevertheless, therapists continue with the process and fill up reams of paperwork based on the undisclosed diagnosis.

But something is wrong here. Our current psychiatric diagnostic system is based on the same medical model that was used to diagnose my friend. But different rules seem to apply. In mental health, patients must rely on their "faith" in the therapist. They must assume that the therapist's clinical judgment is "learned" and somehow "scientific." In many cases, they apparently do not have the right to know their diagnosis or how it was determined. I think, stepping back from the situation, that this would strike most people as highly unusual or even unethical. Infractions of this type seem to occur bit by bit, with one rationalization covering the other. At some point it has been "accepted" that different rules will be applied to mental health care.

But times are changing. With the current crisis in health care and spiraling costs, we can no longer afford to accept diagnostics and treatment on faith. All health care professionals, including psychotherapists, must be held accountable for the services they provide. Insurance and managed care companies must also be held accountable, since they increasingly rely on the initial psychiatric diagnosis to determine the nature and duration of treatment that they will fund.

If mental health professionals accept the validity of their assessment procedures and diagnostic categories, they must be totally open with the lay public about these procedures and categories. If professionals are uneasy about divulging this information, perhaps this indicates that the entire diagnostic system needs to be reexamined. The moral obligation is very clear and simple—people have a right to know how they are being assessed and what the criteria are.

If you have any lingering doubts about this, consider the fact that, until several years ago, thousands of women caught in abusive relationships were routinely given the diagnosis of "masochistic personality disorder." This, of course, implied that they took some pleasure in their pain. Very few women were ever aware that they were given this diagnosis or what it meant. Due to new research findings and political pressure, this diagnostic category was eventually reevaluated. Nevertheless, many women were labeled and treated very unfairly by a system that purported to serve their best interests.

Or consider one of the newest diagnoses to hit the books— premenstrual dysphoric disorder (PMDD). In spite of very shaky, contradictory research evidence, psychiatry has seen fit to officially define a certain type of depression associated with hormonal changes as a "mental disorder." Needless to say, many people take issue with the validity of this diagnosis and fear that it "pathologizes" a normal experience. (You will learn more about this diagnosis in chapter 10.)

The message is clear: mental health consumers need to be actively involved not only in their treatment, but in their own diagnosis as well.

A LOOK AHEAD

Part 1

In part 1 of this book you will learn:

- What a psychiatric diagnosis is and what it is not.
- The advantages and disadvantages of psychiatric diagnoses.
- What the "Bible" of diagnostics is and how therapists use it.
- What to expect during an initial evaluation session.

- What therapists are looking for during an evaluation and what their agenda is.
- How therapists go about getting the information they need for the diagnosis.
- What the Mental Status Examination (MSE) is and what the results may mean.
- Why therapists ask so many questions about past history and what it may mean.
- How therapists go about putting all the information together to arrive at a diagnosis and treatment plan.

Information is presented from the therapist's as well as the patient's perspective, with many case examples and anecdotes used as illustrations. In addition to learning the basic tools necessary for diagnosis, you will also learn:

- How behind-the-scenes bureaucratic gyrations may influence diagnosis and treatment.
- Why all patients must be given a psychiatric diagnosis, even if they're simply upset about work, relationships, or practical matters.
- Why therapists frequently "overdiagnose" patients for insurance purposes.
- How managed care, insurance companies, and health maintenance organizations (HMOs) use and abuse psychiatric diagnoses for the bottom line.
- How therapists and patients are affected by the ever-expanding bureaucracy; why you should care.
- Ten important questions to ask your therapist about your diagnosis.

Part 2

Using the most up-to-date official definitions, part 2 describes over fifty adult diagnostic categories and subcategories in easy-to-understand, nontechnical terms: Major categories include:

- Adjustment disorders
- Mood disorders
- Anxiety disorders
- Dissociative disorders
- Sexual disorders
- Somatoform disorders
- Sleep disorders
- Eating disorders
- Impulse control disorders
- Substance-related disorders
- Schizophrenia and other psychotic disorders
- Cognitive disorders
- Personality disorders

In part 2, you will discover some of the valuable guidelines that therapists use in determining your diagnosis, including:

- The major features of each disorder, in easy-to-follow chart form.
- A checklist of additional symptoms often found with each diagnosis.
- Other important information and clues that therapists look for in making the diagnosis.
- Similar diagnoses that may need consideration.
- Case examples for selected diagnostic categories.
- A "Quick Guide to Selected Diagnoses and Major Symptoms."

In addition, the appendices include a glossary and a resource guide to professional associations, information and referral sources, and self-help groups.

BUT FIRST . . .

Before proceeding, please reread the warning statement at the beginning of the book. As every student of psychology has experienced firsthand, reading diagnostic material inevitably leads to questionable attempts at self-diagnosis and diagnosis of any unlucky soul who happens to cross one's path. A STRONG word of advice—use this book only as an interesting but rough map of the terrain. If you are concerned that you seem to "fit" a particular diagnosis, please consult a professional. Determining a diagnosis can be a very complex process that requires years of training and experience. To make matters more difficult, even highly trained professionals frequently disagree on diagnostics. But after reading this book, you may have a better idea what they are disagreeing about!

HOW
THERAPISTS
MAKE
ASSESSMENTS

1

THE THINGS
THEY NEVER
TELL YOU

A DISCONCERTING SITUATION

Anita finally decided to do it. She had meant to do it for several years but invariably backed away at the last moment. Perhaps there was nothing terribly wrong. Maybe everyone felt this way sometimes. Maybe it would just go away. On the other hand, it could get worse, like before . . . the fleeting thoughts of jumping off the nearest bridge, the angry letter to her lover, the sense of hurtling herself off the cold steel trusses into the oblivion below. But the sheer terror of the thoughts snapped her back into reality. She didn't really want to hurt herself. To some extent the feelings eventually passed, but she continued to be plagued with doubts about her sanity. She was even beginning to feel paranoid around other people. Maybe she *was* going crazy. Maybe she was "schizo" or something. Maybe she had always been messed up but didn't want to face it. This time, something had to be done.

The Plunge

So Anita followed the advice of all the self-help books, swallowed her fear, and reluctantly called the mental health center. Two weeks later, after carefully rehearsing what she would say, Anita found herself sitting in a ten-by-ten room across from an intense, deliberate young woman holding a yellow notepad. The pile of serious-looking textbooks on the therapist's desk was reassuring but disturbing at the same time. One title was particularly intimidating, *Diagnostic and Statistical Manual of Mental Disorders.* It was thick, dog-eared, and occupied a prominent place on the therapist's desk. *Great,* Anita thought. *She's going to look me up in a cookbook and bake accordingly.*

Through the Looking Glass . . .

The therapist began by explaining what she called "the intake process." Today would be an evaluation only, to help determine the nature of Anita's difficulties and the most appropriate therapy. In fact, this particular therapist probably would see Anita for evaluation only, followed by a referral to another therapist within the agency for ongoing therapy.

The therapist asked some rather simple, direct questions about Anita's feelings. To Anita's surprise, she responded with a flood of words. She was shaking inside and felt certain she would lose control. *Why is this happening? I don't even know this woman. She must think I'm really out of it. What if she wants me to be hospitalized? And what is she writing on that pad?* But in spite of her apprehensions, Anita was beginning to feel some relief as the words spilled out. She was finally getting a chance to tell her story.

The therapist looked concerned, said a few reassuring words, nodded her head, and continued to take notes. After about ten minutes she interrupted the flow of Anita's story with very specific questions about possible symptoms: Any changes in appetite or sleep patterns? Any problems concentrating? Feelings of hopelessness, worthlessness? Suicidal feelings? Mood swings? Hear any voices? When did the symptoms start? How long did they last in the past? Anyone in the family with similar symptoms? The therapist also had Anita interpret some proverbs, count backward from one hundred by sevens, calculate a math problem, and memorize the names of several objects to be recalled later in the session.

Anita was taken aback by the barrage of inquiries about symptoms and really just wanted to talk about the on-again, off-again relationship with her lover. But she tried to answer to the best of her ability. The therapist then asked about early family background, relationships, educational and work history, sexual history ... far more than Anita had been prepared to answer. It had all come out in a very disorganized fashion. She wondered how the therapist would make any sense of it.

The session seemed over almost as soon as it began. Anita felt a vague pang of disappointment. Her story had been interrupted by so many nit-picking questions ... maybe the therapist didn't really get the total picture. What difference could it possibly make if Anita interpreted the proverbs in a unique, creative way? And who cared if she was never very good at math? What did that have to do with her problems? Maybe the therapist had other things on her mind, an agenda different from Anita's. After all, she had said it would be an evaluation session, not a therapy session.

The therapist carefully explained her conclusions: Anita was clinically depressed and had some "personality issues" around her dependence on other people. Since clinical depression probably involved biology as well as psychology, Anita needed medication in addition to short-term therapy for the psychological issues. She would set up an appointment for Anita to see the psychiatrist for a medication evaluation.

... and into the Maze

But there was a problem. Anita's insurance only covered seven outpatient visits. The evaluations alone would use two of those visits. In addition, if she were placed on medication, she would need to continue seeing the psychiatrist weekly for the first month to monitor her response. Since the psychiatrist did not provide ongoing psychotherapy, Anita also would need to be followed by another therapist to address the psychological factors contributing to her depression.

The therapist pulled out what she called a "sliding fee schedule" and determined that, based on Anita's income, her fee would be $45 per session after her insurance ran out ... a fee that Anita could hardly afford. Anita doubted that she would be able to pay it, but she had little choice in the matter.

Anita left the clinic with very mixed feelings ... relieved and even hopeful, but disconcerted by the shuffle between therapists as well as the financial issues. She had not expected the bureaucracy. But most of all, she felt shortchanged emotionally. The therapist appeared to be so intent on looking for the signs and symptoms of a psychiatric "disease" that she seemed to miss the range and depth of Anita's anguish and life problems. The session evolved around the therapist's needs more than Anita's. Also, Anita intuitively sensed that she would need more than seven sessions to sort through all of this. *Doesn't the therapist know that I need more than short-term therapy?* she wondered. *Why is she recommending it?*

Behind the Scenes

While Anita waited for her next appointment, the intake therapist wrote a brief evaluation of Anita's difficulties and completed a stack of other forms. She gave Anita two preliminary diagnoses and one rule-out diagnosis, filled out a billing voucher that included the diagnoses, and sent it to Anita's insurance company. She also called them to obtain approval for further treatment. Like most insurance policies, Anita's coverage was only provided if she was suffering from an official "mental disorder." Her diagnostic summary looked like this:

Axis I: 296.32   Major Depression, Recurrent
                 302.71   Rule out Hypoactive Sexual Desire Disorder

Axis II: 301.60   Dependent Personality Disorder, Hysterical Features

Axis III: Chronic headaches, yeast infections

Axis IV: Severity of stressor: 3 (Moderate)
Relationship problems

Axis V: Global Assessment of Functioning (GAF): 55. Serious to
moderate symptoms. Suicidal ideation, denies intent

The therapist knew that most insurance companies print the diagnostic code numbers, not the actual category names, on the billing receipts sent to patients. Sometimes the receipts listed only the Axis I code number, even if additional diagnoses had been given. So the therapist didn't need to worry about upsetting Anita with the Axis II diagnosis or the rule-out. It was for her own good, the therapist reasoned. In fact, Anita would probably never even know about the other diagnoses, unless they were printed and she had access to the codebook.

The therapist also wrote up a preliminary treatment plan, which had to be based on the diagnoses. She realized that Anita needed long-term therapy but also knew that Anita's insurance company seldom approved it except for more serious cases. *The treatment plan had to be modified according to the funding source.* After all, insurance and managed care companies were starting to drop their treatment contracts with therapists and clinics who recommended long-term therapy too frequently. The clinic's administration was more than concerned about this possibility and held tight rein on all treatment plans. Therapists who did not comply were eventually asked to leave.

But, like so many people seeking psychotherapy, Anita knew nothing about any of this. Furthermore, she had no idea that she was given a diagnosis other than depression. Anita didn't know enough to ask. And her therapist was not about to volunteer this information or divulge the diagnostic code numbers. Neither was the therapist likely to tell Anita how she arrived at the diagnoses, what all the questions were about, or what the specific diagnostic criteria were. Nor would Anita be able to find this kind of information in self-help books. And, undoubtedly, she did not have the training or the patience to wade through professional texts.

Becoming an Informed Consumer

Anita's situation certainly is not unique. Mental health professionals have traditionally withheld this kind of information from the general public or, at most, presented it in an extremely simplistic, watered-down version. But enough is enough. To play an active role in your own diagnosis and treatment, you need more sophisticated information.

As a first step, you need to understand the rationale behind the diagnostic system and how it can be of benefit. On the other hand, you should be aware of some of the limitations and abuses of psychiatric diagnoses. These issues are addressed in the next chapter.

2
WHY DIAGNOSE?
THE PROS AND
THE CONS

A LIGHT IN THE DARK

Therapists are faced with a formidable task with each new patient they see. Without some guidelines based on a body of knowledge, experience, and social agreement, the assessment process would be haphazard and nearly impossible. To find their way through the murky puzzle of emotional pain, most therapists rely on the *Diagnostic and Statistical Manual of Mental Disorders*, published by the American Psychiatric Association (APA). This manual is commonly referred to as the *DSM*. The *DSM* lists the usual diagnostic categories found in the United States and describes the symptoms and behavior patterns typically found under each category. Each category is given an identifying number.

To diagnose patients, therapists obtain as much information as they can about the patients' symptoms, behaviors, and personal history. Referring to the *DSM*, therapists then attempt to match this information with the criteria listed for a certain diagnostic category. Quite often, however, patients receive more than one diagnosis. You will learn more about this process in future chapters.

While this might be seen by some as a superficial pigeonholing process, the psychiatric diagnosis can be extremely helpful and valuable. If a patient's behaviors and symptoms are similar to those of other individuals with a known disorder, then therapists can more accurately predict the course of the patient's symptoms as well as the method of treatment. Although the symptoms often overlap and seldom exactly match the categories in the *DSM*, these categories at least give the therapist a starting point from which to begin hypothesizing some ideas about treatment.

For example, if a patient's symptoms more closely match those of obsessive-compulsive disorder (OCD) than those of major depression, medication and psychotherapy recommendations would change accordingly. Anita, the depressed woman described in chapter 1, experienced prolonged depressed moods, loss of interest in daily activities, insomnia, underlying feelings of worthlessness, and problems concentrating. She also had a long-standing pattern of relying on other people for making the simplest decisions of everyday life and did whatever was necessary to win their approval and support. Diagnosed as suffering from major depression (296.32) as well as dependent personality disorder (301.60), Anita was placed on an antidepressant and referred to psychotherapy to address her fragile self-esteem and her pattern of dependent and submissive behavior.

On the other hand, if Anita experiences other symptoms in addition to those described, she might be given an additional diagnosis and different treatment. Suppose she finds herself using up many hours of the day checking repeatedly to see if all her windows are locked. She is aware that the ritual is ridiculous but is totally unable to resist it. She has a persistent feeling that she has forgotten something or done something terribly wrong. The symptoms interfere with her life greatly. In this case, she might receive the additional diagnosis of OCD (300.30). She would probably be treated with a special antidepressant, Anafranil, which is known to be helpful in many cases of this disorder. In addition to the psychotherapy recommended for her depression and personality problems, she also might benefit from behavior therapy to learn some more immediate ways to control her obsessions.

As seen in this example, the diagnosis or diagnoses allow the therapist to make distinctions between different types of behaviors and symptom patterns. They can even help distinguish between emotional symptoms caused by psychological factors and those caused by certain medical diseases. Since diagnoses are now more "scientifically based" than ever before, the therapist and the client can be more confident in the treatment recommendations. As psychotherapy and medication treatments become increasingly specialized, diagnoses become vitally important.

On the negative side, insurance and managed care companies have also learned the value of diagnostics—for their own purposes. Increasingly, therapists must report a patient's diagnosis after two or three sessions and request approval for further treatment. Whether the insurance company approves of long- or short-term therapy is tied in with the diagnosis and severity of the symptoms. Yes, this is a setup for therapists to "overdiagnose" in order to continue treatment. In the worst case, like that of the people who were allegedly kidnapped, improperly diagnosed, and held by a well-known psychiatric hospital chain in Texas, you could end up with a diagnosis you don't deserve. But that is the subject of another chapter.

BUT WHOSE LIGHT IS IT? SOME MAJOR DRAWBACKS

Aside from the hint of impropriety given above, there are other conflicting issues about the subject of psychiatric diagnosis and the *DSM*. These exist on the political, social, and clinical levels. Bear in mind that most psychiatrists are aware of these issues and, at least for the past fifteen years or so, have been giving them much more consideration. Nevertheless, the problems remain.

Politics, Power, and Social Judgments

First, let's consider some of the larger political and social issues. The APA is a professional trade organization for psychiatrists. Like most trade organizations, the APA has political agendas that serve the needs of the profession and, in the APA's view, the needs of the general public as well. Large trade organizations such as the APA, the American Psychological Association, and the National Association of Social Workers have enormous lobbying power and ultimately have the capacity to influence legislation and social policy. This process is an inevitable part of a democratic society.

If you obtain a copy of any edition of the *DSM*, you will notice that the copyright is held by the APA. In essence, the APA owns the framework for the diagnostic categories, their symptom clusters, and the multiaxial system. The APA, a closed professional organization with political power, defines what a particular mental illness is and essentially owns the rights to that definition. Can you imagine this happening with a clearly defined physical illness such as pneumonia? It seems that the mental health industry has a unique set of rules.

By law, facts cannot be copyrighted, although the manner and form in which the facts are expressed can be copyrighted. The APA does not claim that the *DSM* is factual. Wisely, it states that the categories and criteria are simply guidelines. And yet, despite this disclaimer, the *DSM* is generally accepted as the "law of the land" in regard to diagnostics. All mental health professionals in the United States, for legal purposes and insurance reimbursement, use the *DSM*, whether they agree with it or not. It has evolved into an extremely powerful social tool that determines the boundaries of mental illness as well as the activities of mental health professionals.

It would be easy to lapse into conspiracy theories here, attributing all sorts of nefarious motives to the APA and other mental health lobbying groups. But that probably would be more entertaining than factual. Granted, like all professional organizations, the APA is ultimately self-serving. Nevertheless, the *DSM* was developed in response to a great social and clinical need and represents the extensive work of many well-intentioned, dedicated researchers and clinicians. They have done a remarkable job. The problem is that the *DSM* has become institutionalized and accepted as "fact," in spite of the nebulous, ever-changing nature of the field. This is why it must be updated frequently. In the extreme, yesterday's pathology may be today's socially progressive behavior.

Who or What Is Abnormal?

All societies have some agreed-upon guidelines for normal and abnormal or maladaptive behavior, whether formalized in a diagnostic manual or simply implied and understood. Some extreme forms of disruptive, bizarre, impaired behaviors are considered abnormal in most all societies, while other, more subtle behaviors (for example, homosexuality, premenstrual syndrome [PMS], masochistic, self-defeating personality disorder, and so forth) have been the subject of much disagreement. Whether or not these different behaviors constitute "mental disorders" becomes a value judgment.

Ultimately, all diagnoses of mental disorders are social and value judgments based on "scientific" data and socially agreed-upon criteria. This is unavoidable. But a problem inevitably occurs when a single group becomes powerful enough to identify and determine these boundaries. Although the APA has been increasingly more responsive to minority perspectives, female psychology, and alternative viewpoints, the fact remains that their professional group holds some rather unique but pervasive social powers.

SOME CLINICAL PROBLEMS WITH DIAGNOSIS

Labels

The major drawback of any diagnosis is that it labels someone. Being labeled can distort other people's perception of you as well as your own self-image. People tend to see what they expect to see, therapists included. So once you receive a diagnosis, there is an increased possibility that other therapists will perceive you in a similar light. And once you learn of your diagnosis, the possibility increases that you may start to define yourself in those terms. You might see yourself as very different from other people, even though it may be only one part of your thinking or feeling that differs significantly.

The diagnosis can become a self-fulfilling prophecy or even a shared misconception between client and therapist. Consider this example:

At age twenty-two, John began to hear voices and was convinced that coworkers were plotting to kill him. At times he experienced periods of elation, while at other times he became seriously depressed. He also had increased difficulty concentrating and remembering. A trusted friend suggested to John that he might be suffering from manic-depressive disorder. The friend's uncle had this disorder and was helped immensely by Dr. Boggs, a psychiatrist widely known for his book on the treatment of manic-depressive disorder. John avidly read Dr. Boggs's book and suspected that he did indeed have the disorder. He went to see Dr. Boggs.

Dr. Boggs agreed with John's self-assessment, since his stated symptoms met all the criteria for manic-depressive disorder and did not seem to suggest anything else. He treated John with lithium and other antipsychotic medications over the next six months. John hated the medications and eventually refused to take them. He engaged in frequent verbal battles with Dr. Boggs over the medication issue. Dr. Boggs threatened to terminate therapy if John continued his noncompliance. John became progressively worse and eventually had to be hospitalized.

The hospital staff did not question Dr. Boggs's diagnosis and continued to reinforce his treatment recommendations. John was rehospitalized three more times with the same diagnosis. Perplexed by John's lack of improvement, Dr. Boggs eventually ordered a complete neurological evaluation, including a CAT scan of John's brain. Dr. Boggs was shocked to find a small brain tumor. He changed the diagnosis to organic mood disorder. Fortunately, the tumor was operable and John improved significantly after it was removed.

Although trained to look beyond biases, therapists can fall victim to their own expectations and categorical thinking. As discussed earlier, mental disorder diagnoses are not necessarily facts or firm categories—some are quite fluid and subject to frequent revision. Nevertheless, for practical purposes, therapists often treat them as facts.

Fads

But there is another problem, something therapists do not like to admit. Like everyone else, they are subject to fads. Strange as it may seem, a certain diagnostic category or "syndrome" suddenly becomes the object of ten zillion professional seminars and journal articles. Needless to say, the rate at which the disorder is diagnosed increases dramatically. And by the time it reaches Geraldo or Oprah, a large segment of the population suspects they have the disorder. You may remember the "Satanic ritualistic abuse syndrome" that swept through the United States in 1992.

Another recent "disorder of the year" has been multiple personality disorder (MPD). Others have been OCD, post traumatic stress disorder (PTSD), bipolar (manic-depressive) disorder, and the various "syndromes of addictive behavior." While these are important difficulties worthy of serious attention, the fact remains that social consensus and expectations shape the way all of us see things. In spite of the heroic efforts to "pin down" diagnoses with very specific criteria, even the "objective" experts are subject to very biased interpretations. This is an unavoidable quirk of being human. Although science has come a long way, we should never forget that the Salem witch trials were based on *Malleus Maleficarum*, a diagnostic handbook held to be truth for over two hundred years.

Avoiding Responsibility—Victims

Being assigned a diagnosis can be a very confusing situation. Suddenly you are John Smith, suffering from intermittent explosive disorder, *DSM* category 312.34. The diagnosis becomes both a description of you and some sort of entity that seems to be separate from you. This can be hard to reconcile. "If I could only get rid of this intermittent explosive disorder, I would stop beating my wife. How about giving me some medication to fix it?" So, is the disorder actually you, something you have, or both? Are you a "victim" of some disorder or do you play a part in it?

A talk show host recently interviewed a group of women who

considered themselves "victims of compulsive shopping." Might their next step be to sue store owners for selling to them in spite of their obvious "affliction"? While this may seem ludicrous, it illustrates a disturbing public trend that is a direct outgrowth of labeling people with diagnoses. And the pervasive tort attorneys are all too willing to cash in on these misguided notions.

To a lesser extent, this is even happening in self-help groups that use even broader, benign, "unofficial" categories, such as Adult Children of Alcoholics. While this is an extremely valuable, helpful group, it is made up of many different people with many different personalities who may be similar in some respects because of experiences with alcoholic parents. Yet some people will define themselves in terms of the category. Others will rationalize and subtly excuse their behavior because of their parents' behavior. While this is certainly not the objective of the self-help group, it is an unavoidable consequence of labeling and categorical thinking. The following is an example of this kind of thinking:

Steve, a twenty-seven-year-old married truck driver with a sporadic work history, returned home after spending six months in Saudi Arabia during the Persian Gulf War. During his tour of duty, he was not exposed to direct combat but could hear explosions in the distance. Most of his time was spent waiting in anxious anticipation of an invasion that never came.

Steve was elated by the homecoming parades and his newly acquired status as a war veteran. Unfortunately, he was returning to a very unhappy marriage. To make matters worse, his wife had taken a job as a waitress while he was in the Gulf . . . something Steve had always prohibited. Steve became physically abusive, controlling, suspicious, demanding, anxious, and depressed—as he frequently did throughout his five-year marriage when his wife went against his wishes.

To escape the home situation, Steve hung around with other veterans and eventually attended a support group for Persian Gulf and Vietnam vets. The vets used the group to discuss the impact of war on their lives and to help readjustment back to civilian living. Some of the vets exposed to heavy combat in Vietnam suffered from PTSD. Listening to their symptoms, Steve was convinced he also had PTSD and insisted that his relationship with his wife had deteriorated because of it.

A local TV news station did a feature story on the group. Steve, a vocal member with a new cause and sense of purpose, spoke convincingly about his PTSD, the effect the Persian Gulf War had on his marriage, and his subsequent inability to hold a job. He failed to mention that his problems had existed long before the war. Steve intended to apply for disability benefits but stated, "The VA screws vets and probably won't give me anything." The reporter accepted Steve's laments at face value and suggested that Steve was yet another victim of a heartless government.

Running Amok

Another problem with diagnosing mental disorders is that they can be culturally determined. Although many kinds of mental illness are recognized universally, others occur only in certain cultures. A psychiatrist from Thailand might have great difficulty diagnosing an abnormally thin American female who is preoccupied with food and determined to stay that way. The disorder, anorexia, is found most frequently in the United States and seems to be tied to certain American expectations about female physiques.

There are many other culturally bound syndromes. *Amok* is a behavior found primarily in Malaysia and involves a sudden homicidal killing spree by a male following a personal humiliation. The frenzied attack seems to follow a prescribed pattern. Asian males might suffer from *koro*, a fear that the penis will withdraw into the abdomen, resulting in death, while certain Native American Indians experience *windigo*, the fear that they will be turned into cannibals by an evil spirit. Spirit possession is quite common in certain African groups and includes hallucinations and clairvoyant experiences that might be seen as psychotic in the United States. In the group context, however, they reflect shared beliefs that are quite normal.

In many instances there indeed may be an underlying psychiatric disorder, but the manner in which it is expressed varies according to cultural expectations. In many areas of Africa, a variety of disorders, including major depression, generalized anxiety, and even schizophrenia, are expressed through unusual physical symptoms rather than the symptom patterns typically seen in the United States. On the other hand, sometimes an illness or emotional problem is not simply the expression of a known psychiatric disorder, but is instead a unique interaction between culture and biology.

Looking at these examples and others, it becomes evident that individual pathology cannot be determined or categorized simply by the symptoms or the nature of the behavior. Context and culture must be considered. As the United States becomes increasingly diverse in its ethnic cultures, the problems of cross-cultural diagnosis are amplified.

WHAT'S THE SOLUTION?

Some psychologists, and psychiatrists as well, argue that people should not be given an all-encompassing diagnosis but should be assessed according to their strengths and weaknesses in a variety of areas, including thinking abilities, coping skills, and personality patterns. From this perspective, people are seen as constellations of factors and potentials that don't necessarily add up to single definable entities. Assessments would describe these constellations without giving them a larger label.

This may be an enlightened, insightful way of looking at things, but unfortunately, it is not very practical and overlooks our natural tendency to categorize anything and everything. Like computers, our minds fall into these patterns regardless of our best intentions. But even if clinicians didn't assign categories, the administrators, lawyers, and accountants would. They need something to label and measure. Concepts alone are a little too diffuse for their purposes.

It is likely that we will always be stuck with diagnostic categories. As discussed previously, they can be extremely valuable and useful. The important thing to keep in mind about psychiatric diagnoses is that they are very rough maps of an ever-changing terrain. And they do not point to single causes of behavior. While some factors may be more important than others in certain cases, behavior (and disease) results from a complex interaction between biological, psychological, and social factors. The relationship among these factors is much more complex than we ever imagined.

Table 1 summarizes some of the advantages and disadvantages of the *DSM* diagnostic system.

TABLE 1:   SOME PROS AND CONS OF PSYCHIATRIC DIAGNOSIS

Advantages
- Makes sense out of a vast array of symptoms.

- Serves as a special language to organize and convey information among therapists, patients, and administrators.

- Helps distinguish between different disorders, including psychiatric disorders and medical illnesses.

- Helps therapists organize and standardize their assessment procedures.

- Can be used to predict the course of an illness.

- Can be used as the basis for treatment decisions.

- In most cases, labels symptoms and signs of illness rather than the person.

- By focusing on symptoms and signs, the *DSM* system claims to avoid conflicting theories about causes of behavior.

Disadvantages
- Creates many artificial boundaries that have not been validated scientifically.

- Limits perspective to the medical model, oversimplifies.

- Focuses on pathology. Does not indicate relative strengths and weaknesses.

- Labels patients. Therapists and patients can jump to conclusions and organize their perceptions to fit the categories. The diagnosis can be self-fulfilling.

- Diagnoses can be used to avoid personal responsibility.

- Many of the categories do not apply in different cultures. The signs and symptoms that diagnosis is based on can vary from culture to culture.

- The medical model of diagnosis has been developed by a professional guild with strong vested interests. Objectivity may be compromised.

- The categories are easily abused for administrative, financial, and legal purposes.

3
BEGINNING
THE
ASSESSMENT

OVERCOMING OBSTACLES

How does a therapist go about getting very personal, sensitive information in one or two sessions without alienating the patient? Since all patients consciously or unconsciously resist therapy on some level, how does the therapist cut through the defensive obstacles? At the same time, how does the therapist separate his or her own hang-ups from those of the patient?

To begin to answer these questions, let's look at the general process of a typical assessment session. Although therapists are trained in many different schools of therapy and have their own personal styles, most follow very similar steps in gathering diagnostic information. Some may go about it in a loose, unstructured manner, while others may cling to a certain order and framework. In either case, they must come up with very specific information in order to make the diagnosis using the *DSM*.

BUILDING RAPPORT AND GATHERING INFORMATION

Cold Feet: What Am I Doing Here Anyway?

Imagine, if you will, that you are the patient coming in for the initial assessment session with a skillful therapist. Although the basic process of building rapport and gathering information is the same regardless of the sex of the therapist, for our example, assume that you are seeing a woman. In any case, stepping into a strange office and facing an unknown therapist for the first time is a little like diving from a sheer cliff into an unknown pool of water. You hope that you don't look like a fool going down, that the water is deep enough, and that you remember how to swim. Everything seems to grow in magnitude and importance, including that minuscule bump on the therapist's nose that suddenly protrudes like a treacherous boulder from the water.

The therapist may also feel some anxiety. You are an unknown entity and she really doesn't know what to expect. Perhaps someone is forcing you to come to therapy. Perhaps you've had bad experiences with therapists and are coming in simply to please your spouse. Or perhaps you are explosive, threatening, and eat therapists for breakfast. In any event, the therapist has a very complex task ahead of her. And, like any other professional, she wants to come across as knowledgeable and helpful. To varying degrees, she cares how you feel about her but is ready to shoulder any negative feelings you might have—including your unnerving preoccupations with her nose.

Putting You at Ease

The therapist's first goal is to put you more at ease, allay your anxieties, and build rapport. She knows, in most cases, that the quality of the patient-therapist relationship has a greater influence on diagnostic and treatment success than all the technical knowledge in the world. The interaction between the patient's personality and the therapist's personality, coupled with the therapist's skill and knowledge, sets the stage for change. In fact, without such a relationship, diagnosis and treatment hardly get off the ground.

Asking the Right Questions, Gently

In order to help you, to get the information she needs, your therapist will approach questions from many different angles if necessary. And she will listen intently. She may pull back from questioning at times when she senses that you are resisting too much, or she may feel confident in pressing you a bit. For the most part, however, if she is a skillful interviewer, her questions won't seem terribly invasive. In fact, you might even find the direction of her questions quite informative. Even in the first session, she can help you clarify feelings and issues.

The Therapist's Agenda

While the therapist may appear to be casual and spontaneous, she has a very complicated agenda in mind, to be accomplished in a short time. At the same time that she is tailoring her manner and responses for your needs, she is observing and noting many things about you, including your appearance, behavior, attitude, affect and mood, manner of speech, orientation, the appropriateness of your emotional responses to the matters being discussed (for example, laughing while talking about the death of a loved one), and other facets of your thinking.

These observations and others help determine your current *mental status*, or current level of functioning, which plays an important role in your diagnosis. Your therapist determines your mental status during the natural course of the interview and by asking some very specific questions related solely to mental status. Known as the *Mental Status Examination (MSE)*, it consists of all the impressions and observations made by the therapist during the session. You will learn detailed information about the MSE in chapter 5.

Your therapist is also looking for very specific information that helps her to understand who you are, what you are presently experiencing, and the effect of past experiences. Psychiatrists refer to this as a *psychiatric history*, even if the patient has never had psychiatric or psychological help before. Psychologists and clinical social workers might refer to it as a *psychosocial history*. At minimum, the history contains information about the patient's chief complaint, current situation and stressors, past psychiatric and medical illness, developmental history, family history, educational and occupational histories, and relationship history. The psychosocial history is discussed in chapter 4.

The therapist's agenda may be clear, but as you may have guessed, it is easier said than done. After all, you do have a complicated agenda of your own, some of which may be beyond your immediate awareness. If it were simple, you probably wouldn't have come to therapy.

BRICK WALLS AND OTHER COMPLICATIONS

While ferreting out the necessary information may seem like a straightforward task, it is more like a mystery novel, full of pitfalls, dead ends, red herrings, and complicating factors. These complications are often quite puzzling and difficult, but they lie at the heart of all therapist-patient interactions, including the initial assessment.

As you will see, patients may consciously or unconsciously resist the therapist in different ways, distort the information, experience difficulty putting their feelings into words, contradict themselves, or even fake symptoms. In order to overcome these obstacles, therapists have devised all sorts of techniques and strategies. But before learning about techniques, you need to be able to identify and understand some of the complications that inevitably occur in the assessment process and in therapy.

HELP ME, BUT LEAVE ME ALONE

As strange as it may seem, all patients *resist* the therapist's efforts, in many subtle and not so subtle ways. Anxiety and tension trigger a wide variety of resisting maneuvers during the evaluation and during therapy as well. Avoiding topics, changing the subject, talking about irrelevant matters, giving one- or two-word answers, focusing on the therapist, acting seductively, speaking in a highly intellectual fashion, and claiming a sudden cure are just some of the many ways that patients resist the therapist.

Fortunately, in most cases, another part of the patient does indeed want help and usually ends up in direct conflict with the resisting forces—which is why therapy can be such an exhausting process for patient and therapist alike. Among other things, it is the job of the evaluator/therapist to create an alliance with the patient to overcome the resisting forces.

Problem? . . . What Problem?

Often patients will talk freely about some problems but conceal what's really bothering them. There may be many reasons for consciously resisting the therapist. Lack of trust, uncertainty about the therapy process or confidentiality, embarrassment, desire to maintain an image, avoidance of emotional pain, and fear of the therapist's response are common reasons for willful resistance.

Sometimes the resistance is so deliberate and contrived that it threatens to undermine the evaluation and therapy. This is often the case when people are coerced or forced into therapy by partners, family members, or the courts. Whether or not the resistance can be overcome depends on the therapist's ability to gain rapport and the patient's desire to be understood, to tell his or her side of the story—even if the blame for problems is placed on others. If the therapist is unable to tap into some kind of pain or conflict that the patient wishes to resolve, therapy becomes a game to appease others.

Here are two brief examples of willful resistance seen during evaluation sessions:

1.   Stan, a thirty-seven-year-old attorney with a history of physically and verbally abusing his girlfriends:

     She told me she'd press charges if I didn't come. That would ruin me. I know what the problem is and, with all due respect, don't need therapy to fix it. For some reason I keep choosing women who are beneath me intellectually. When they can't compete with me they start to nitpick, complain, and even flirt with other men. I get fed up when they won't listen to reason. I'll admit I get angry, but I never really hurt them. From now on, I'll look for more intelligent, perceptive women.

2.   Elizabeth, a fifty-two-year-old college professor, complaining of depressive feelings that do not meet the diagnostic criteria for a major clinical depression:

     From what I've read, my clinical symptoms are not necessarily the manifestation of underlying conflicts but have something to do with neurotransmitter levels in my brain. I just need an antidepressant to kick them back to normal. The stress of my divorce six months ago probably messed up the balance, but that's all over now. How about writing me a prescription for Prozac and I'll see you next month?

Unconscious Obstacles or Defenses

This complication is beyond the patient's general level of awareness and voluntary control. He or she may be totally unaware of using certain defensive patterns. Defenses such as denial, projection, rationalization, repression, acting out, and others all put a distorted twist on the way the patient sees him- or herself and others. Usually this is the stuff of psychoanalysis and psychodynamic therapy, but it does pop up in the evaluation session. If it interferes with the evaluation, the therapist must deal with it. Otherwise, it is simply noted for the treatment plan.

An example will illustrate this complex problem. Here is a woman who desperately wanted help but found herself running away from change:

By age twenty-three, Stephanie had been sexually abused by an uncle, raped at a party, beaten up by two boyfriends, and fired from three jobs because of absenteeism. By the time she decided to seek therapy for depression, low self-esteem, and self-destructive thoughts, she was convinced that a black cloud hung perpetually over her life—that she was somehow "tainted" from birth. Feeling she had little to lose, she often engaged in humiliating, self-defeating behavior. This led to a further sense of shame, feeding the negative cycle endlessly.

But Stephanie told little of this to her therapist, a young, rather attractive male social worker. In spite of her past, Stephanie believed she could relate more easily to men and had requested a male therapist. She knew what men expected and believed that she had a stronger sense of herself around them—or so it seemed. And most men liked and paid attention to her. So it seemed only natural to see a male therapist.

On one level, Stephanie sincerely wanted help. On another, perhaps unconscious level, she sensed that she could fall into a familiar, comfortable role with the male therapist. Like most men, he undoubtedly would be attracted to her. Her superficial, rather seductive demeanor during the sessions would guarantee it. She would be the one in control.

Needless to say, the sessions went nowhere, in spite of the therapist's best efforts. Stephanie's pattern of avoiding, resisting, denying, and playing out roles was at the core of her unhappiness, yet she was unable or unwilling to move beyond it. Not ready for real change, she essentially sabotaged her own therapy.

Intruders from the Past

Another complicating factor concerns the feelings the patient may have toward the therapist. Some of these feelings are based on the reality of the therapist-patient relationship, but others are not. These other, often unconscious feelings are based on the patient's past experiences with other significant people—particularly if the therapist looks or acts like these significant people in any way. The feelings are then displaced or transferred to the therapist. Therapists refer to this process as *transference*. In transference, the patient may attribute all sorts of qualities, positive and negative, to the therapist even though they may not exist to the degree that the patient imagines. Although this may seem like some kind of craziness (it can, in fact, reach that level), all human beings experience transference to varying degrees, particularly with authority figures.

During an assessment and even more so during intense, longer-term therapy, the therapist must be able to distinguish between the "reality base" of the patient's reaction to him or her and the patient's possible "illusions" about certain aspects of the relationship. This is easier said than done. As you will see, sometimes the therapist's own feelings get in the way and complicate the situation even further.

As the water gets murkier, therapists look for various clues that help identify transference feelings. Although this can be very complicated and beyond the scope of this book, there are three basic signs that are suggestive of transference:

1. The patient overreacts or underreacts to circumstances in a manner that would generally be seen as inappropriate.
2. The patient may realize that his or her response is unusual but is unable to say what is causing it.
3. The patient has very strong but conflicting feelings about the therapist.

Although transference feelings do not have much time to develop during assessment sessions, they frequently show up there and continue to intensify during the early stages of therapy. If transference is evident during assessment, the therapist will identify it as a possible area of conflict and target it in the treatment plan. In most forms of psychotherapy, transference feelings are seen as important sources of information about early experiences and ultimately, the emotional development of the patient. In fact, the patient may continue to play them out with people throughout his or her life unless these feelings are seen for what they really are.

Unfortunately, the current trends toward brief forms of therapy do not allow for in-depth explorations of transference feelings. On the other hand, some therapists focus on them almost entirely, at the expense of other important issues.

Bill, a thirty-eight-year-old carpenter in therapy for panic attacks, explains his transference feelings this way:

It was really crazy and it took a long time to figure out. The therapist seemed like a decent guy, but he wore this three-piece suit, sat in a high-backed leather chair, rubbed his chin a lot, and just sat there looking superior. He seemed like a pompous ass. From the beginning I had lots of trouble being myself around him. To make matters worse, I kind of felt like scum, coming in off the job in my work clothes.

But when he spoke, he seemed to be a down-to-earth guy. I couldn't figure it out. He was actually helping me, but part of me couldn't stand him. I felt like puking on his suit, punching him out, smacking him with a two-by-four. I even started making fun of his feedback, even though I knew he was right. Once, I nearly jumped down his throat, called him an incompetent, pompous ass. He had suggested that part of me was still an insecure little boy inside, out to prove something.

I didn't go back for two months. It was weird, though, because my wife said the same thing to me and it didn't really get to me. I knew it was true. She convinced me to go back. You wouldn't believe the anger and other crap I threw on that poor therapist. Over the next month, I told him everything I thought and felt about him and everyone else. God, where was it all coming from? After a while I realized that he really hadn't done anything to bring it on. I knew it but couldn't seem to stop myself. It made me wonder if I had done this to other people, particularly if I felt they were more successful or powerful than me.

The Imperfect Therapist

Another very basic complicating factor in the therapist-patient relationship is *countertransference*. This is the therapist's bugaboo, the emotional reaction related to his or her own issues. Like transference, it involves the displacement of feelings—but this time the therapist transfers feelings about a person or persons in his or her past onto the patient. This and other unresolved issues experienced by the therapist can create "therapeutic blind spots." Experienced therapists can generally sense when this is happening and consult with colleagues to sort through it.

Obviously, the therapist's level of personal awareness and development is crucial to the therapeutic process, including the evaluation. You can imagine how messy things might get if the therapist has distorted perceptions in certain areas. It can and does happen ...

therapists are not perfect. But the best ones are nondefensive, receptive to feedback from their patients, and seek consultations when necessary.

There are, of course, a thousand other things about therapists that can get in the way: obnoxious mannerisms; a rigid, controlling role; an ingratiating, condescending attitude; an inability to really listen; boredom or anxiety; inability to see the problem from the patient's perspective; impatience; and so forth. All therapists make mistakes and have bad days. For some therapists, every day is a bad day.

In other words, many unsuccessful evaluation sessions may have more to do with the therapist than the patient. Unfortunately, the therapist rarely finds out what goes wrong in these instances. The patient simply doesn't come back ... and it's all too easy to blame the patient or shrug it off.

This brings us back to the role of the therapist. Let's take a look at some of the very basic techniques and strategies that may be used to build rapport, reduce resistance, and gather the information necessary to make the diagnosis. Although complex cases require techniques and approaches that are beyond the scope of this book, the basic principles are the same.

TECHNIQUES

An Important Word about "Technique" and Manipulation

The idea of having to resort to "techniques" to build rapport and gather information may seem contrived and manipulative to many people. After all, rapport should flow from the natural give-and-take in an honest relationship, right? Unfortunately, it is not that simple, particularly since therapists must be able to relate to a wide variety of personalities in many different situations. Therapists use whatever approaches they can as long as they are within the bounds of their own personalities, their emotional resources, and their professional standards.

Although resorting to particular techniques does smack of manipulation, please remember that the ultimate goal is to help the patient. When it comes right down to it, all forms of therapy involve manipulation, power, and control—even if the therapist just sits and nods his or her head. It's the nature of the beast, although some therapists would adamantly deny this.

Experienced therapists generally don't turn techniques off and on like switches. The techniques become a natural part of their therapeutic repertoire and tend to flow on the intuitive level, along with a genuine sense of compassion and caring. Many top-notch therapists can't even identify the techniques they may be using.

On the other hand, some therapists do indeed get carried away with techniques and become extremely manipulative and patronizing at the patient's expense. But such a blatant exercise in self-importance is usually a sign of an incompetent or insecure therapist, no matter how fancy the office. Let's hope such therapists are in the minority.

Techniques for Building Rapport

To illustrate these techniques, let's go back to your session with the evaluating therapist. You can easily imagine how you might feel if she behaved like a computerized robot—probing with a series of rote questions, nodding on cue, and maintaining a cold aura of indifference. You might be tempted to kick her, scramble her programming, or pull the plug.

Sharing personal information may be easy for the guests on "Geraldo" or "Oprah," but if you are like most people, certain conditions need to exist before you are willing to do this, even in a therapy session. In order to feel more comfortable, open, and honest in telling your story, you need to sense certain qualities about your therapist and her manner of relating:

1. She is a caring, compassionate person who is interested in your problem.

2. She is able to listen carefully.

3. She does not seem to be judging you.

4. She seems able to understand your point of view, your experience.

5. She respects you as a person and sees that you have some good qualities and strong points, in spite of your problem.

6. She seems to know what she is doing and has seen this kind of problem before—but she also knows that you are not necessarily like everyone else with this problem. She doesn't jump to conclusions.

7. She seems to have a sense of authority without being domineering. You can probably depend on her.

While you might not be totally aware of these conditions, you would sense if something was amiss. It follows, then, that good therapists attempt to fulfill these conditions, without coming off as contrived and artificial. Some therapists never really get the hang of it. Others have a natural ability and could probably do it with very little training.

To convey these conditions and build rapport, your therapist will use a variety of techniques, including:

- Focusing on the feelings behind the events that you report. This brings feelings to the surface and conveys a sense of caring.

- Listening intently without getting in the way of your story. On the verbal level, she might repeat something you have said to convey attentiveness.

- Avoiding subtle verbal and nonverbal expressions of disapproval.

- Interjecting comments that are on target with your level of understanding and insight. She will also summarize her understanding of what you have reported.

- Providing you with an initial framework for ordering and

understanding your difficulties without being unduly authoritative.

Techniques for Gathering Information

Even if you are totally open and cooperative, the therapist must guide much of the interview in order to get specific diagnostic information. By matching the nature and timing of her questions with your needs, she is able to gather information without reducing the session to an inquisition.

Your therapist probably will start the evaluation by asking *open-ended questions* that require more than one- or two-word answers. Questions like "What brings you here?" or "Why does your lover think you need therapy?" (if relevant) invite you to present your perception of the problem. As a certain problem area is identified, the therapist will begin to ask very direct questions to target in on specific symptoms. Some of these questions may be *closed-ended*, such as "How many weeks have you felt this way?" or "How many panic attacks have you had in the past month?"

Since answers to the open-ended questions are often very complicated and confusing, the therapist must help *clarify* them. If your answers are too detailed while ignoring the bigger picture, she will work to broaden your report. If your complaints are very vague, she will *focus* on them with closed-ended questions or, at the risk of putting words in your mouth, directly ask if you have particular symptoms. She may even *probe* for your understanding of the reasons behind your behavior. The goal is to get a very clear picture of your presenting complaint, your symptoms, and the context in which they are occurring.

If you are on the right track, at least in her mind, she will *encourage* you to continue by nodding, saying "Uh-huh," or using other gestures of approval. If you tend to ramble on, get lost in irrelevant detail, or talk around a subject, she will be much more *directive*. To subtly change your focus, she might choose and *repeat a particular word or statement* you say, even though that was not your intended direction. Or, if that fails, she may *interrupt* and steer you to another topic. However, different types of patients need different approaches. For example:

Obsessive patients often get off the track and bury themselves in irrelevant details. They need clear, direct questions, along with frequent steering back to the subject at hand.

Depressed patients can be very vague in describing their feelings and often need more help clarifying the symptoms.

Defensive, suspicious patients usually give very brief answers to closed-ended questions and are much more comfortable with less confining, open-ended questions.

Patients who deny many of their problems, such as substance abusers, require very specific, closed-ended questions.

Patients who may attempt to lie to or deceive the therapist for secondary gain (for attention, to please the court, win a financial settlement, compensation, and so forth) need to be asked similar questions in different ways and orders throughout the interview. This helps to expose inconsistencies and contradictions.

Techniques for Reducing Resistance

As you have seen, resistance is a natural part of the therapy process and occurs within and beyond your level of awareness. Painful emotions can be very difficult to talk about or even admit to oneself. During the initial evaluation, the therapist needs to reduce your resistance only to the extent necessary to obtain diagnostic information. With experience, a good therapist acquires a sense about this and is very careful not to push too hard in areas the patient may not be ready to address. As in ongoing therapy, timing is very important.

If you think about it, it's easy to see that your relationship with the evaluator/therapist is the most important ingredient in allaying your fears and setting the scene for open communication. You have already seen some of the conditions necessary for a good rapport. If there are major problems with rapport, you are likely to dance circles around the plodding therapist. And if he or she is obtuse enough to attempt some fancy techniques to reduce resistance, you would probably declare war. The important point here is that a good rapport is the first and sometimes the only step necessary in reducing resistance during the evaluation.

But things aren't always so simple. In spite of a reasonably good rapport, patients often need help getting beyond obstacles. Rather than going through a laundry list of techniques, let's look at three typical cases and ask an evaluating therapist how he might initially approach them. The names of some basic techniques are italicized.

Problem 1: Forty-nine-year-old male, referred by the court after he was arrested for exposing himself and masturbating while sitting alone in his car. One prior arrest for exposing himself. Patient denies purposefully exposing himself in both instances but acknowledges open masturbation. Denies any problem other than "poor judgment and an overactive sex drive." He is pleasant but guarded. No previous therapy.

Therapist's approach: "This is common in court referrals—they often minimize or deny the emotional aspects that underlie the behaviors that led to their arrest. They often claim that the only problem that bothers them is the arrest. In this case, he is probably embarrassed and ashamed on several levels and is fearful of judgment and ridicule—the therapist might think he is a 'pervert.'

"My approach would be to avoid any moral judgments and convey a sense of *acceptance* without necessarily condoning his behavior. I would also *confront* how he minimizes the impact of the problem. After all, he has been arrested twice. To engage him emotionally, I would try to *change the focus* to the pain his 'poor judgment and overactive sex drive' have caused him."

Problem 2: Twenty-three-year-old female, feeling very depressed, overwhelmed, hopeless. Crying constantly during the session, says she is worthless, weak, a perpetual failure. Most of her statements are self-denigrating. Although quite verbal and animated, she has difficulty providing specific information about her life. No previous therapy. Denies thoughts of harming herself.

Therapist's approach: "She obviously is feeling very overwhelmed and needs to cry, but I get the feeling she is avoiding issues by falling into a self-punishing stance, which could be a pattern for her. But rather than focusing on that, I would simply give her a lot of *support*, point out her strength in coming to therapy, *reassure* her, and so forth. This might allay her anxiety, *offer hope*, and engage her more in the process. If I were to confront her too much or press for the information, she would probably tune me out."

Problem 3: Twenty-eight-year-old mother of two children, ages four and two. Very anxious, upset, says she doesn't know how to be a good parent. "They're driving me crazy and I have horrible thoughts about them and what I might do. I love them but can't handle them. I don't want to be like my own mother." When asked, patient won't say what her horrible thoughts are or what her mother is/was like. "I don't want to talk about that. Besides, what do you do with the information?"

Therapist's approach: "This is a rough one, because she lacks trust and seems to have a lot of guilt about her perceived failures as a parent. I have to wonder about her "horrible thoughts" and any actions she may have already taken on those thoughts. Perhaps she has abused the kids. Perhaps her own mother was abusive. She is probably aware that, by law, I would have to report any abuse—yet at the same time, she obviously wants help. A real dilemma, but it shows strength on her part.

"I wouldn't confront her on her avoidance of the topic. Instead, I would focus on the pain she is feeling, the guilt, the feelings of failure. I would approach the issue of possible abuse in a roundabout way, from a *different angle*, after she is engaged emotionally. I suspect she really wants to tell me but feels too guilty and is worried about the legal consequences. I would *discuss her expectations* about this and *clarify* what therapists must do if abuse is involved. I would *praise* her strength as a caring parent, to come to therapy in spite of possible consequences."

So now that you have a better idea how a therapist goes about getting information, it is time to look at the nature of the material that is needed for the diagnosis. What is the therapist looking for?

4
YOUR
PERSONAL
HISTORY:
WHAT THE
THERAPIST
LOOKS FOR

YOU ARE YOUR PAST . . .
AND MORE

Hazy Snapshots

At first glance, mapping and making sense of the vast and complex labyrinths of personal experience might seem like an impossible, mind-boggling task. After all, biographers spend years researching a particular subject and often arrive at similar yet very different pictures. Anyone who has read the various biographies of John Lennon, Elvis Presley, or Marilyn Monroe knows how this can happen. The final portrait is a mixture of fact, hearsay, conjecture, and subjective interpretation.

So how can a therapist possibly compile an "accurate" historical profile of his or her patient after one or two evaluation sessions? Or fifty sessions, for that matter? Isn't the information presented by the patient biased or subject to distortions in memory? And doesn't the therapist impose his or her own biases on the information? Can't some patients' memories be twisted and shaped by leading questions from the therapist? Aren't records of prior treatment also biased?

Unfortunately, the honest answers to these questions are not terribly reassuring, although many grandiose or narrow-minded therapists might suggest otherwise. Common sense tells you that there is no magic here. Therapists encounter the same kinds of difficulties faced by biographers. In addition, therapists run the risk of influencing the patient's account by the nature of the questions asked.

While there is no perfect solution to this dilemma, enlightened therapists acknowledge the pitfalls and limitations of history taking, particularly during the initial evaluation. Rather than seeing the psychosocial history as an all-encompassing portrait of the patient, they are more inclined to see it as a series of small, somewhat hazy snapshots that will probably evolve as therapy progresses. Along with other, more concrete historical information, the subjective snapshots are very important and provide clues for diagnosis and treatment.

THE PSYCHOSOCIAL HISTORY

So what kind of information is the therapist looking for? In gathering the information, most therapists rely on a basic format, referred to as the *psychosocial* or *psychiatric history*. Although therapists don't necessarily follow the format verbatim, they use variations of it to organize their own thoughts, formulate questions, and write up the evaluation. Without guidelines, important information can be overlooked.

The psychosocial history is not a separate, distinct part of the initial evaluation. The information is gathered throughout the interview as you tell your story, along with observations about your mental status. (See chapter 5 for details of the MSE.) As certain aspects of your past and present life come to light, the therapist will ask questions to obtain more specific information. This can jog your memory and perhaps even lead you to unexplored areas. Although it may not be readily apparent, there are reasons for every question the therapist asks. Table 2 shows the basic parts of the psychosocial history.

By exploring the eight areas listed in the psychosocial history format, the therapist gains insight into your personality development, character traits, self-image, strengths and weaknesses, coping patterns, and styles of relating to others at various points in your life. Since most of this information is expressed in your own words, the therapist also learns about your particular point of view. With your permission, additional information may be gathered from family members and any past treatment records.

To understand how this works, let's look at each part of the psychosocial history in more detail. This will be followed by an actual psychosocial write-up.

Identifying Data

This information is sometimes collected over the phone when you make your first appointment, particularly if you are calling a mental health center or clinic. It includes basic demographic data (name, address, phone, age, occupation, marital status, referral source, and so forth) as well as your insurance information. While the purpose of this is obvious, it may also determine which therapist you see at the clinic. And, as you will see in chapter 7, the nature of your insurance coverage plays an important role in your treatment plan, even if you are seeing a private practitioner.

Presenting Problem or Complaint

If you are like most people seeking therapy, you have a number of problems and complaints, rather than a single concern. However,

---

TABLE 2: THE PSYCHOSOCIAL HISTORY

1. **Identifying Data:** Name, date of birth, address, marital status, source of referral, and so forth.

2. **Presenting Problem or Complaint:** This briefly describes, in your own words, why you are seeking help; e.g., "I've been feeling really down and can't seem to get anything done."

3. **History of Complaint:** An in-depth description of the complaint, when it started, what may have triggered it, current life circumstances, effect on work, relationships, and so forth.

4. **Past Psychiatric History:** Previous emotional difficulties, diagnoses, treatments, hospitalizations, medications.

5. **Childhood History (Birth to Puberty):** Developmental history, family history, family relationships, emotional climate in family, trauma, behavior problems, personality traits, peer relationships, school history, and so forth.

6. **Adolescent History:** Personal identity, self-esteem, independence, reactions to sexuality, peer and family relationships, attitude toward adults, social behavior, drug and alcohol abuse, impulse control, ways of handling conflict, and so forth.

7. **Adult History:** Interpersonal relations, intimate and family relationships, educational and occupational history, military history, legal history, risk behaviors, drug and alcohol abuse, coping styles.

8. **Medical History:** Past and present illness or symptoms, physical traumas, treatments, past and present medications, adverse reactions to medications.

---

when the therapist asks, "How may I help you?" or "What brings you here today?" you are likely to start with a very broad, general statement. You have probably thought about it for weeks before coming in. The statement usually says something about symptoms you might be experiencing, relationship problems, stressful situations, or long-term personality characteristics that interfere with your life:

> It's probably nothing, but every time I go out of the house I start to feel like something terrible is going to happen. My heart beats fast and I get so dizzy. I try to fight it, but nothing helps.

> My mother is driving me crazy. I'm thirty-three years old and she still treats me like a child, interferes with my marriage, and takes over with my kids. And I let her get away with it. I need help dealing with her.

> I don't believe this is happening. It's tearing me up, I'm going nuts, getting really paranoid. The Department of Social Services is sending me here. My daughter's therapist filed a sexual abuse charge against me, but I haven't done anything wrong! Either way, I still need help with this; it's driving me over the edge.

> For some reason, I keep getting hooked up with these real losers. It's happened again even though I was really on the lookout this time. Maybe all men are losers. Or maybe I keep screwing myself for some reason. Is it me? What am I doing wrong?

The presenting complaint is important since it indicates which problem you have chosen to focus on, how you see it, and how it is affecting you. Even if it is only the tip of the iceberg, it says something about you.

In reading each of the above examples, even an untrained individual can begin to make some initial conjectures about the person behind the statement. And if you could see and hear the person making the statement—watching the facial expressions and mannerisms and listening to the intonations—you would have an even better sense of him or her.

Therapists try to write down the presenting complaint verbatim, since the way it's phrased may be significant. Saying, "My wife is driving me to drink," is vastly different from saying, "I have a drinking problem." The first may suggest denial and avoidance of personal responsibility, while the second is a more straightforward self-appraisal. Either way, each statement leads the way toward a more in-depth look at the perceived problem, even if it is distorted, exaggerated, or minimized.

History of Complaint

Once you have presented a particular problem, the therapist will want to know your symptoms as well as all the life circumstances that you feel are related to your problem. Since psychiatric diagnosis follows the "medical model," much attention is paid to symptoms, even if they are vague, e.g., "I'm generally unhappy about the direction of my life and want to find out why." The therapist will work to pinpoint and refine what you mean by "generally unhappy." Whether you like it or not, the therapist will have to redefine "generally unhappy" until it fits into an acceptable diagnostic category.

This part of the psychosocial history provides the therapist with a wealth of information about the nature and duration of your symptoms (depression, general anxiety, compulsions, irrational thinking, mood swings, explosive behavior, panic attacks, social avoidance, and so forth), the pressures that may trigger or perpetuate them, and the social context in which the symptoms are occurring.

In order to complete the history of your problem, the therapist is looking for answers to a number of questions, including:

- When did the problem or complaint start?
- What was going on in your life when it started? Did something trigger it or has it been a vague problem going on for a long time? What's going on in your life now?
- Why did you decide to come to therapy now?
- What kind of symptoms are you experiencing? How long have they been going on? Do they come and go or are they with you constantly? What have you tried to do about them?
- How has the problem and/or symptoms affected your work, your relationships, or your feelings about yourself? In what way? What do other people in your life say about it? Is there anyone you can rely on?

- How have you tried to handle the problem?
- Are there any other problem areas that you are concerned about?

As you will see in chapter 6, "Putting It All Together," this information, along with information gleaned from the MSE (chapter 5), is extremely important in identifying the specific symptom patterns that must be matched up with the diagnostic criteria listed in the *DSM*.

Past Psychiatric History

The therapist will want to know the dates of any previous inpatient or outpatient treatments, length and type of treatments, reactions to any medications, and treatment results, as well as your feelings about the experiences. If you have had previous therapy, and depending upon your problem, the therapist may ask you to sign a release to obtain records from your former therapist.

Some patients vehemently object to the release of prior records, particularly if they feel the former therapist was inadequate or wrong in his or her assessment. They worry that past treatment records might bias the present therapist and the evaluation. Without a doubt, this can and does happen. But the potential benefits generally outweigh the risk of bias. With the prior records, the new therapist can see what worked and what didn't, what the triggering events were, what your symptom and coping patterns were at that time, and how they compare with your present difficulties.

In addition, the present diagnosis sometimes depends upon the existence of past episodes of one type or another. For example, if a patient has suffered a manic episode in the past (see part 2 for a description of this diagnostic category) and now, one year later, experiences all the symptoms of a major depression without the manic symptoms, the present diagnosis, according to the *DSM*, would be bipolar disorder, depressed, rather than major depression.

Not knowing about the manic episode, the therapist would make the incorrect diagnosis and treat with an antidepressant alone. This could trigger a manic episode. (Bipolar patients in the depressed phase are usually treated with lithium as well as an antidepressant to avoid triggering mania.) In this instance, information about previous illness is crucial.

Childhood History (Birth to Puberty)

As strange as it might seem, it is possible to make many adult diagnoses with very little information about childhood history. (See chapter 6.) But in order to better understand their patients, most therapists gather more than the minimum information needed to make the diagnosis. They look for a well-rounded picture of the patient's psychosocial development and the major influences on his or her early life.

Good therapists also want to know how their patient understands his or her childhood, since *it is a person's understanding, past and present, that shapes his or her experience of emotional and physical events.* A painful, destructive experience for one person might be a difficult but enlightening experience for another.

Depending upon a therapist's theoretical orientation and training, he or she will place different degrees of importance upon the patient's childhood history. This is true for the initial evaluation as well as ongoing therapy. Some therapists take great pains in exploring details about birth, toilet training, feeding habits, patient's hatred of his or her father, and so forth, while others give these and related developmental features a more cursory glance. Either way, most look for important clues about the patient's past that may have some relationship to his or her emotional problem. Even if aspects of your childhood have not "caused" your problem, they may be influencing how you perceive and deal with your problem.

Here are some, but not necessarily all, of the important things therapists look for in your childhood history. Since this list and the ones covering the adolescent and adult years are quite detailed, you may wish to simply scan them, using them for reference purposes only:

A. Family Background

1. Nature of relationship between parents or other caregivers.
2. A brief history of each parent.
3. Evidence of drug or alcohol abuse in the family.
4. Separations or divorces.
5. Mental health and medical problems in parents and siblings.
6. Your relationship with each parent or other caregiver.
7. Your feelings about each parent or other caregiver.
8. Emotional climate of the family unit(s).
9. Relationship with siblings.
10. Physical and/or sexual abuse involving you or other family members.
11. Other major traumas.
12. Cultural, economic, religious aspects of family.

B. Behavioral Problems

1. Bed-wetting, stuttering, phobias, nightmares, persistent fears, clinging behavior.
2. Temper tantrums, hyperactivity, fire setting, cruelty to animals, stealing.

C. Problems with Intellectual or Motor Development

1. If known, delivery problems at birth, birth defects, delays in walking, talking, carrying out age-appropriate tasks.
2. Problems paying attention, concentrating, thinking logically, learning to read, and other learning disabilities.
3. Problems with physical coordination, motor control, hand-eye skills.

D. **Personality**

Outgoing, withdrawn, shy, friendly, aggressive, demanding, passive, and so forth.

E. **School History**

1. Chronology of school history.

2. Difficulties or successes with particular subjects.

3. Relationships with teachers, attitude.

4. Behavioral problems at school, problems with attendance, following rules.

5. Feelings about school.

F. **Nature of Relationships and Manner of Relating**

1. Ability to develop close friendships.

2. Ability to function in groups.

3. Problems getting along with peers or adults.

4. Adequacy of social skills.

5. Predominant manner of relating to others—aggressive, passive, anxious, manipulative, uncaring, and so forth.

6. Regard for the rights and feelings of others, a sense of right and wrong.

Adolescent History

Since adolescence is often a mass of conflicting forces involving physical growth, sexuality, and the search for personal and social identity, it is a rich area for exploration by the evaluating therapist. Many of the questions applied to the childhood history also apply to adolescence, but your answers may be different for this stage of your life. These additional questions only scratch the surface but open up areas for further exploration if relevant:

A. **Family**

1. What was your family situation during adolescence? Who provided discipline and how did you react to it? Which

parent or other caregiver were you closest to, if any? How did either parent, or caregiver, seem to react to your growing up?

2. How did you relate to siblings, extended family members, or other caregivers?

3. Any physical or sexual abuse, in or out of the family?

B. Personal Identity, Sense of Self

1. Did you have any role models to follow?

2. What were you like?

3. How did you feel about yourself? Anything you particularly liked or disliked? How did you want to be?

4. Did you ever think of hurting yourself? Any attempts? What happened?

C. Sexuality

1. How did you feel about your developing sexuality?

2. Was your attitude about sexuality different from your family's? How did you handle it?

3. What were your feelings about dating and/or sexual activity? How did you handle them? Any problems?

4. How did you relate to the opposite sex or, if you had homosexual feelings, the same sex?

5. Any sexual trauma, rape, incest, molestation?

6. Any other concerns about sexuality—sexual identity, sexual practices, sexual problems?

D. Relationships

1. How did you get along with peers during this period? What kind of people did you choose as friends? How did they react to you?

2. How did you handle group situations? Did you have a sense of who you were in the group, how you fit in?

3. How did you relate to adults and other authority figures? Any problems? How did adults seem to feel about you?

4. Any serious love relationships during this period? How did you handle them? How did they affect you? How do you feel about them now?

E. Coping Skills, Emotional Problems

1. How did you handle stress and conflict then? Did you withdraw, resort to fantasy, or detach emotionally? Did you run away, have tantrums, destroy property, steal things, hurt yourself or others, abuse drugs and/or alcohol, or engage in unrewarding sexual relationships?

2. How did conflict affect you emotionally? Did you have periods of depression? Anxiety? What did you do about it? Any emotional symptoms that you particularly worried about?

Adult History

In exploring the patient's history, many therapists don't actually follow a strict chronology. Instead, they first ask about the patient's adult history and then move back and forth to related topics in adolescence and childhood as the story progresses. For instance, if you report that you are currently being abused by a lover, the therapist is likely to ask about childhood abuse before jumping to a different adult topic. Or you may want to head off in that direction on your own.

The point is that most therapists would use a great deal of flexibility in gathering your history. After all, it is *your* story. And you certainly don't need to be constrained by any of the formats you see here! If you do happen to get way off track, the therapist will gently bring you back. With that said, let's look at the typical parts of the adult history:

A. Interpersonal Relations

1. How do you relate to people in general? Do you have close friends or do you tend to avoid people? If you avoid them, why? Fear of rejection? Lack of trust? Do you dislike most people or any type in particular? Do you feel you have

problems getting along with others? How do people feel about you? Does race or culture play a part?

2. How do you relate to authority figures? With apprehension? Hostility? Distrust? Submissiveness?

B. Intimate Relationships and Family

1. Are you currently in a long-term relationship? What are your feelings about it? Is it emotionally and sexually fulfilling? Have you had other long-term relationships? Why did they end? If you are not currently involved and wish to be, what are you looking for?

2. Do you have children? How do you feel about them?

3. Do you still see your parents? What role do they play in your life? How do you feel about them?

C. Occupational History

1. If employed, how long have you worked at your job? Do you like it? How do you feel about your occupation? What other jobs have you held? What other work would you like to do? Has work or lack of work been a major problem?

2. How do you get along with other people at work, including bosses? Any problems in the past with this?

D. Educational and Military History

1. How far did you go in school? Any problems? What is your attitude toward school?

2. Any time spent in the military? What was your reaction to it? Were you in or near combat situations? Has that affected you? Do you still think about it? What was the nature of your discharge?

E. Legal History

1. Any arrests for violations like auto theft, larceny, robbery, shoplifting, gambling, prostitution, and so forth? What is the disposition? Any time served? Are you on probation?

2. Any arrests for assaulting, injuring, or threatening other people?

3. Have you been arrested for dealing drugs? Possession? Driving under the influence?

F. Drug and Alcohol Abuse

1. How many drinks do you have on an average day? Do other family members drink? Has anyone ever suggested that you had a drinking problem? Has drinking ever interfered with your work or with relationships? What is your history of alcohol use? Any treatment?

2. Do you presently use any drugs? How much? How often? What is your past history of drug use? Any problem with prescribed medications? Do other family members use drugs?

G. Risk Behaviors

1. Have you ever tried to hurt yourself? How? Cutting yourself? Taking pills? What happened? If not, have you ever thought of hurting yourself? Do you think about that now? If so, how would you do it?

2. Have you ever lost control and hurt other people? How? What were the circumstances? Do you have a problem controlling your temper? Do other people think you do?

3. Do you put yourself at risk in other ways, such as having unprotected sex with different partners, driving recklessly, or placing yourself in potentially dangerous situations?

H. Attitude toward Yourself

1. How would you describe yourself?

2. What do you feel about that person?

3. Specifically, what do you like and dislike about yourself? What would you like to change?

I. Coping Styles

1. What do you do when under stress? Withdraw? Become irritable? Strike out at others? Punish yourself? Eat too much? Become physically sick? Depressed? Suicidal? Resort to drink, drugs, or other risk behaviors? Or do you simply try to ignore conflict?

2. Are the above styles working for you or would you like to learn other ways of handling stress and conflict?

Medical History

When you appear for your initial evaluation appointment, don't be surprised if the therapist asks you to complete a one- or two-page form covering your medical history, as well as your current health habits—smoking, coffee consumption, hours of sleep you get, alcohol consumption, and so forth. You may also be asked to sign a release allowing your medical doctor to send your latest physical report as well as other records that may be relevant. So, you might feel, why all the fuss, particularly if you're feeling as healthy as a horse and just want help learning to relax?

When it comes to the relationship between mind and body, nothing is simple or clear-cut. Emotions affect physical health and physical health affects emotions. If you are seeking help for anxiety, it would be foolish to overlook the amount of caffeine you feed your jangled nerves each day. It would also be foolish to overlook any past history of hypoglycemia. Taking a routine medical history can be extremely valuable in identifying any toxic or biological contributions to your emotional symptoms.

Many physical diseases are associated with feelings of depression, anxiety, mood swings, disorientation, delusions, and personality changes. (See table 3 for some examples.) With this in mind, the therapist will want to know all major illnesses, surgeries, hospitalizations, medications, and physical traumas you may have experienced. You might also be asked about a variety of symptoms such as headaches, allergies, intestinal problems, backaches, rashes, asthma, nausea, dizziness, and so forth. Although certainly this is not always the case, many of these symptoms can be an indication of emotional stress.

TABLE 3: SOME MEDICAL PROBLEMS THAT MAY HAVE PSYCHIATRIC SYMPTOMS

Disease	Possible Psychiatric Symptoms
Multiple sclerosis	Depression, mood swings, personality changes
Temporal lobe epilepsy	Delusions, confusion, depression, angry outbursts, personality changes
Brain tumor	Depression, memory loss, personality changes
Alzheimer's disease	Depression, delusions
Hyperthyroidism	Depression, anxiety
Hypothyroidism	Irritability, delusions, confused thinking, hallucinations
Anemia	Anxiety, depression, guilt
Electrolyte imbalance	Depression, delusions
AIDS	Anxiety, depression, mental slowing, disorganization, psychosis
Systemic lupus	Anxiety, depression, confusion, delusions, psychosis
Vitamin deficiencies	Anxiety, depression, delusions
Hypoglycemia	Anxiety attacks, depression, feelings of impending doom, confusion
Congestive heart failure	Delusions
Chronic infections	Anxiety, depression, delusions
Wilson's disease	Explosiveness, mood swings, delusions

CASE EXAMPLE

This is a very abbreviated version of an actual psychosocial history, but it will give you the general idea. Since the patient was cooperative and motivated, all the information was gathered in a single evaluation session. You will notice that the write-up does not follow the exact format previously described and does not delve into some of the deeper psychological issues, but it does contain the basic information necessary for the initial assessment. Additional details did surface as therapy progressed, but the clinical picture remained essentially the same.

A diagnosis cannot be made from this information alone, since it does not include the results from the MSE. In chapter 6, "Putting It All Together," you will see how this patient is actually diagnosed.

IDENTIFYING DATA—RONALD T.

Forty-two-year-old white Catholic male. Married nine years, two children, ages nine and seven. Works as a night security supervisor. Appeared for session with wife.

PRESENTING PROBLEM

Insists that his wife has been cheating on him for past eight months but has no evidence. Recently exploded, breaking windows, furniture. Denies ever hitting her. "I love her, but I'm afraid I'm going to hurt her. She says I'm crazy."

PRECIPITANTS, HISTORY OF COMPLAINT

Ron promoted to night supervisor one year ago. Began to suspect wife was having an affair in his absence. Led to confrontations, shouting matches, "uncontrollable rage." Ron frequently drove home on breaks, hid in bushes under bedroom window. Never saw anything. In morning, would check sheets for evidence. Eventually installed a voice-activated tape recorder in bedroom. No evidence, but ripped up house anyway. "He's absolutely obsessed with this and will not listen to reason." Wife gave him ultimatum to attend therapy.

PAST PSYCHIATRIC HISTORY

In therapy ten years ago. Lasted two months. Related to explosive outbursts during first marriage, which lasted three years. "Unfortunately, I only went to therapy to make her happy."

RECENT BACKGROUND INFORMATION

Ron and wife describe nine-year marriage as "very good" until his job change last year. Wife is sober alcoholic, fifteen years. Says she had a series of brief affairs when drinking, before meeting Ron. "He used to drill me about the intimate details, over and over again." She says he has never been controlling in other areas of their life—"it's only been around the jealousy thing." Ron has been steadily employed. Most of time is spent working or attending to tasks. Has few friends, no hobbies. Depends mostly on wife for emotional support. Described as a good father but says he is uncomfortable in that role.

EARLY HISTORY

Younger of two children. Father, an alcoholic, abandoned family after Ron's birth. Mother worked as a waitress, barely supporting the family. Mother had a string of brief relationships. Ron remembers hearing the noisy bedsprings, amorous groans, through thin walls. "It was very confusing for me." She was eventually hospitalized—apparently grew paranoid, felt all men were trying to kill her. Ron also lost a beloved aunt during this time. "I cried but quickly shut it all down."

Ron and brother lived with an uncle during adolescence. Uncle approached Ron sexually but withdrew. "I almost killed him." Ron says he learned to avoid older males, a pattern he still follows. "I kept active in work and sports and tried not to think about things." Older brother was in and out of juvenile detention. "I didn't want to go that route."

Ron supported his mother after her hospitalization, living with her until age twenty-two. She has remarried and lives in Florida. "We have a good relationship, but I still have very mixed feelings about her."

EDUCATION AND VOCATIONAL HISTORY

Completed high school, in spite of a reading disability. Several special classes throughout school history. Good attendance, but was suspended many times for fighting. Has worked steadily at a variety of blue-collar jobs. With current employer for ten years. Indicates some hostility toward "authority types" but has learned to "gloss over my hostility with niceness." Enjoys his work, but performance has been deteriorating over past months.

ALCOHOL AND SUBSTANCE ABUSE

Drank one and one-half cases of beer weekly in his twenties. Has limited himself to one beer daily for past twelve years. "It just made my explosions worse." Denies any other drug use, past or present.

LEGAL HISTORY

Arrested at age twenty-five, driving under the influence. Attended alcohol awareness course. No other legal charges.

RISK BEHAVIORS

Denies thoughts of hurting himself but fears he could hurt others. Denies hitting anyone since adolescence. "I just make threats and destroy things—but even that is very rare."

MEDICAL HISTORY

Head trauma, age four. Fell off swing, hit head. Followed by seizurelike episodes for one year—"spacing out, rolling my eyes." Placed on unknown medication at the time. Seizures stopped by age six. No other medical problems other than chronic low back pain. Drinks five cups of coffee daily; trying to cut down. Does not smoke. Last physical one year ago.

Before Ron can be given an initial diagnosis, the information collected for his psychosocial history needs to be combined with the results of the MSE. The next chapter (chapter 5) explains each part of the exam and what different responses might mean for a patient's diagnosis. You will find the results of Ron's MSE and his diagnosis in chapter 6.

5

HOW THE
THERAPIST
ASSESSES
YOUR MENTAL
STATUS

THE MENTAL STATUS
EXAMINATION (MSE)

Closely Held Diagnostic Secrets

Of all the diagnostic tools that therapists use, aside from psychological testing, the MSE is probably the most closely guarded secret. Although many therapists will vehemently object to the release of this information, you have a right to know what it is and what it means. After all, it is you and your life that are being evaluated.

The moment the therapist lays eyes on you, he or she is collecting impressions that will be used in the diagnosis. While this may seem unnerving, remember that you are also sizing up the therapist: clothes, manner and attitude, the way he or she chews on a pencil or nervously taps a foot. It's a natural, inevitable thing to do. Somehow you end up with an initial impression of the therapist, but you

TABLE 4: PARTS OF THE MENTAL STATUS EXAMINATION (MSE)	
Appearance	Thought Content
Attitude	Perception
Psychomotor Behavior	Attention and Concentration
Alertness	Memory
Orientation	Abstract Thinking
Speech	Intelligence
Mood and Affect	Impulse Control
Thought Process	Judgment and Insight

may not be able to put your finger on all the factors that influenced the picture. You might even attribute your assessment of him or her to an "intuitive sense" about people.

While the therapist also may have an intuitive sense, he or she must be able to justify conclusions. Furthermore, the therapist needs to know some very specific information about your current mental functioning. In order to gather this information, if he or she is like most therapists, your therapist will rely on the format provided by the MSE. As with the psychosocial history, the therapist won't follow the format verbatim but will use it as a guide to organize important thoughts and questions. A reliable *DSM* diagnosis cannot be made without this information.

So what is the MSE? Quite simply, it is a detailed profile of your appearance, speech, thinking pattern, and behavior observed during the interview. Table 4 shows the basic information collected for the MSE, and the pages that follow include a full description of each part.

The MSE was originally developed by psychiatrists. Other mental health professionals have criticized the MSE, stating that it follows the "medical model" too closely and may be demeaning to patients. However, since all therapists must use the diagnostic system developed by psychiatry, they have little choice in the matter—at least in theory. (As you will see in chapter 7, there is often a wide gap between how diagnoses are supposed to be made and the way they are actually made.)

While the MSE is referred to as an "examination," most of the information is actually gathered while you are telling your story. The therapist looks for certain clues that are related to your current mental status and weaves the exam in with his or her questions about your story. You may not even be aware of it. Sometimes, however, the questions are very direct and you will know that you are being "tested."

Some patients are completely put off and offended by the more blatant questions posed by the MSE, particularly if they have to go through the same obnoxious process every time they see a different therapist. This often happens at clinics or hospitals where a patient may see three or more different professionals—an intake evaluator, an ongoing therapist, and a psychiatrist. The patient may feel a bit dehumanized and angry as he or she fends off the routine litany of questions.

Sometimes this can't be avoided. But most of the time, complaints about the MSE can be traced to an insensitive, mechanical, self-important, or hurried therapist. Should you find yourself in that unfortunate situation, voice your concerns! And if you have a choice, why should you pay to be treated like an automaton?

For each part of the exam, the therapist looks for indicators of "abnormal," impaired, or unusual behaviors and responses. An abnormality in any single part lays the groundwork for building a diagnosis or ruling out others; however, *the MSE must be evaluated as a whole,* along with the results of the psychosocial history and other information, before the initial diagnostic impression can be formulated. Although it looks overwhelming, the MSE often can be completed by the therapist using a simple checklist. Most people coming to therapy have only a few problem areas that stand out, so a whole range of diagnoses can be ruled out quickly.

The remainder of this chapter is a reference section describing each part of the MSE and the diagnostic clues that therapists look for. This is followed by some real-life examples. Again, keep in mind that the MSE must be evaluated as a whole. Please refer to part 2 of this book for descriptions of the diagnostic categories mentioned.

1. Appearance

What this part describes: overall physical appearance, including race, body type, grooming, clothing, posture, poise, eye contact, and so forth.

   Clues the therapist looks for: disheveled dress, grossly mismatched or "inappropriate" attire, meticulous neatness, poor hygiene, sickly appearance, particularly youthful- or old-looking, obesity or low body weight, tense or slumped posture, excessive perspiration, avoidance of eye contact.

   What the clues may suggest: Since the assessment of someone's appearance varies with the eye of the beholder, therapists rarely use appearance as a basis for diagnosis unless it is particularly extreme or bizarre. Even then, it's a risky business.

- If a person's hygiene and dress start to go downhill for no apparent reason, it could indicate the beginning of clinical depression, drug or alcohol abuse, a cognitive disorder related to a medical condition such as Alzheimer's disease, or the onset of schizophrenia.

- Grossly inappropriate clothing (e.g., wearing a heavy winter coat in summer, showing up in a swimsuit, wearing only one sock, and so forth) can be a sign that the person is psychotic, or out of touch with reality.

- A sudden uncharacteristic change to flashy, gaudy clothing or excessive makeup can signal the start of a manic episode in some individuals.

- On the other hand, fastidious dress and grooming may point to obsessive-compulsive traits, while seductive manner and dress might suggest a histrionic personality disorder.

- Poor physical health can indicate many disorders, including disease, alcohol or drug abuse, anorexia, bulimia, depression, and schizophrenia.

2.   Attitude

What this part describes: how the patient relates to the therapist.

Clues the therapist looks for: degree of cooperation, friendliness, attentiveness, hostility, suspiciousness, remoteness, apathy, evasiveness, defensiveness, helplessness, apprehension, arrogance, impatience, seductiveness.

What the clues may suggest: The patient's attitude can be influenced by many factors, including the therapist's attitude toward the patient—a fact overlooked by some therapists. Past experience in therapy, the patient's general level of anxiety, and the traffic jam on the way to the session all can influence how the patient might relate to the therapist. Nevertheless, there are certain pervasive attitudes that may indicate a diagnosable problem.

- Overt hostility is found in many disorders, depending upon circumstances, but is frequently seen in patients with antisocial personality disorder, borderline and narcissistic personality disorders, and substance abuse problems. Of course, if someone is evaluated against his or her wishes, hostility is almost guaranteed.

- Apathy and helplessness can be a sign of depression as well as dependent personality disorder. Lethargy is found in some patients with cognitive disorders and other brain dysfunctions with known medical causes.

- Suspiciousness and evasiveness can suggest paranoid tendencies, but when mild they may indicate realistic concerns about confidentiality and/or the therapy process.

- Apprehension, beyond what normally would be expected, is found in many disorders, but patients with generalized anxiety disorder, panic disorder, phobia, PTSD, or OCD are particularly prone to this.

- Remoteness, emotional detachment, and lack of emotional expression are common in schizophrenia.
- Arrogance is often seen in narcissistic personality disorder and in patients with paranoid traits.
- Impatience and distractibility can be signs of a manic episode.

3.   Psychomotor Behavior

What this part describes: any unusual movements, mannerisms, or levels of physical activity.
   Clues the therapist looks for: pacing, agitation, restlessness, hyperactivity, repetitive gestures, aimless activity, slowed responses, stiffness, waxy flexibility, low energy level.
   What the clues may suggest:

- Restlessness, pacing, and agitation can be an indication of an agitated depression or anxiety.
- Hyperactivity in adults may signal the start of a manic episode.
- Slowed responses and low energy level are frequently seen in clinical depression.
- Stiffness, waxy flexibility, no movement, or repetitive movements are seen in various types of schizophrenia.
- Various tics, tremors, and uncontrolled activity may indicate neurological problems or reactions to certain psychiatric medications.

4.   Alertness

What this part describes: level of awareness of the environment and external stimuli, level of consciousness.
   Clues the therapist looks for: a reduced awareness or "clouding" of consciousness, lethargy, stupor, "spells," trances.

What the clues may suggest:

- Drug and/or alcohol ingestion.
- An organic, medical brain disorder such as epilepsy.
- A dissociative or trance disorder.

5. Orientation

What this part describes: the patient's ability to correctly identify the date and time of day, the place he or she is in, his or her name or the names of other people in the area.

Clues the therapist looks for: gross errors in any of the answers describing time, place, or person, including a lack of understanding of the current situation.

What the clues may suggest: Many therapists do not ask direct questions about orientation unless there is good reason to suspect some impairment. Orientation often can be determined during the general conversation.

- Disorientation can be a sign of many psychiatric and medical disorders, including but not limited to substance abuse disorders, cognitive disorders (dementia, delirium, amnestic disorder, and so forth), mental retardation, depression, and schizophrenia.

6. Speech

What this part describes: all aspects of the patient's speech, including speed, flow, volume, nature of speech, and any impairments.

Clues the therapist looks for: All qualities of speech are noticed—for example, rapid or slow, loud, soft, emotional, mumbled, nonstop or pressured, stuttered, spontaneous, hesitant, argumentative, dramatic, and so forth.

What the clues may suggest:

- Depressed patients may speak in a monotone, slowly, and with great effort.

- Anxious patients are more likely to speak continuously and are more difficult to interrupt. Or, depending upon personality, they may speak softly, with much hesitation.

- The speech of manic patients is often rapid, frenzied, and very difficult to interrupt. This may also be true with certain substance abusers.

- Suspicious, paranoid patients may lack spontaneity and respond with very brief, controlled sentences.

- Loud speech can indicate a lack of inhibition or control. Or the patient may have a hearing problem.

- Some schizophrenic patients speak in repetitive rhymes or phrases, often in a monotone. They may combine or make up new words and meanings. Some psychotic patients won't speak at all.

- Problems with rhythm and articulation often point to brain dysfunctions resulting from disease, head trauma, or stroke.

7. Mood and Affect

What this part describes: *Mood* is the general emotional state reported by the patient, such as irritable, anxious, depressed, and so forth. It can last hours or days and influences the way the patient sees the world. *Affect* refers to the outward expression of emotion observed by the therapist and covers the whole spectrum of emotions, including, but not limited to, fear, anger, shame, sadness, suspicion, and joy. Affect can change quickly according to the questions asked by the therapist, even though the underlying mood may remain the same. Affect is shown by facial expressions, body movements, and tone of voice. Sometimes mood and affect don't jibe with each other, as with a patient who reports feeling depressed but smiles throughout the session.

Clues the therapist looks for: Any sustained mood state that the patient reports is important—depressed, anxious, angry, fearful, guilty, elated, confused, hopeless, and so forth. The therapist needs to know how long the mood lasts, how intense it is, if there are any fluctuations, and if the mood changes when life circumstances change.

Affect is also evaluated for its range of expression: either normal, constricted, blunted, or flat. Most people have a wide range of expressions for their feelings—eyes light up or cry, faces scowl, hands move in an animated way, and the voice takes on different pitches. Someone with a constricted affect, however, shows a reduced range of expression, while someone with a blunted affect shows very little emotion. Flat affect is exactly that: the patient may appear robotlike, with no external expression of feelings.

Therapists also look to see if the patient's emotional expression is appropriate to the subject being discussed or the mood reported, e.g., showing no feeling when talking about the recent death of a loved one, and so forth.

What the clues may suggest: The duration of a mood is extremely important for diagnostic purposes. For many disorders, the *DSM* clearly spells out how long a particular mood must last to meet the diagnosis. Here are some examples. Refer to part 2 of this book for specifics.

- For a diagnosis of major depression, the serious depressive symptoms must last for at least two weeks. The mood usually does not change, even for normally pleasurable activities.
- For dysthymia (depressive neurosis), there must be a depressed mood most of the time for at least two years. Pleasure may be experienced from time to time, depending upon circumstances.
- For generalized anxiety disorder, the patient must experience unrealistic worry or excessive anxiety for at least six months.

- For PTSD, the symptoms must persist for at least one month.
- An unpleasant, disturbing mood can last hours or days in the personality disorders and is often tied in with social/relationship problems.
- Pronounced mood shifts can be found in substance abuse, borderline and histrionic personality disorders, brief psychotic disorders, cognitive disorders, and other mental disorders related to certain medical conditions.
- Blunted affect is frequently seen in major depression, PTSD, schizoid personality disorder, and schizophrenia. Flat affect is found most often in severe schizophrenia, although it can also be a side effect of psychiatric medications.
- Constricted, suspicious affect is often seen in obsessive-compulsive and paranoid disorders, while elated, effusive affect may be found in mania, substance abuse, cognitive disorders, and certain medical conditions.
- Lack of agreement between mood and affect might simply mean that the patient is consciously or unconsciously trying (unsuccessfully) to cover his or her symptoms, or it could indicate a more serious problem in the patient's thinking process.

8. Thought Process

What this part describes: This is an extremely important part of the MSE since, along with thought content (no. 9), it helps to determine the presence of a "thought disorder," a disturbance in thinking found in psychosis and certain organic conditions. An evaluation of thought process describes the way a person thinks, how he or she puts ideas together, whether the thinking is logical or illogical, whether the associations make sense, and whether or not the thinking is relevant and directed toward a goal.

Clues the therapist looks for: Since evaluating thought process is quite complex, therapists rely on several very specific signs (table 5):

TABLE 5: PROBLEM SIGNS IN THE THINKING PROCESS	
Loose associations	Word salad
Flight of ideas	Clanging
Circumstantial thought	Neologisms
Tangential thought	Concrete thinking
Thought blocking	Retardation of thought
Perseveration	Vague thought

The presence of any one of the signs does not necessarily mean that the patient has a thought disorder; rather, it is the *degree* of impairment that's important. Let's look at the signs and some examples. (In the examples, each patient has been asked: "What brings you here?")

- **Loose associations:** The ideas expressed do not appear to be connected or related. Or they may be marginally related with a peculiar connection. Either way, the patient jumps from one subject to another, unaware that the associations are loose:
  My brother's one crazy dude. Same as the bitch, that bitch. But you just never know. I mean, it just ain't worth it, man. Just can't do it anymore. All it takes is money. I know. It's screwed.

- **Flight of ideas:** The patient jumps rapidly from one idea to another without reaching a goal. Although the ideas seem to be loosely related, the only connection between the thoughts may be certain words or chance associations.
  I'm fine; how are you? Always the questions, with that cold tone. Florida may be nice, warm. I love the warmth. The Sundance Kid. Do you ever think about skin cancer? Lithium may hurt my kidneys. Those drug companies really make out like bandits.

- **Circumstantial thought:** The thoughts are connected to varying degrees, but the patient is sidetracked by irrelevant details. Many of his or her sentences contribute very little toward reaching a goal. However, the patient eventually makes his or her point, but in a very roundabout way.

Well, I have this thing about the baby, these fears. But I must tell you that I'm not a clumsy person. I've always been coordinated and even played tennis in college. I had so much confidence in those days. I worked nights and graduated with a business degree, A-minus average. True, I would worry about tripping then, but I would just put it out of my mind. Now I find that hard to do, to keep the thoughts out of my mind. I could never hurt my baby, but God, what if I dropped her?

- **Tangential thought:** This is similar to circumstantial thought, but the patient never reaches the point or goal. He or she gets sidetracked by irrelevant details or thoughts and never finds the way back.

She says I'm crazy, with crazy talk. Just because she can't hear him like I do. Some people are just deaf. So she sends me to you or out on my butt I go. One hell of a hard lady. She'll never change. I remember when she hit me with a bottle. Nearly busted my skull. Then we made love. Those were the days, but they wore me out. So what do you want to talk about?

- **Thought blocking:** The flow of thought or speech suddenly stops, often in midsentence. The patient may continue after a pause or lose the thought altogether. Usually the patient can't explain why it happened.

I keep having upsetting dreams about my father. I don't think he would ever do ... do anything, like, I mean ... he never ... [long pause]. Sorry, I can't seem to remember what I was going to say.

- **Perseveration:** The patient seems to get stuck on a certain word, phrase, or idea. He or she may even give the same response to different questions.

I've got this thing about people. With this thing, I'm lonely without people, but I don't want to be with them. That's what the thing is, the thing that bothers me. It's hard to know what to do about this thing I've got.

- **Word salad:** This is an unconnected mixture of words and sentences with no meaning or logic.

Mish mash, I will not, go, go go, Goodyear, ramshackle, hackles, shrinko, shrinkle. Hah! The better for me. Pee pee.

- Other disturbances in thought include:

  Clanging: Connecting thoughts by rhymes.
  Neologisms: Creation of new words.
  Concrete thinking: Does not understand symbolic, abstract meanings.
  Retardation of thought: Slowing of speech and thought.
  Vague thought: Overly abstract, conveying little information.

  What the clues may suggest: An evaluation of the thought process alone cannot lead to a diagnosis. The degree of disturbance must be considered, along with all the other signs and symptoms. Nevertheless, thought process disorders are more commonly found in schizophrenia, manic episodes of bipolar disorder, other psychotic disorders, and cognitive disorders.

- Bipolar patients in the manic phase typically show a flight of ideas.
- Although not all schizophrenic patients have a problem with thought process, nearly all the disturbances above can be found in the various forms and stages of schizophrenia. But none are unique to schizophrenia.
- Patients with OCD may be very circumstantial in their thinking. Anxious patients may also be circumstantial, but this generally improves as they become more comfortable during an evaluation. They may experience mild thought blocking as well.
- Depressed patients may have a retarded thought process, perseveration, or blocking.
- Patients with cognitive disorders and organic brain syndromes in various stages can show evidence of any number of the disturbances listed above.

9.   Thought Content

What this part describes: In contrast to thought process or form, this part describes the predominant themes in the patient's thinking, particularly if the themes are "disturbed" or unusual.

Clues the therapist looks for: Typically, disturbances in thought content are evidenced by the following signs (table 6):

TABLE 6:   SIGNS OF DISTURBANCES IN THOUGHT CONTENT

Delusions	General paranoia
Obsessions	Persistent suicidal or homicidal thoughts
Compulsions	Preoccupations
Phobias	

- **Delusions.** Delusions are evidence of psychosis. They are strongly held but false beliefs that the patient clings to in spite of obvious evidence that the beliefs are not true. No amount of reasoning, logic, or incontrovertible evidence will convince the patient otherwise. The beliefs or ideas are not consistent with the patient's educational or cultural background. Delusions can be nonbizarre (based on things that could actually happen in real life) or bizarre (totally unbelievable, unrelated to reality as we know it). There are several different types of delusions, including:

  Delusions of persecution: The patient insists he or she is being harassed, cheated, followed, spied upon, conspired against.

  Delusions of grandeur: The patient is convinced of his or her great importance, unrecognized powers, talents, or discoveries.

  Delusions of being controlled: These are more bizarre. The patient insists that others are controlling his or her thoughts and actions through radio waves, evil looks, possession, special forces, and so forth.

Delusions of reference: The patient is convinced that the actions or words of others have special meanings directed at him or her. For example, the patient may wrongly believe that the television news is about him or her or giving a personal message.

Delusions of worthlessness, guilt: The patient believes he or she is worthless, evil, wicked, or weak and deserves to be punished to allay guilt.

Other delusions include: jealous, erotic, and somatic (fixation on body defects, odors, and so forth).

- **Obsessions:** These are persistent, intrusive thoughts, feelings, or impulses that are unacceptable to the patient. They are not influenced by logical reasoning.

- **Compulsions:** In contrast to obsessions, compulsions are repetitive, intrusive, unwanted actions that the patient feels compelled to perform. They are often carried out in response to an obsession. Examples include counting, checking, and hand washing.

- **Phobias:** These are persistent, unrealistic fears of certain things or situations. Exposure leads to overwhelming anxiety. The patient may also experience great anxiety anticipating the object or situation.

- **General paranoia:** Some people have a very suspicious, defensive view of the world and persistently misinterpret the benign actions of others as threatening or demeaning. Such people often feel harassed or persecuted and are quick to take offense. This form of paranoid thinking usually does not reach delusional intensity: the person is not psychotic and can listen to reason, although he or she is likely to maintain a suspicious outlook.

- **Persistent suicidal or homicidal thoughts:** With certain individuals, these thoughts can be persistent and recurring. Many patients have suicidal or homicidal thoughts but no intention of acting on them. Others fear they will lose control and act on the impulses. Therefore, it is extremely important that the therapist ask about plans and intentions.

- **Preoccupations:** Typically, these center around unexplained physical symptoms or body defects. Although there is no evidence of physical illness or a pronounced defect, the patient has an exaggerated concern about health and may be preoccupied with certain body organs or serious diseases. Sometimes the preoccupations turn into rigid, fixed beliefs that reach delusional intensity.

What the clues may suggest: As with the disorders of thought process, an evaluation of the thought content alone cannot lead to a diagnosis. Also, some patients become very adept at hiding their more questionable thoughts. Through experience, they have learned what others might regard as "crazy." In those instances, a perplexed therapist might request psychological testing.

- The *DSM* has a category called delusional disorder, which covers most of the nonbizarre delusions listed above, including persecutory, grandiose, jealous, erotic, and somatic. However, schizophrenia, mania, and major depression must be ruled out first to make the diagnosis. (See part 2.)
- Most of the delusions, bizarre and nonbizarre, can be found in various forms of schizophrenia, although not everyone suffering from schizophrenia experiences delusions.
- Delusions can also be found in cognitive disorders and other medical diseases.
- Patients suffering from major depression can experience delusions of worthlessness and guilt, or even delusions of persecution and control. This is known as major depression with psychotic features.

- Manic patients may experience delusions of grandiosity or persecution.
- Obsessions and compulsions are usually found together in OCD. Sometimes the patient no longer rejects the obsessions and compulsions as unreasonable. At that point, they become more like psychotic delusions.
- Phobias are not a sign of psychosis. In the *DSM*, they are classified as anxiety disorders.
- General paranoia is most often seen in patients with paranoid or schizotypal personality disorders. It can also be a part of certain cognitive disorders, medical diseases, and substance abuse disorders.
- Persistent suicidal or homicidal thoughts can be found in a wide variety of emotional disorders and do not point to any particular diagnosis. However, a mood disorder and/or personality disorder may be the first suspect(s).
- Somatic preoccupations with no known physical evidence can be symptoms of a somatoform disorder such as hypochondriasis or body dysmorphic disorder (BDD). (See part 2.) These are not psychotic disorders. However, if the patient is unable to consider the possibility that the preoccupations are exaggerated or unrealistic, a somatic delusion (psychosis) may be indicated.

  Diagnoses involving somatic preoccupations are particularly tricky because of the complexity of the mind-body relationship and the possibility that a medical diagnosis has indeed been missed. Traditionally, it has been too easy for many physicians and therapists to write off certain physical symptoms as psychological.

10. Perception

What this part describes: any distortions in the way the patient perceives "reality," either through sight, hearing, smell, taste, or touch. Whether or not a perception is seen as a pathological distortion depends upon cultural norms and the prevailing view of reality. The more serious distortions take the form of illusions and hallucinations.

Clues the therapist looks for:

- **Illusions** are distortions of reality based on a
  misinterpretation of things and experiences that actually
  exist: the sound of rain may be misinterpreted as applause,
  shadows seen as monsters, sounds of the wind interpreted
  as voices. Most people have experienced brief illusions when
  tired, anxious, or expecting to see or hear something, but
  they quickly correct themselves as they investigate the source
  further. Problems arise when the illusions are frequent,
  persistent, and accepted as reality in spite of evidence to the
  contrary.
- Unlike illusions, which are based on actual stimuli,
  hallucinations are sensory perceptions that are not based
  on any known, real stimuli in the physical world. Examples
  include: hearing voices when no people are around, seeing
  hatchets floating in the air above the head, feeling nonexistent
  bugs crawling under the skin, smelling pungent burning
  rubber when no one else smells it, and tasting all food as bitter
  poison.
- **Depersonalization** is a feeling of strangeness, unreality, and
  detachment. The patient may feel like he or she is outside
  his or her own body or observing him- or herself as if in a
  dream. This is often accompanied by **derealization**, a
  feeling that reality has changed, perhaps in shape or size. The
  patient is aware of the distortions and usually is distressed
  by them.

What the clues may suggest: Traditionally, psychiatry has seen almost all illusions and hallucinations as indicators of "abnormal" mental states. The narrow-mindedness of this position is evident when one stops to consider that various cultural groups all over the world experience "hallucinations" as part of their normal religious ceremonies. Hearing the voices of dead spirits or seeing visions is not out of the ordinary for many cultures. Hence, judging whether or not a perceptual "distortion" is an indication of "pathology" involves a close examination and understanding of the patient's cultural base, as well as his or her philosophical and metaphysical beliefs.

A mental disorder may be indicated if the hallucinations or illusions differ significantly from the cultural/consensual reality and if the patient has the other signs and symptoms required to make the diagnosis. Many of these disorders, such as schizophrenia, manic-depressive (bipolar) disorder, and perhaps major depression, are found in all cultures.

- Illusions are often seen in various drug-induced states, schizophrenia, organic brain syndromes, and schizotypal personality disorder. Patients with PTSD and other anxiety disorders may also experience illusions.

- Auditory hallucinations are the most common perceptual disturbances. They are most prevalent in schizophrenia but are found in other disorders as well.

- Patients suffering from a major depression may also experience auditory hallucinations, as might manic-depressive (bipolar) patients.

- Stress can induce hallucinations. People with certain personality disorders (borderline, narcissistic, paranoid, histrionic, and so forth) appear to be more vulnerable to stress-induced hallucinations.

- Hallucinations involving sight, smell, touch, and taste are less frequently found and may be signs of alcohol and/or drug ingestion or withdrawal, epilepsy, or other medical conditions.

- Some hallucinations, such as the kind experienced midway between wakefulness and sleep, are common and rarely indicative of a problem.
- Auditory and/or visual hallucinations sometimes are experienced after the death of a loved one and may be a normal part of grieving for some people.
- Feelings of depersonalization and derealization alone are not symptoms of psychosis, even thought the person may feel like he or she is going crazy. Anxiety and stress can trigger these feelings in many people, or they can be brought about by deep meditation and other trance-inducing procedures. Organic disorders, such as epilepsy, can also give rise to depersonalization. If the experiences are distressful, persistent, severe, and appear with no other disorder, the person may be suffering from a "depersonalization disorder." (See part 2.)

11.   Attention and Concentration

What this part describes: Attention and concentration go hand in hand but have slightly different meanings. *Attention* refers to a person's ability to focus on specific things that are generally outside of him- or herself, as in listening to directions or watching a movie. *Concentration* is the ability to focus on internal tasks and thought processes, such as those involved in completing a mathematical problem or writing a poem. Both concentration and attention are required for most tasks.

   Clues the therapist looks for: Generally, the therapist can assess attention and concentration by the way the patient handles the interview. If the patient seems particularly distracted, has difficulty filling out the forms, or has trouble focusing on and answering questions, the therapist may have him or her do some brief tasks:

- To test attention, the therapist might have the patient listen to and repeat a list of seven digits, both forward and backward.

- To measure concentration, the therapist might ask the patient to subtract a certain number repeatedly downward from 100.

What the clues may suggest: Concentration and attention may be diminished in many disorders, including anxiety disorders, mood disorders, substance abuse disorders, adjustment disorders, developmental and childhood behavioral disorders, and cognitive disorders. These abilities can also be impaired if the patient is preoccupied with internal hallucinations. Since so many disorders have impaired concentration and attention, the therapist must determine the degree of impairment and identify those factors (anxiety, depression, a thought disorder, and so forth) that may be getting in the way. The other parts of the MSE may provide the clues.

12. Memory

What this part describes: *Immediate memory* is the ability to recall information after five to ten seconds. *Recent memory* involves recall after several minutes to several months. Most activities of daily living depend on recent memory. *Remote memory* is the ability to recall information after many months or years.

Clues the therapist looks for: Therapists can get a general idea about the patient's memory abilities just by listening and asking a few questions. However, since many patients with memory problems try to hide them by talking around questions or making up answers, the therapist has to keep an eye out for evasive answers and inconsistencies. Further testing may be necessary.

- A patient with problems in immediate recall may repeatedly forget the therapist's name within seconds of being told. Or the patient may forget what he or she has just spoken about. To test further, the therapist can have the patient repeat four words (e.g., *ball, jump, red, large*) several seconds after hearing them.
- Problems in recent memory may show up as the patient speaks about his or her current life situation. The patient may have

difficulty describing how he or she got to the therapist's office or may forget what happened in the news yesterday. The therapist can further test this by asking the patient to repeat the four words again after thirty minutes.

- If the therapist has access to verifiable information about the patient's past history, he or she can use it to test remote memory. If this is not available, the therapist can ask the patient about well-known, popular events from the distant past.

What the clues may suggest:

- Anxiety and depression can temporarily interfere with memory. This should improve as the depression and/or anxiety decrease(s).
- Memory disturbances occur in the dissociative disorders, including amnesia, fugue, and MPD. In these disorders, the memory loss is usually triggered by traumatic events and can be treated. Memory impairment also can be seen in PTSD. (See part 2 for specifics.)
- Memory deficits are commonly associated with substance/ alcohol abuse or withdrawal.
- In alcohol-induced amnestic disorder (Korsakoff's syndrome), brought on by years of alcohol abuse, immediate memory is intact but deteriorates after a few minutes. The patient has problems remembering events occurring within the past several minutes to several months. Memory for remote events (months or years ago) remains intact. The condition is chronic.
- Severe memory impairment is almost always seen in the cognitive disorders, such as Alzheimer's disease. Recent memory is usually the first to deteriorate. As the disease progresses, the patient has difficulty learning new

information. Remote memory is impaired in the advanced stages of Alzheimer's.

- Brain tumors, head trauma, and certain diseases can all lead to varying degrees of memory impairment.

13.   Abstract Thinking

What this part describes: the ability to grasp and use concepts and ideas.

Clues the therapist looks for: Some patients show concrete thinking; they miss the overall idea and interpret things literally. For example, if the therapist asks such a patient to explain the meaning of the saying "Sticks and stones may break my bones, but words will never hurt me," he or she may respond, "Sticks and stones are hard and can hurt you, but words are just sounds." While the answer is not incorrect, it misses the larger meaning. On the other hand, some patients are overly abstract and general.

The patient may also have difficulties understanding the relationship between concepts. To test for this, the therapist may use the similarities test. The patient is asked to explain how certain things, such as a bicycle and a bus, are similar. The answers can indicate various levels of abstract thinking: "both have wheels"; "you ride on both"; "both are means of transportation."

As seen in the examples, therapists sometimes use proverb interpretation and the similarities test to assess levels of abstract thinking. More often, however, the levels can be picked up in normal conversation with the patient. Language and cultural differences must be taken into consideration.

What the clues may suggest:

- Impairments in abstract thinking are primarily related to low intelligence and/or cognitive mental disorders such as alcohol-related dementia and Alzheimer's disease.
- Average and above-average levels of abstract thinking are generally required for insight-oriented psychotherapy.

14.   Intelligence

What this part describes: *Intelligence* is a very broad term that is used to describe the sum total of a person's capacity to learn, understand, and apply knowledge. Intelligence is made up of many different parts.

    Clues the therapist looks for: The therapist usually can get an idea of the patient's general level of intelligence without doing any formal testing. The patient's knowledge about the world, vocabulary, and ability to understand and use concepts become apparent during the conversation. In sizing this up, the therapist must take into account the patient's educational and cultural background.

    What the clues may suggest:

- Impairments in intelligence are often related to mental retardation and other developmental disorders, as well as the cognitive disorders. If the patient's intelligence has deteriorated markedly over time, the therapist may suspect an organic mental disorder such as dementia. Further testing will be necessary.
- Emotional problems such as depression can also interfere with a person's intellectual performance. In spite of this, the therapist can still get a good idea of "pre-illness" intellectual level by looking at the patient's vocabulary and his or her general fund of information. Unless some memory impairment is involved, these two parts of intelligence are the least vulnerable to illness.

15.   Impulse Control

What this part describes: the patient's ability to control aggressive, sexual, suicidal, or any other impulses that may be harmful or seen as socially inappropriate.

    Clues the therapist looks for: The therapist can assess degree of impulse control by looking through the psychosocial history, observing the patient's behavior during the session, and asking direct questions. Research has shown that someone who has lost control in the past is more likely to lose it again under stressful circumstances, although this is not always the case. If there have been suicide attempts or assaults on others in the past, the therapist must weigh this against the feelings currently reported by the patient.

What the clues may suggest:

- Lack of impulse control can be seen in a wide variety of disorders ranging from the cognitive/organic disorders, to the psychoses, to the personality disorders, to the substance abuse disorders.
- In the personality disorders, patients with antisocial or borderline disorders show a higher incidence of destructive and/ or self-destructive, impulsive behaviors.
- Patients with major depression may also have suicidal impulses, although not all suicidal patients are clinically depressed.
- PTSD can also involve reduced ability to control impulses.
- Other very specific impulse disorders include intermittent explosive disorder, kleptomania (impulsive stealing), pathological gambling, pyromania (fire setting), and trichotillomania (hair pulling). See part 2 for further discussion of these disorders.
- If a patient appears to be in imminent danger of seriously hurting him- or herself or others, the therapist is legally obligated to intervene. This kind of decision is seldom clear-cut and places an enormous burden of responsibility upon the therapist, not to mention the additional stress on the patient.

16. Judgment and Insight

What this part describes: *Judgment* refers to the patient's ability to assess social situations, understand the consequences of his or her behavior, and work toward realistic goals.

For the purposes of the MSE, intellectual *insight* is seen as the patient's ability to acknowledge and understand that something is wrong, that he or she may be ill. True psychological insight goes beyond this definition and involves knowledge of thoughts, feelings, motivations, and defenses that may be contributing to the distress.

Clues the therapist looks for: To assess judgment, therapists often ask patients about their future goals and how they will go about attaining them. This gives the therapist an idea how a patient sees his or her abilities against the realities of the social world. Goals may be grossly understated, overstated, or totally unrealistic: a depressed but very successful physician planning on leaving his practice, convinced that he is inept; the young woman who expects every man to fall in love with her and bases her life on that premise; or the patient who feels called by God to save the world. Therapists also assess judgment as the patient reports his or her handling of current life situations.

Insight exists on several different levels. The man who adamantly believes he is Superman and denies that anything is wrong with his thinking has no insight (unless he can leap tall buildings in a single bound). The patient who hears voices and knows he is sick but blames it on the devil has partial intellectual insight. The woman who compulsively washes her hands but knows it is irrational has good intellectual insight—even though she may not understand why she washes her hands.

What the clues may suggest:

- In most people, judgment is extremely vulnerable to emotional distress. Ideas about ourselves and others can change subtly or dramatically according to the degree of depression and anxiety experienced. We all know people, if not ourselves, who have been through this.
- Judgment tends to deteriorate according to the severity of the psychiatric disorder.
- Unless they are experiencing delusions and hallucinations, most patients with mood and/or anxiety disorders have

fair to good intellectual insight about the nature and extent of their illness. However, this does not mean that they necessarily have good psychological insight.

- Psychological insight may be more limited in patients with personality disorders, but this can often change with therapy.

- Therapists gear the level of therapy to the level of insight shown by the patient.

CASE EXAMPLE

Patricia, a twenty-seven-year-old teacher, was eventually diagnosed with bipolar disorder, manic, based on the MSE and the psychosocial history. She was told to come to therapy by her husband. Here is the mental status part of her evaluation:

Appearance: Short, somewhat overweight white female. Wearing a sequined evening dress, heavy makeup. Appears self-assured, effusive. Says she feels good in the dress. "I wore it to celebrate this occasion." Carried in two bags of groceries. "It's too hot to leave them in the car."

Attitude toward examiner: Overbearing, invasive, but in a friendly, good-natured way. Placed grocery bags on examiner's desk without asking, knocked off pile of papers. Asked many personal questions about the examiner, reached over, patted his hand repeatedly. Tried to be cooperative, but too easily distracted.

Psychomotor behavior: Very active, rarely able to sit still. Stood up several times to make a point. Had to be directed back to the chair. Laughed, apologized, and sat down.

Orientation: Accurately described time, place, person.

Manner of speech: Loud, emotional, pressured. Very difficult to interrupt.

Mood and affect: Says she feels great, can't understand why her husband thinks she needs help. Says everything is going "wonderfully" in her life, except that her husband doesn't want her to enjoy herself. "He's just a couch potato. If I'm not depressed, he thinks there's something wrong." Says she was hospitalized for depression two years ago. Mood is elated, expansive. Affect is consistent with mood. For the past week, has been sleeping only three to four hours nightly. Drinks rarely. Denies substance abuse.

Thought process and content: Process marked by flight of ideas, jumping from subject to subject, but associations are fairly logical. Says it feels like her thoughts are flying. "But there are so many wonderful things to think about." Patient says she is making plans to travel to Hong Kong, London, "then maybe to Nice." Says money is no object (contrary to financial info). Content focused on travel, great accomplishments.

Perceptual disturbances: Denies hallucinations, illusions. No evidence during interview.

Attention and concentration: Poor. Highly distractible. Very brief attention span—three digits forward and backward. Not able to do serial 7s. Kept laughing, saying it was silly.

Memory: Hard to test since she is so distracted, but appears to be intact.

Abstract thinking: Intact, but tends toward vagueness.

Intelligence: Appears to be above average, consistent with her education and accomplishments.

Impulse control: Denies any suicidal or homicidal thoughts or intentions, denies any history of impulsive behavior "except I love spending money."

Judgment and insight: Judgment is impaired. Her life is becoming increasingly disorganized. Has unrealistic plans, no means to attain them. Plans change from moment to moment. Impaired judgment leading to consequences, i.e., threat of dismissal from job. Insight is poor. She acknowledges feeling elated but denies it's causing any problems or that she is in need of treatment. "It's really no one's business but mine. They're just jealous of my freedom."

CASE EXAMPLE

Rhonda, age twenty-one, had been married for three months when she came in for therapy. She was initially diagnosed as having a generalized anxiety disorder. However, as more information from her history became available, she was given the additional diagnosis of dependent personality disorder.

Appearance: African-American female, very neat, conservative dress. Extremely polite, poised. Good eye contact, but seemed to be looking everywhere at once.

Attitude toward examiner: Very cooperative, perhaps too eager to please. Asked permission to sit, apologized profusely if she felt she was unable to answer all questions. Kept asking for reassurances about her responses. "What do you think?" and "What should I do?" were frequent questions. Had a clinging quality. Difficulty ending the session.

Psychomotor behavior: Very tense, constricted, hands shaking. When asked about this, she replied, "If I let it loose, I'm afraid I'll pass out or have a heart attack. I almost always feel tense like this." Appeared to be hypervigilant.

Orientation: Intact.

Manner of speech: Articulate, soft-spoken, hesitant. But at times seemed to "burst forth" with emotional material.

Mood and affect: Describes her mood as "total anxiety all the time." Experiences dizziness, heart palpitations, feelings of suffocation, restlessness, irritability, hot flashes. "I worry myself sick about absolutely everything—money, whether I'm good enough for my husband, that he'll leave me, that I'm stupid, that my parents will die, that the house will burn down, you name it. My husband says it's crazy and he's right, but I can't stop." Says the anxiety is making her depressed. Anxiety symptoms have persisted for the past year. Affect appeared very tense, fearful, vigilant, although patient worked hard to maintain a poised stance.

Thought process and content: Thought process appears to

be intact, logical, although somewhat circumstantial. Mild thought blocking at times. Content is focused on unrealistic fears, physical symptoms of anxiety. Predominant themes are fears of abandonment, inability to make decisions on her own, helplessness, need for approval.

Perceptual disturbances: None, but says she is quick to misinterpret noises and shadows as lurking danger.

Attention and concentration: Attended to examiner's questions but couldn't do digit span—threw her hands up, saying she was too nervous, didn't want to try again. Very apologetic. Concentration poor, says her mind goes blank. "But I do better at home."

Memory: Intact, but immediate recall limited by anxiety.

Abstract thinking: Good.

Intelligence: Appears to be average or above.

Impulse control: Good, past and present. Denies suicidal, homicidal ideation. "But sometimes I'm afraid I'm just going to scream and cry and come unglued in front of everyone."

Judgment and insight: Both good, although she doesn't seem to be aware at this point of the extent of her dependencies or her approval-seeking behavior.

CASE EXAMPLE

Phil, age twenty-two, came into therapy because he couldn't stand looking at his own face. Although he still lived with his parents, he had become increasingly isolated, rarely leaving his room. He eventually lost his job as a paralegal. His preliminary diagnosis was body dysmorphic disorder (BDD).

Appearance: Tall, well-built, athletic white male. No remarkable features. Eye contact poor, as if shy, but general manner was outgoing.

Attitude toward examiner: Cooperative, friendly,

spontaneous—but acknowledged that he feels uncomfortable showing his face.

Psychomotor behavior: Unremarkable.

Orientation: Intact.

Manner of speech: Tends to give detailed account, but otherwise unremarkable. Articulate.

Mood and affect: Patient describes feeling increasingly sad, depressed, and trapped because of his isolation, recent loss of his job. The sad mood comes and goes, but he still feels hopeful. Affect appears sad, particularly during silences. Normal range of affect.

Thought process and content: Logical, but some perseveration when discussing his face. Patient is preoccupied with the size of his nose, feels it is grossly disproportionate to his face. "I became aware of it about six months ago. If I look down, I see this thing jutting out from my face; it's absolutely gross and I don't want anyone else to see it. And God, it's something else again if I have to blow it in public." (His nose is slightly large but hardly noticeable.) Patient is considering surgery, although his parents tell him he's being crazy. He can give no explanation for the sudden focus on his nose. "It never bothered me before, but now the damned thing is driving me crazy." Patient says he tends to get obsessive about things. Currently no signs of other obsessive thoughts or behaviors. Patient can consider the possibility that his concerns are exaggerated. No delusional intensity.

Perceptual disturbances: None other than perceiving his nose as very large.

Attention and concentration: Good.

Memory: Intact.

Intelligence: Above average.

Abstract thinking: High level.

Impulse control: Appears to be good, past and present.

Judgment and insight: Patient's judgment is influenced by his preoccupation—social and vocational areas beginning to deteriorate as a result. He is aware that something may be wrong but can't break away from the preoccupation. He is still considering surgery. "What harm could it do? At least I would stop worrying and get on with my life."

As you can see, the MSE can provide important information. It is most useful in sorting through or ruling out the more serious psychiatric problems, as well as certain emotional problems related to medical diseases. Unfortunately, some therapists (usually psychiatrists) rely on it far too much and, in their diagnostic zeal, gloss over the context and depth of a person's life. Other therapists, in their efforts to understand and "connect" with a person's experience, sometimes minimize the MSE and miss important diagnostic clues that could lead to more successful treatment.

To make an official diagnosis using the *DSM*, therapists must combine the results of the MSE with information gleaned from the psychosocial history. This often tenuous process is described in the next chapter.

6

PUTTING
IT ALL
TOGETHER

MAKING THE
DIAGNOSIS

After submitting yourself to dozens of probing questions and examinations of your behavioral, thinking, and feeling patterns, the time has finally come for the official label that may somehow provide an explanation for your emotional pain. From the therapist's perspective, this can be a daunting experience, as he or she wades through reams of notes and reports, particularly since the entire process must be completed in one or two sessions.

How in the world can it all be reduced to a single diagnostic summary? A diagnostic category is defined by perhaps three short paragraphs of symptoms and behavioral signs in the *DSM* ... how can it possibly reflect the subtle complexities of a life story?

The truth of the matter is ... it can't. As you may recall from chapter 2, diagnoses are seldom definitive and are subject to many, many pitfalls. It is important to remember that they have been developed by the APA and reflect a particular way of viewing and ordering the mind-body complex. Diagnoses evolve or even regress as society changes. For example, if certain politicians have their way, homosexuality, whether or not it has biological origins, would once again be classified as a psychiatric illness.

And if we believe the spiraling statistics presented by the professional organizations, all of us are likely to be diagnosable and in need of therapy at some point in our lives—particularly as researchers work fast and furiously to develop diagnostic categories for an incredible array of human behaviors. If nothing else, this is certainly good for business. With that said, it is time to see how therapists put together the diagnostic puzzle.

Pieces of the Puzzle

As you saw in chapters 3–5, therapists try to collect a vast array of very detailed, specific information. When diagnosing adults, this information usually includes:

- The psychosocial history, including a medical history.
- Results of the MSE.
- Information from interviews with family members or friends, if available and agreed upon. (Emergency situations have different rules about this.)
- Results of any psychological testing.
- And, last but not least, the degree of insurance coverage.

Therapists use a variety of strange and unusual methods to sort through and make sense of this information. If you believe the textbooks and the promotional material of the various mental health professional organizations, diagnosis should be a fairly clear-cut process using the latest research and some keenly developed, objective techniques.

Unfortunately, in most cases, this is simply not true. The ballyhooed "cutting edge" is dulled by the vagaries of human perception, cultural fashion, and administrative brickwork. But before elaborating on this state of affairs (see chapter 7), it is helpful to know how the diagnosis is *supposed* to be culled, clean and neat, from the above information. The key to this, as you already know, is the *DSM*.

USING THE BIBLE OF PSYCHIATRIC DIAGNOSIS

Searching for Symptoms and Signs

The *DSM* has been revised several times since it was first published in 1952. Many diagnostic categories have come and gone over the past forty years, just as they are likely to come and go in the future. In early editions, the categories were poorly defined and grouped according to the possible "causes" of the distress. More often than not, the diagnosis indicated more about the therapist and his or her particular theoretical orientation than anything about the patient.

The more recent editions of the *DSM* (*DSMIII-R*, 1987, and *DSMIV*, 1994) rarely address the possible psychological or sociological causes of distress. Instead, each category is simply a descriptive list of certain *symptoms and signs*, along with criteria concerning their onset and duration. *Symptoms* are the distressful feelings reported by the patient—anxiety, inability to sleep, feelings of worthlessness, frequent crying, and so forth. *Signs* are the behavioral observations made by the evaluating therapist—poor hygiene, hyperactivity, monotonous, flat speech, illogical thinking, attitude, and so forth. Part 2 of this book provides many examples of diagnostic criteria based on signs and symptoms.

For a diagnosis to be made, the patient's symptoms and signs must match the very specific criteria listed in the *DSM*. You might be surprised to learn that most diagnoses, other than the "personality disorders," can actually be made with little or no regard for the range and depth of the patient's life experience. The subtle complexities of his or her life story may be important for most forms of therapy, but they play a limited role in determining the diagnosis. This can lead to some of the difficulties you read about in chapter 2, particularly since signs and symptoms may mean different things in different ethnic groups and cultures.

The *DSM* system of looking for signs and symptoms is based on a medical perspective, the same theoretical model used to diagnose medical diseases. This explains why all the categories are referred to as "disorders," even if they are simply adjustment problems related to a particular situation. Although many disorders do indeed appear to have strong biological features, these account for a relatively small portion of the *DSM* categories. As a result, there is much debate within the field about the merits of using such a cut-and-dried medical model for diagnosing all varieties of emotional distress—but most therapists find it useful as a general guide. More important, they must use the *DSM* for insurance and administrative purposes, whether they agree with it or not.

Sifting, Sorting, and More Sorting

To understand how a therapist might arrive at a diagnosis, you must know how the *DSM* is organized. This is important, since most therapists now tend to shape their interview questions according to the information required to make a match with the *DSM* categories. So, for better or worse, the therapist's thinking is strongly influenced by the *DSM* organization. (Since the *DSM* is "reorganized" every few years, you can imagine how confusing this can be to therapists. Many cling to the older categories and definitions in spite of changes.)

The *DSM* uses what is known as a "multiaxial system" to evaluate a patient on five different levels. Each level is called an "axis." It is not as intimidating as it sounds. You saw an example of this in chapter 1 of this book. This was Anita's five-level diagnostic picture:

Axis I: 296.32 Major Depression, Recurrent
302.71 Rule out Hypoactive Sexual Desire Disorder

Axis II: 301.60 Dependent Personality Disorder, Hysterical Features

Axis III: Chronic headaches, yeast infections

Axis IV: Severity of stressor: 3 (Moderate)
Psychosocial stressor: Relationship problems

Axis V: Current Global Assessment of Functioning (GAF): 55
Serious to moderate symptoms. Suicidal ideation, denies intent

During the interview, the therapist gathers as much information as he or she can that will allow some sort of decision to be made for each axis or level. Sometimes one or more diagnoses are placed on each axis. The signs and symptoms experienced often overlap more than one diagnostic category, just as a medical patient can suffer from migraine headaches and epilepsy at the same time. This is particularly true of Axis I, since the disorders listed there are the most prevalent. Axis II disorders are not nearly as common. Often there is no diagnosis given on that axis.

Axis I—Mental Disorders

Axis I is used to list any mental disorders found, except the personality disorders, which are reserved for Axis II. Table 7 shows the Axis I major diagnostic categories used in the *DSM*.

Each major category is divided into subcategories or "clinical syndromes." It is the clinical syndromes that are actually listed on Axis I. Major depression is a syndrome of the mood disorders, as is bipolar disorder (manic-depression). Panic disorder is a syndrome of the anxiety disorders, and so forth. Each syndrome is given an identifying number.

There are approximately two hundred syndromes that can be listed on Axis I. It might be helpful to refer to part 2 of this book to see how some of the major categories and syndromes are organized. You will also find the code numbers used for insurance purposes.

Axis II—Personality Disorders

"Personality disorders" are certain maladaptive personality traits and behavioral patterns that persist throughout an individual's life. They are ingrained, characteristic ways of thinking and behaving that repeatedly result in social impairment. Often, however, the behavior causes more distress to family, friends, and coworkers than to the individual. More than other diagnostic categories, the diagnosis of

TABLE 7: MAJOR *DSM* DIAGNOSTIC CATEGORIES FOR AXIS I	
Disorders first diagnosed during infancy, childhood, or adolescence	Somatoform disorders
Cognitive disorders	Factitious disorders
Mental disorders due to medical conditions	Dissociative disorders
Substance-related disorders	Sexual disorders
Schizophrenia and other psychotic disorders	Gender identity disorders
Mood disorders	Eating disorders
Anxiety disorders	Sleep disorders
	Impulse control disorders
	Adjustment disorders
	Other miscellaneous conditions

a personality disorder is ultimately a social statement about a person's behavior. This can vary from culture to culture.

The personality disorders found in the *DSM* are listed in table 8. All involve certain extreme ways of seeing, behaving, and relating to the world, resulting in social difficulties.

The personality disorder categories labeled as "needing further study" were included in the appendix of the *DSMIII-R*, but because of inadequate research data supporting their "existence," they were not given an official number. Nevertheless, therapists used them frequently and included them in a catchall category: 301.9, personality disorder not otherwise specified (NOS). (Refer to part 2 for details.)

Although self-defeating and sadistic personality disorders have mysteriously disappeared from the new *DSMIV*, it is likely that therapists will stick to old habits—at least for several years. *DSMIV* has also demoted passive-aggressive personality disorder to the appendix, where it rests in limbo with a slew of other "unofficial" disorders. As you can see, these things come and go. . . .

TABLE 8: *DSM* PERSONALITY DISORDERS FOR AXIS II

Group A
Paranoid personality disorder
Schizoid personality disorder
Schizotypal personality disorder

Group B
Antisocial personality disorder
Borderline personality disorder
Histrionic personality disorder
Narcissistic personality disorder

Group C
Avoidant personality disorder
Dependent personality disorder
Obsessive-Compulsive personality disorder
Passive-Aggressive personality disorder (*DSMIII-R*)

Categories Needing Further Study
Sadistic personality disorder (*DSMIII-R*)
Self-defeating personality disorder (*DSMIII-R*)

Axis III—General Medical Conditions

This axis is used to list any current medical and physical conditions that may be related or relevant to the emotional disorder. Since there are many medical conditions that can cause or contribute to psychiatriclike symptoms, it is important to fully explore these possibilities.

Axis IV—Psychosocial and Environmental Problems: Stressors

The *DSMIII-R* uses a 6-point scale to rate the severity of psychosocial stressors in the patient's life according to certain criteria: 1 = none, 2 = mild, 3 = moderate, 4 = severe, 5 = extreme, and 6 = catastrophic. As an example, "moderate" might be the loss of a job or a marital separation, while "extreme" might be the death of a spouse or rape.

Obviously, therapists differ widely how they might rate these stressors, in spite of vague guidelines offered by the *DSM*. Because of these difficulties, the rating scale has been dropped from the *DSMIV*. Instead, the therapist simply lists the areas of stress.

Axis V—Global Assessment of Functioning (GAF)

For this axis, the therapist judges the patient's current functioning as well as the highest level of functioning over the past year. A 90-point scale is used, based on a continuum of mental health to mental illness, with 90 indicating good functioning in all areas, including social, occupational, and psychological functioning. Ideally, the therapist uses a *DSM* table for these purposes.

As an example, a score of 50 is used for someone with serious symptoms (suicidal ideation, obsessive rituals, and so forth) or serious difficulties in social functioning, while a score of 10 might be given to someone who is in persistent danger of hurting him- or herself or others or is not able to care for him- or herself.

TRIMMING, MIXING, AND MATCHING

To see how all of this works, at least in theory, it is helpful to look at a real-life example. Bear in mind that therapists are trained in many different orientations and use a wide variety of techniques and personal styles in gathering the information. But, in the end, they are all expected to use a similar mix-and-match routine to ferret out the diagnostic picture.

However, as you know, life is never so simple, consistent, or clear. Reality tends to twist and turn according to the eye of the beholder. As you will see in chapter 7, a very disconcerting view of reality emerges as the psychiatric eye peers through the rather messy, confusing mazes of the mental health and insurance systems. Things get a bit hazy, if not downright obscured.

But for now, our focus is on the *DSM* ideal. Let's start with a fairly straightforward case that a beginning therapist could diagnose easily. Each step of the process is described in detail so that you will see how a person's story is actually translated into a diagnostic picture.

CASE 1:
Pollution Control

Mary's Story

Mary nervously greets the therapist with a smile, but her eyes dance furtively around the room. As the therapist extends his hand to introduce himself and put her at ease, Mary suddenly drops the handbag that had been clutched so tightly under her arm. She is a tall, thin, neatly dressed fifty-three-year-old woman. It is a very warm day, but Mary is wearing a rather bulky sweater. Before sitting, she quickly runs her hand over the seat, as if brushing off dust.

Mary is very articulate and presents her story in a logical manner. Although anxious and initially hesitant, she clearly understands the therapist's questions and is able to carry on with the normal give-and-take of conversation. She is guarded but is obviously trying to be pleasant and cooperative.

With a very heavy sigh, Mary explains how difficult it was for her to come to therapy. Her twenty-three-year-old son had been urging her to do so for the past year, but she was hoping she could control these distressing things herself. It all started a year ago at her office, where she had worked for ten years as an administrative assistant. Some renovations were being done to the ceiling, and white particles kept falling on her desk. Mary was afraid they might contain asbestos and complained to her boss.

In spite of his reassurances, she persisted with her complaints, long after the renovations were done. Mary began to worry that every bit of dust contained asbestos and found herself wiping her desk constantly. After several months she realized that her actions were ridiculous but simply couldn't stop herself. Unable to function effectively at work, she eventually quit and withdrew to her home, where she lives by herself.

The symptoms became worse. Soon she was washing fruits and vegetables over and over again, rubbing away the skins, cleaning away the poisons. Eventually, she refused to eat anything that she could not wash. She even felt compelled to walk on certain floor tiles, avoiding others. Sometimes she had to count the tiles before she would allow herself to eat. Her weight dropped dramatically. She seldom left the house for fear of air pollution. She wore heavy clothing to block the pollution and hide her thinness.

Mary began to cry, saying that all this was driving her crazy and that she was becoming increasingly depressed. Intellectually, she knew her fears were irrational, but giving in to them was less anxiety-provoking than trying to suppress them.

Mary's past history is, for the most part, clinically unremarkable. She describes a relatively happy childhood and remains very close to her parents to this day. She did well in school, had many friends, and eventually married at age twenty-one. She and her husband divorced five years ago after he ran off with a younger woman. While this was a major blow, Mary soon found that she enjoyed the freedom of dating other men. Apparently, she and her husband had long ago lost interest in each other, sexually and emotionally. She has not dated for the past year and finds herself very isolated and lonely, particularly since her son moved out after she quit her job.

Mary has never been in therapy before and, until now, has never felt the need. There is no family history of emotional problems, although she describes her mother as "a very nervous, apprehensive person who worries about everything." Mary used to drink three or four glasses of wine per week prior to her present symptoms but now drinks only bottled water. She denies any substance abuse, past or present. Other than weight loss, she has no known medical problems. She realizes that she is too thin and is trying to eat more. Her appetite is good. She suffered a ruptured appendix ten years ago but otherwise has been very healthy.

Looking for Clues

Before anything else is done, it is helpful to look at a brief summary of Mary's MSE. The therapist collected most of this information while Mary was talking, without having to directly ask many of the "test questions" you learned about in chapter 5. Mary's mental status is trimmed and translated into the following summary:

Appearance and behavior: Tall, thin, well-groomed, appears stated age. Clothing inappropriate for warm weather. Visibly anxious, limited eye contact.

Attitude toward examiner: Initially guarded. Appeared to drop handbag to avoid shaking hands. Cooperative, pleasant as session progressed. Readily volunteered information.

Psychomotor behavior: Rigid body posture, hands clasped tightly on lap, crossing and uncrossing of knees. Wiped off seat of chair before sitting.

Orientation: Intact. Accurately describes time, place, person.

Manner of speech and thought, thought content: Articulate, coherent, somewhat pressured. Thoughts logical, but tended to give unnecessary details, at times drifting from the point. Obsessional thoughts about cleaning, washing, pollution, as well as compulsive behaviors and rituals around those issues. One-year duration, getting worse. Sees them as irrational. No evidence of psychosis.

Mood and affect: Depressed mood off and on for past year, getting worse, but reports no difficulty sleeping, little loss of energy. Appetite is good, in spite of weight loss. Has some pleasurable activities. Denies any thoughts of suicide but acknowledges feelings of hopelessness. Apprehensive. Affect appears to be predominantly sad. Cried during session but was also able to laugh appropriately, sometimes at herself. Normal range of expression.

Perceptual disturbances: None. Denies hallucinations, illusions.

Attention: Good. Concentration: fair, had some difficulty subtracting serial 7s from 100. Said she was anxious. Memory, remote and recent, is intact. Intelligence is average to above average.

Impulse control: Good at present. No known history of problems.

Judgment: Good, understands consequences of her behavior, effect on others.

Insight: Good, realizes she needs help, accepts that feelings and behaviors are irrational. Appears to be a reliable informant.

Since Mary's reported psychosocial history appears to be unremarkable—"happy" childhood, normal cognitive, emotional, and social development, and so forth—the MSE provides most of the information necessary to make the diagnosis. Even though Mary does have some concerns she wishes to address in therapy, e.g., relationships with men and a lack of future goals, these issues do not appear to have a direct bearing on the *DSM* diagnosis. As stated before, this is often the case with *DSM* diagnoses, which are based mostly on the signs and symptoms, past and present.

Putting It All Together

To understand how the therapist might do this, follow the steps below. Using the information collected by the therapist and the diagnostic categories listed in part 2 of this book, you will see how a diagnostic picture comes together. Be aware, however, that most therapists have developed their own methods and styles to accomplish this.

> **Important Note: The steps described below, as well as the diagnostic descriptions referred to in part 2, have been simplified to give you a general idea of the process and are not intended for self-diagnosis or diagnosis of others! Leave that to the professionals. To make an actual diagnosis, the *DSM* must be used.**

Axis I

1. Therapists first look for the most prominent symptoms. In Mary's case, these are anxiety, obsessive thoughts, compulsive behaviors, and depressed mood. This serves as a starting point. Looking at the major categories (see table 7), you and the therapist might conjecture, at least for now, that Mary is suffering from an anxiety disorder or a mood disorder. Another way to do this is to look at the "Quick Guide to Selected Diagnoses and Major Symptoms" in part 2 of this book. You will find an abbreviated list of selected diagnoses that typically include the particular symptom or symptoms. The therapist has access to a more extensive symptom list in the *DSM.*

2. To see if Mary might have an anxiety disorder, the therapist turns to the "Anxiety Disorder" chapter in the *DSM* and looks over the very specific diagnostic criteria listed for each of the anxiety disorders. (An experienced therapist quickly zeros in, without thumbing through all the disorders.) You can follow a similar procedure by turning to chapter 11, which describes five different kinds of anxiety disorders. Looking through them quickly, you will find that one in particular captures your attention: OCD.

3. The therapist carefully matches Mary's signs and symptoms with the *DSM* criteria and conditions listed for OCD. Although the *DSM* is needed to make the actual diagnosis, the descriptions listed in chapter 11 will give you the general idea. Mary experiences obsessions and/or compulsions as described, recognizes that they are unreasonable, and is considerably distressed by them. There appears to be a match.

4. But before deciding on this diagnosis, the therapist must rule out other disorders that might have similar symptoms. The *DSM* lists some alternative diagnoses that must be considered. After carefully eliminating these possibilities, the therapist writes the diagnosis on Axis I of the diagnostic summary.

5. The therapist now turns to the other major symptom, depressed mood. Since the *DSM* has a major diagnostic category for the mood disorders, it is reasonable to start there. The therapist narrows down the diagnosis by following the same procedures as he or she did for the anxiety disorders.

You will find some of the mood disorders listed in chapter 10. Major depression will probably catch your eye first. To make the diagnosis using the *DSM*, Mary's depressive symptoms must last for two weeks minimum, match at least five of the symptoms listed (depressed mood or loss of interest, significant weight loss or gain, sleep problems, physical slowness or agitation, low energy, guilt or worthlessness, indecisiveness or problems concentrating, repeated thoughts of death or suicide), and meet several other special considerations. They do not. Although Mary has a depressed mood, it appears to be related to the distress of her other symptoms. It is not severe enough to warrant a separate diagnosis.

This should complete the diagnosis for Axis I. Mary has no other obvious symptoms—drug abuse, erratic moods, psychosis, sexual problems, distortions about her body as found in anorexia, problems with impulse control, known medical problems, and so forth.

Axis II

The therapist will now look for Axis II disorders. As you remember, these are the personality disorders; they can be more difficult to determine, particularly after meeting with a patient for only one session. The signs and symptoms are not always immediately apparent. Since the personality disorders involve long-term patterns, the therapist must have a complete psychosocial history available before determining the diagnosis. Some therapists choose to write "Deferred" on Axis II until they are more certain.

1. As a first step, look over the thirteen disorders listed in table 8 (page 104) and described in chapter 21. It is helpful to be familiar with the basic nature of each one. The disorders are divided into three major groups, according to the way the individuals tend to appear or behave:

   Group A: People with paranoid, schizoid, or schizotypal disorder often appear odd and eccentric.

   Group B: Those with antisocial, borderline, histrionic, or narcissistic personality disorders all have issues with emotional control and often appear very erratic, attention-seeking, impulsive, and dramatic.

Group C: People with avoidant, dependent, obsessive-compulsive, or passive-aggressive personality disorders generally are more anxious and apprehensive.

2. Referring to Mary's MSE and her history, the therapist finds no evidence of any long-standing personality issues that have interfered with her social functioning or her personal relationships. Although her behavior has been unusual for the past year, she has no history of being odd or eccentric and has no apparent problem with emotional control. However, she is anxious and apprehensive and may fit in with group C.

3. The therapist then turns to the third group of personality disorders listed in the *DSM*. You will find these in chapter 21. Your eyes will immediately land on obsessive-compulsive personality disorder. But read it carefully before jumping to conclusions. Although it has a similar name, it has nothing to do with Mary's symptoms. The therapist comes to the same decision using the *DSM*. So much for that category. None of the other categories match either. Axis II is left blank or "None" is written in. If there are still doubts or questions about it that need to be determined in time, "Deferred" is usually written on Axis II.

Axis III

In Mary's case, this axis appears to be clear-cut—no obvious medical problems have been reported. However, the therapist will send a request to Mary's physician for further information. To highlight a potential problem, "Weight loss" might be written on this axis. If her weight drops below a certain level, medical intervention may be necessary.

Axis IV

For this axis, the therapists chooses to use the *DSMIII-R* stressor rating scale. Mary's level of psychosocial stress would probably be rated a 3 or 4, moderate to severe, on the 6-point scale. Within the last year she lost her ability to work, and she is having financial difficulty. Her son also moved out, which left her alone and isolated. Her symptoms are further sources of stress.

Axis V

Her current GAF, on a scale of 1 to 90, would fall in the 50 range, since she has serious symptoms leading to serious problems in social and occupational functioning. The therapist does not rate her lower than this because she communicates well, is in touch with reality (even though she acts otherwise), and is able to care for herself and others.

Mary's estimated GAF before the onset of illness would probably be 80 to 90, with few symptoms of any kind other than those normally expected from daily stressors. Generally, the higher the number, the better the prognosis for recovery—but this is not necessarily true in all cases.

The Diagnostic Picture

Mary's final diagnostic summary would look like this:

Axis I: 300.30 Obsessive-Compulsive Disorder
Axis II: None
Axis III: None other than weight loss, secondary to obsessive-compulsive symptoms
Axis IV: Severity of stressor: 3–4 (Moderate to Severe) Psychosocial stressor: Occupational and financial problems, social isolation
Axis V: Current Global Assessment of Functioning (GAF): 50
Highest GAF in past year: 80–90

Complicated Steps for More Complicated Cases

Most cases are much more complex than Mary's. Her case, as presented, is easy to diagnose because her symptoms were relatively clear-cut. Her MSE was positive for only three symptoms: depressed mood, mild anxiety, and obsessive-compulsive thoughts and behaviors. And only one of these was severe enough to meet diagnostic requirements. In addition, her psychosocial history did not suggest any complicating factors.

So how do therapists handle the more complicated but everyday cases involving many different symptoms, multiple diagnoses, and convoluted personal histories? More often than therapists would care to admit, the answer is simple: *with great difficulty*. To see how complex the process can be, refer to tables 9 and 10. Both tables are very technical and are presented here merely to show you what therapists face. If you find the steps confusing or vague, you are not alone. You can see how the process, at its worst, could deteriorate into a hit-or-miss affair. But for now, let's assume the positive. After all, your insurance company does take the diagnosis seriously.

TABLE 9: STEPS THERAPISTS FACE IN MAKING THE AXIS I DIAGNOSIS (All Mental Disorders except Personality Disorders)

---

1. Identify and focus on all the symptoms underlying the chief complaint.

2. Look for the most serious or prominent symptoms: psychotic symptoms, mood symptoms, anxiety symptoms, physical complaints, or organic symptoms (brain impairment such as Alzheimer's). This gives a general idea where the diagnosis might be found, since the *DSM* is organized around these symptoms—psychotic disorders, mood disorders, anxiety disorders, and so forth.

3. Make a list of *all* diagnoses that include the most serious symptoms. Use the clues suggested by the MSE. The list may be quite lengthy. For example, depression would first suggest a mood disorder, but it can also be found as part of many other disorders, including organic disorders. List all possibilities.

4. Determine how long each major symptom has lasted, the severity of the symptom, what may have triggered it, and if it occurred with any other symptoms. Use the psychosocial history for a complete overview of symptom history and the context in which it occurred.

5. Go back to the list of possible diagnoses and match the information from step #3 with the *defining* symptoms for each disorder. Defining symptoms are those that *must* be present to make the diagnosis, e.g., panic attacks in panic disorder, obsessions or compulsions in obsessive-compulsive disorder, two weeks of depression in major depression, and so forth. Exclude the diagnoses that don't match the defining symptoms.

6. Identify the less prominent but *associated* symptoms such as irritability, insomnia, fatigue, depressed feelings, mild anxiety, minor headaches, fear of going crazy, inability to concentrate, and so forth. Refer to the MSE. Associated symptoms are found in many disorders and, by themselves, do not determine a diagnosis. A diagnosis must be made using defining and associated symptoms.

7. Compare the associated symptoms with the *DSM* criteria for each of the disorders listed in step #5. If a sufficient number match a particular disorder, a tentative diagnosis can be made.

8. Follow this process for each of the prominent symptoms, since more than one diagnosis can be given on Axis I.

9. Pay attention to the "diagnostic hierarchies" that the *DSM* follows: the presence of some diagnostic categories may exclude others, with the more serious disorders (such as schizophrenia, cognitive disorders, or medical diseases) taking precedence in many cases.

10. If the symptoms are lifelong or have a pattern of popping up again and again in response to certain aspects of personal or social relationships, an Axis II personality disorder should be considered.

TABLE 10: STEPS THERAPISTS FACE IN MAKING THE AXIS II DIAGNOSIS (Personality Disorders)

1. Look for long-term patterns that create conflicts in personal, social, or work relationships. People with personality disorders repeatedly misinterpret and overreact to certain subtle aspects of relationships or social rules. They may experience distressing emotional symptoms when coping skills fail. Look for the patterns that trigger the symptoms.

2. For every area of conflict reported, trace it back to childhood, adolescence, and early adult history to see if similar patterns and symptoms existed. For example, if a person is currently

experiencing anxiety and depression due to social isolation, look for a possible pattern of social avoidance, timidity, and excessive fear of disapproval beginning in late adolescence. The pattern could suggest an avoidant personality disorder.

3. If a pattern is found, assess the severity by looking at the effect on relationships or the frequency of related conflicts. If it affects all relationships—personal, social, and work—it is severe.

4. To narrow down the diagnosis, look for appearances and behaviors that fit the three personality groups discussed earlier: (A) odd and eccentric; (B) erratic, attention-seeking, impulsive, and dramatic; (C) anxious and apprehensive. The personality disorder section of the *DSM* is organized around these three groups.

5. Turn to that group of personality disorders in the *DSM*. Look for matches with the diagnostic criteria listed for each disorder. Since more than one Axis II diagnosis may be given, check other groups if indicated.

6. If the pattern does not fully meet the diagnostic criteria for any one personality disorder but causes significant distress or problems in social functioning, the diagnosis of personality disorder NOS may be given.

CASE 2:
Raging Jealousy

Ronald T.

You read this patient's psychosocial history in chapter 4. Ron is the forty-two-year-old male who was convinced, against all reason, that his wife was having an affair. He resorted to nightly spying and tape-recorded surveillance. When his wife denied the accusations, he ripped up the house in a blind rage.

Before discussing Ron's diagnosis and the rationale behind it, let's look at his MSE:

Appearance and behavior: Average height, husky build, bearded. Well-groomed. Very intense, distraught.

Attitude toward examiner: Cooperative, volunteered information freely, but angered quickly if his perceptions about his wife's alleged infidelity were questioned. Able to calm himself down.

Psychomotor behavior: Tense at times, particularly when discussing infidelity. Subdued when discussing childhood history.

Orientation: Intact.

Mood and affect: Says mood is generally depressed or angry; particularly after he began suspecting his wife. Sleep is okay, as is energy level. Is able to enjoy some activities. Past history is negative for significant depression. Range of affect is normal. Although he says he usually comes across as calm, he was quite emotional and intense today. "Discussing this stuff gets me going—I usually stay away from too many feelings."

Thought process and content: Thought process intact, logical. No incoherence or loosening of associations. Concerning content, patient is preoccupied with wife's alleged affairs. He is insistent about this and angrily dismisses the possibility that it's not true. He can cite no supporting evidence, although he has been looking diligently for the past nine months. "I just know it's going on." Wife is extremely upset and adamantly denies any affairs.

Perceptual disturbances: Denied. No evidence of hallucinations or illusions.

Attention and concentration: Good.

Memory: Intact.

Intelligence and abstract thinking: Average intelligence. Tended toward more concrete thinking but not impaired.

Impulse control: Patient has history of explosive outbursts, serious destruction of property. Denies hitting people since adolescence. He says he has had approximately six explosive episodes as an adult. Prior to his recent outbursts, the last one was ten years ago. Rages are usually out of proportion with the stressor. Patient says he is generally an easygoing person. (Confirmed by spouse.) Presently he fears he could lose control. "I'm afraid I'm going to kill her when I flip out." Denies any intent. "I love her too much to hurt her." History is positive for head injury, seizures. Alcohol abuse a problem in the past, denies at present. Denies suicidal thoughts, past or present.

Judgment and insight: Judgment is impaired. Patient is acting on his suspected delusion. Judgment in other areas of his life is relatively intact. No insight into illness. Acknowledges problems with anger control but denies possibility that his preoccupations are a sign of illness.

Axis I Diagnosis—Psychiatric Disorders

Ron has two major symptoms that need consideration for Axis I— preoccupations with infidelity and explosive outbursts. Although all the facts aren't available during the evaluation, it appears that his preoccupations have reached a delusional level. In spite of evidence to the contrary, he tenaciously holds to his beliefs and has gone to extremes in making his case—all to no avail. His persistence has grossly interfered with his job and jeopardized his marriage. Most people suspicious of a spouse would not go to these extremes, particularly for eight months without any evidence whatsoever. By that point, they could at least consider the possibility that the charges were unfounded. Ron cannot acknowledge the possibility.

Ron's "craziness" appears to be limited to issues of infidelity. In all other respects (except for his rages), he acts and appears normal. His thinking process is intact. The *content* of his thinking, however, is delusional.

Looking through the quick guide in this book, you will find several diagnoses that include delusions. Checking these out, you will see that he clearly meets the criteria for delusional disorder, jealous type. For this disorder, delusions are the defining symptoms. Schizophrenia and the other psychotic disorders are ruled out because, among other things, Ron does not experience hallucinations, illusions, bizarre, impossible delusions, or problems with his thought process. Major depression with psychotic features is ruled out because he is only mildly depressed, perhaps as a result of the delusions. Drug abuse is not a factor, and his mental status shows no evidence of an organic disorder. Also, although it may or may not be a contributing factor, it is notable that Ron's mother was hospitalized several times with paranoidlike symptoms. There may be an inherent proclivity for mental illness.

The other prominent symptom is severe explosive behavior, which occurred frequently as a child but diminished as Ron matured. He claims that he has had six explosions as an adult, with nine years separating the last two episodes. Explosive behavior can be a part of many disorders, but Ron's may be a bit different since he has a history of head injury and seizures at age four, followed by frequent fighting at school. Look at the impulse control disorders and you will find intermittent explosive disorder, which seems to describe the nature of Ron's explosive outbursts. These types of outbursts are sometimes seen in people with early head trauma, learning disorders, and "soft" neurological signs. Pending further neurological investigation, Ron is given a rule-out diagnosis of intermittent explosive disorder.

Ron also experiences some associated symptoms and signs like mild depression, significant tension, avoidance of feelings, some social isolation, and excessive caffeine consumption (five cups of coffee daily—which may be aggravating his explosive behavior). However, none of these is sufficient to warrant another diagnosis, although they should be considered in therapy.

Axis II Diagnosis—Personality Disorders

Ron has several long-term patterns: explosive behavior, avoidance and denial of feelings, distrust of older males and authority figures, lack of trust in intimate relationships, and some conflicts with dependency.

Ron's early history is quite chaotic and traumatic—an absentee alcoholic father, head trauma and school problems, the sudden death of a beloved aunt, exposure to his mother's sexual activities, his mother's "nervous breakdown," breakup of the family, sexual advances by an uncle, a delinquent older brother, and so forth. Ron's manner of handling stress was to shut out his feelings or keep himself preoccupied with other activities such as sports. This worked to some extent.

As a young adult, he worked steadily to support his mother and, unlike his brother, avoided problems with the law. Although there were some problems with authority figures and alcohol abuse, he showed many good coping skills.

As an adult, he has worked steadily and maintained long-term relationships. The reasons behind the failure of his first marriage are unclear other than his propensity to explode, which he tended to blame on his wife's provocations. This suggests some denial of personal responsibility, although he presently acknowledges the explosive behavior as totally unacceptable and feels extremely remorseful about it. "I can't stand thinking of myself as a violent person." He avoids close social relationships and relies almost exclusively on his wife for emotional support. He is uncomfortable being a father, although he feels close to his kids.

So what does all this mean for Axis II? Looking at the three groups of personality disorders, he does not seem to fall under any one group, if any. Nevertheless, it is wise to look through them. Although Ron has had a traumatic history and some specific behavioral and emotional patterns, he does not appear to meet the criteria for any of the personality disorders. He does have psychological problems that may be contributing to his Axis I diagnoses, but the long-term personality patterns apparently have not been pervasive or severe enough to cause significant distress or impairment in social functioning. A closer look at the triggers behind his rages might be enlightening, but there are no personality disorders listed in the DSM with explosive behavior as the defining symptom. Some therapists might play it safe and write "Deferred" on Axis II, suggesting that further digging might unearth some classifiable patterns.

Ron's Diagnostic Picture

Axis I: 297.10 Delusional Disorder, Jealous Type
312.34 Rule out Intermittent Explosive Disorder

Axis II: Deferred

Axis III: History of head trauma, seizures—age four

Axis IV: Severity of stressor: 4 (Severe)
Psychosocial stressor: Stress secondary to delusions

Axis V: Current Global Assessment of Functioning (GAF):
30
Behavior influenced by delusions
Highest GAF in past year: 70

Even if you're not ready to diagnose the cat, you can probably see how the whole diagnostic process is often held together by wishful thinking. It's the best diagnostic system we've ever had, but that may not be saying much. It looks good on paper and could work reasonably well if all therapists were extremely objective, capable of following directions, and tireless in their pursuit of the "correct diagnosis." Sometimes it does work well. But with two hundred thousand therapists out there making diagnoses under the watchful eye of bottom-line administrators, something is bound to go wrong—and it does. The next chapter discusses some complicating realities that influence your diagnosis.

7

BEHIND THE
SCENES:
THE THERAPIST'S
HEADACHE ...
AND YOUR
HEADACHE

WHEN A ROSE IS
NOT A ROSE

So you finally have a diagnosis. If we believe the statistics of a 1988 study by the National Institute of Mental Health, one in three American adults will have a diagnosable mental or substance abuse disorder in his or her lifetime. While the figures are compelling, one must keep in mind that the statistics are based on the categories and definitions cited in the *DSM*. As new categories are developed or "identified," cynics might argue that more and more individuals will slip into the "diagnosable disorder" arena, oiling the wheels of the mental health industry. Others will argue that the maladies have always been there in one form or another, awaiting definition by the psychiatric eye.

Whatever the case may be, the definition of your emotional problem will have major implications for you and for your therapist. Your diagnosis affects who pays for your treatment, how much, and for how long. In turn, your treatment will be influenced by financial considerations. It doesn't take any great leap in logic to conclude that financial considerations might also influence the diagnosis. In fact, it happens all the time.

But before pointing any fingers, let's look at some of the forces at work in a convoluted, deeply troubled system historically mired in questionable practices, grandiose claims, turf battles between professionals, and, now, managed care mismanagement. In most cases, there are no clear-cut bad guys in this mess; all parties feel trapped in a no-win situation. Nevertheless, these factors undermine "objectivity" and will affect your diagnosis and treatment.

INTENTIONAL MISDIAGNOSIS

Diagnosing for Maximum Profit

The headline in the *New York Times* on November 24, 1991, came as no surprise: MENTAL HOSPITAL CHAINS ACCUSED OF MUCH CHEATING ON INSURANCE. The article continues: "Investigators looking into psychiatric hospitals that are operated for profit have uncovered evidence of fraud and abuse in the filing of insurance claims that could run into millions of dollars." Written by Peter Kerr, the extensive story details the federal and state investigations that unearthed a variety of unsavory practices including:

- Inflated bills for medications and services.
- Billings for services never rendered.
- Unnecessary hospitalizations.
- Financial relationships between the hospitals and referral sources such as schools.

• Altering diagnosis and treatment to fit insurance policies.

Newsweek, reporting on the same story in a November 4, 1991, article titled "Money Madness," went on to cite other abuses, including kidnapping of patients to fill beds, dumping patients when the insurance ran out, and charging exorbitant fees to substance abuse patients recruited from Canada.

While most of the investigations were centered on the Psychiatric Institutes of America (PIA), a seventy-four-hospital chain operating throughout the United States, other major for-profit chains were also implicated.

Although a spokesman for the National Association of Private Psychiatric Hospitals disputed that the practices were widespread, a study by the Health Insurance Institute of America suggested otherwise. Cited in the *New York Times* article, the study investigated fifty thousand psychiatric and medical cases between 1987 and 1989. Fraudulent diagnosis or data was found in 32.6 percent of the cases. "Deliberate misdiagnosis and changing of dates of service are among the more common types of all medical insurance fraud. . . . But proving a diagnosis was altered to increase insurance reimbursement is often extremely difficult, particularly in psychiatry, where definitions are vague."

How had this come about? The *Newsweek* article points to the phenomenal growth of private psychiatric hospitals during the free-spending days of the early 1980s. It was an extremely lucrative business. As health care costs increased, however, insurers began limiting hospital stays to weeks instead of months. Suddenly hospitals were left with empty beds. Since survival depended on keeping the census up, aggressive marketing plans were instituted, based on the bottom line. According to one PIA psychiatrist, "the whole place was census driven . . . if your [referring to staff members] census dropped and stayed that way, you were out the door."

Smaller Transgressions

Most of the "transgressions" in the mental health industry are not as outrageous or blatant as the ones cited above. And they are not necessarily motivated by profit. Although perceptions and actions may be subtly twisted and rationalized by financial considerations, most therapists would argue that transgressions, such as exaggerating a diagnosis, are carried out to ensure adequate treatment.

Why is this so? The answer lies with the reimbursement system. Although the problem has been around ever since insurance companies began providing mental health benefits, it has gotten worse in recent years as insurers have legitimately attempted to cut back on costs. In response to the health care crisis and the uncontrolled abuses found in the health care industry, most insurance companies have now hired management companies (at *great* expense) to review, approve, modify, or disapprove individual treatment plans. Under this managed care system, each patient is assigned a manager who communicates directly with the therapist. Based on the information provided by the therapist, the manager ultimately decides the type and duration of treatment. And, more often than not, the treatment promoted is short-term and designed to relieve the most immediate symptoms.

Offhand, this would seem like a good solution, since traditionally it has been too easy for therapists and patients to lapse into unfocused, expensive, long-term therapy. But things are seldom so simple, particularly when vague, poorly defined entities are involved.

Unappetizing Cookbooks

Since the goal of managed care has been to contain costs, the management companies naturally shoot for the shortest treatment plan, with only secondary concern for the quality of care. (This may be changing since corporate America is finally complaining about treatment effectiveness under managed care.) To make their treatment determinations as "scientific" and "empirical" as possible, many managed care companies have developed treatment "cookbooks" *based on diagnosis*; four outpatient sessions allowed for an adjustment disorder, twelve sessions for major depression, and so forth. Unfortunately, in their search for pragmatic, expedient measures of human behavior, the managed care companies have erroneously come to regard psychiatric categories with the same degree of certainty as medical diseases.

Needless to say, this frequently forces therapists to overdiagnose in order to provide what they feel is adequate treatment. An "adjustment disorder with depressed mood (309.0)" might shift into a "major depression (296.20)"—on paper. In addition, more and more managed care companies are limiting coverage to those services deemed to be "medically necessary"—services that provide immediate relief of symptoms caused by "disorders"—without looking at longer-term solutions or family contexts.

Under managed care, more than ever, the definition of what constitutes a disorder becomes very important. Services such as marriage and family therapy are seldom covered, since the problems are not considered disorders. To get around this, therapists will often give a spouse or family member the diagnosis of dysthymia or adjustment disorder to justify treatment. And most patients willingly go along with this or even suggest it, since they want the therapy.

For many therapists, this is a strange turn of events—patients actually requesting a more severe diagnosis in order to pay for therapy. Some therapists have consistently underdiagnosed patients in the past to avoid the labeling inherent in the system. However, today they are at great risk if they do so. A hot new area for litigation centers around underdiagnosis—patients are actually suing their therapists, claiming that their treatment was limited by the more benign diagnosis!

Misdiagnosis and Ethical Dilemmas

Although the prevalence of deliberate misdiagnosis has not been established, one study carried out in the earlier days of managed care gives a general idea. Researchers S. Kirk and H. Kutchins surveyed clinical social workers and found some rather startling results ("Deliberate Misdiagnosis in Mental Health Practice," *Social Service Review* 62 [1988]). They found that 59 percent of the social workers surveyed said that they used Axis I diagnoses for insurance purposes even when unwarranted clinically. Not surprisingly, 72 percent said they were "aware of cases where more serious diagnoses were used to qualify for reimbursement," and 86 percent said that they diagnosed individual family members even though the primary concerns were family or marital issues.

This situation most certainly is not limited to social workers or even to individual therapists—the author knows of mental health clinics where every therapist has been instructed to avoid certain diagnoses. The administrators of one such clinic, a very large non-profit organization near Boston, disallowed the adjustment disorders and some of the anxiety disorders. Therapists were instructed to upgrade to dysthymia or other diagnoses. The rationale behind this blatant distortion apparently rested with the limitations imposed by a major funding source. The funding source had determined that the clinic had used the diagnoses of adjustment disorder and the anxiety disorders more frequently than would be expected statistically. The clinic administrators were left with a terrible dilemma: distort the diagnosis or cut off service to a wide range of patients. As this was one of the last clinics in the area committed to providing extremely low-cost mental health services, the administrators opted for the distortion. Technically, this is fraud.

As managed care grows, the situation will undoubtedly become worse. All therapists are faced or will be faced with nagging ethical dilemmas about the misuse of diagnostics. And in spite of the fact that the managed care companies essentially define the rules and dictate the course of therapy, the burden of responsibility, both legally and ethically, is dumped on the shoulders of therapists.

A Dubious Task

But it would be unfair to blame all of this on managed care. As stated earlier, the problem has been around in varying degrees for many years. Managed care companies have the dubious task of defining and containing the amorphous winds behind emotional suffering—in the most cost-effective manner. Why should we expect administrators and accountants to be any better at it than therapists? Therapists have enough problems of their own trying to make sense of the human psyche. The "experts" come and go, and new treatment modalities, geared to the financial climate, are rationalized and hyped with the same zeal as "new and improved" laundry detergents. Economics, as much as clinical research, determines the state of the art.

UNINTENTIONAL MISDIAGNOSIS

The Eye of the Beholder

Since you now have a general idea how the diagnostic process works, it should be evident that it is extremely easy to misdiagnose even moderately complex cases. Considering that there are over two hundred thousand therapists in the field, representing different theoretical perspectives, practice styles, and personalities, it's a miracle there is any consistency in diagnostics. Couple this with the bureaucratic misuse of diagnosis, and you have a major problem.

How does this type of misdiagnosis happen? Although the researchers behind the *DSM* work hard to make the diagnostic categories "reliable" in field studies (e.g., many different therapists will come up with the same diagnosis when evaluating the same patient), the reliability is often undermined in actual practice.

For the most part, therapists are not researchers, nor do they think like researchers. Often they do not have the time or the patience to sort through all the necessary steps and the long lists of diagnostic criteria; they are pressed to get something down on paper after the first session, perhaps with the intention of clarifying it later. More often than therapists would care to admit, the diagnosis is made on the basis of a single major symptom, without considering the vast array of associated symptoms. For example, if a patient is experiencing auditory hallucinations, it is all too easy to diagnose schizophrenia. (People with major depression sometimes have auditory hallucinations also.) This happens with less severe cases as well.

In addition, many therapists gloss over the MSE because they feel it is too mechanical, intrusive, and demeaning to their patients.

Since the *DSM* is built around the MSE, this can be a problem. Other therapists have mixed feelings about the validity and usefulness of diagnostic categories in the first place, so they may evade or minimize the formal diagnosis. The treatment they provide may be very effective, but it is not necessarily based on *DSM* criteria or the medical model.

Other factors also come into play. Therapists are subject to the same human biases as everyone else. Researchers have shown time and time again that diagnoses are influenced by racial, sexual, and class biases. Short of the day when all diagnoses are reduced to measurable biological phenomena (not likely), diagnoses will be influenced by the eye of the beholder. Anyone who has attended a diagnostic case conference in a major teaching hospital can attest to the obnoxious bickering and power plays that occur in ferreting out the "correct" psychiatric diagnosis. ...

TURF BATTLES AND YOUR DIAGNOSIS

The Frenzied Dance of the Professionals

Speaking of obnoxious power plays, the war between the professional guilds has heated up considerably as they chase the dwindling therapy dollars. Although the vast array of mental health professionals—psychiatrists, psychologists, social workers, psychiatric nurses, family and marriage counselors, and mental health counselors—generally work together amicably, their trade organizations are scurrying about to justify their members' existence to the managed care companies. This often means waging war with and pushing out competing therapists.

Managed care companies strike terror in the hearts of therapists and the professional organizations, since they pick and choose who will belong to their list of service providers and who will not. How they choose is anybody's guess and varies as much as the weather. Sometimes, as ridiculous as it may sound, the choices are made according to the therapists' "proven ability" to consistently alleviate patients' suffering in seven sessions or less. (And once the lucky therapist wins the managed care contract, he or she risks a swift kick into obscurity if the therapy pattern changes significantly.) At other times the managed care companies prefer one breed of therapist over another, particularly if they can get away with paying that particular breed less. As you might imagine, psychiatrists aren't faring very well under this system, since they are too expensive and don't necessarily offer better services. For some, private practice is going the way of the fondue pot.

In an effort to pare down the supply of eligible mental health professionals and gain illusory control over the slippery whimsies of the human mind, some managed care companies have resorted to a new gambit: requiring therapists to obtain "certification" in numerous "specialty areas" before they can provide a particular type of therapy or see a particular type of patient—even if they have been doing it well for years. One well-known psychologist, a noted expert on alcoholism, was denied reimbursement for alcoholic patients since he lacked the new certificate. The course required to get the certificate—150 hours plus a practicum—was something he easily could design and teach. While certification might seem like a good idea for "quality control," there is absolutely no evidence that additional credentialing, above and beyond the extensive training and continuing education already required of therapists, is of any benefit. *Reducing mental health care to a disarray of specialty areas based on diagnosis also reduces patients to a diagnosis*—and you know how shaky that is. Mental health treatment is not nearly as mechanistic or divisible as most forms of medicine. Nevertheless, the professional organizations have responded with a frenzy of certification courses, and therapists are frantically jumping through hoops. Where it will end is anybody's guess.

Psychiatry's Sleight of Hand?

To see how politics and money affect diagnosis, let's look at psychiatry's response to the dwindling dollar. Although all mental health guilds overstate the case for whichever service they happen to provide, the psychiatry associations could write the headlines for the *National Enquirer*. Perhaps you've seen the media blitz—

---

*Amazing new biological breakthroughs in
treating mental disorders!* [or]
*Revolutionary psychiatric findings changing the
face of mental health treatment!* [or]
Miracle drug cures depression!

The argument here, at least from this author's perspective, is not whether or not there have been advances, but how they have been oversold and hyped to the public and the managed care companies. Indeed, new medication such as Clozaril (an antipsychotic medication) and Prozac (an antidepressant also used to treat some of the anxiety disorders) have greatly helped many individuals where previous treatments have failed. And as neuroscience works to identify particular cellular processes that influence neurotransmitters (chemicals believed to play a role in psychosis, depression, and anxiety), medications may be developed that are much more specific and have fewer side effects. *This author has no doubt that certain mental disorders are associated with brain abnormalities and may benefit by medical treatment.* The contributions of psychiatry are extremely valuable and worthy of the utmost consideration.

So what's the problem? Other than the usual chicken-or-egg arguments (e.g., which came first?—the stressful emotional problems triggering abnormal brain activity or the brain abnormality triggering the emotions, and so forth) and the fact that *many* people are not helped at all by medications (just as many people are not helped by talking therapy), the problem lies in just how far psychiatry is willing to go to label all emotional problems as "biological" or medical. As you know, the diagnostic categories in the *DSM* are already referred to as "disorders." If you see a therapist and your insurance company pays for it, you have a "disorder"—at least on paper.

Because of its medical tradition, it is not unreasonable or unexpected that psychiatry might interpret everything from a medical perspective. However, there are other motives involved—the same motives that underlie the activities of the other professional groups. As psychiatry fights for its diminishing market share of patients, it must make itself indispensable. There are many ways to do this; unfortunately, most involve manipulation of public perception (convincing people that their problems require medical solutions), redefining what's biological and what isn't, demeaning or minimizing the work of other professionals, and promising quick-fix solutions.

If other professional groups are going through similar gyrations, why pick on psychiatry? Because psychiatry is in the unique position of determining what is and isn't normal, as well as the nature and definition of diagnostic categories. The profession is hardly objective in these determinations. As of this writing, many state psychiatric associations are pushing for "biologically based" psychiatric disorders to be reclassified for insurance purposes as medical disorders, thus overcoming the more restrictive financial limits imposed on the treatment of mental disorders. (Many insurance companies limit outpatient mental health treatment to five hundred dollars yearly, versus thousands of dollars for medical treatment.) So what's wrong with this suggestion? Wouldn't it help a lot of people?

Keep Your Eye on Your Wallet

At first glance, the plan could be a boon for individuals suffering from schizophrenia or other severe mental disorders—as well as a financial boon for psychiatrists. Since the conditions would be considered medical, psychiatrists would be required to make the diagnosis and provide or supervise most of the treatment. Many therapists would argue that psychiatrists are necessary for prescribing the medication, but not for diagnosis or therapy supervision. Either way, the problem goes beyond such a simplistic solution and becomes one of definition—where do you draw the line between biology and psychology for all the other diagnostic categories?

To see how such a division is influenced by culture, politics, the theories of the observer, and the beliefs of the patient, we can look at an example from China. Arthur Kleinman is an American psychiatrist who has done extensive field research in China and other Asian countries. In his highly recommended book, *Rethinking Psychiatry: From Cultural Category to Personal Experience* (New York: Free Press, 1988), he describes an official Chinese psychiatric diagnosis known as "neurasthenia." In China, neurasthenia is seen as a biologically based illness attributed to a brain malfunction in the cerebral cortex. It is marked by chronic fatigue, nervousness, headaches, various physical complaints, and depressed mood.

After studying one hundred patients, Kleinman found that most met the diagnostic criteria for the American *DSM* category of major depression. However, "unlike the majority of chronically depressed patients, these patients responded only partially to antidepressant medications ... their chief somatic complaints and medical help seeking ended only when they were able to resolve major work and family problems" (p. 13).

Kleinman concluded that belief in the biological diagnosis avoided the mental illness stigma feared by the Chinese. It was also a way to avoid psychological interpretations and personal responsibility. Since neurasthenia is a very popular diagnosis, Chinese patients, in making sense of their symptoms, "select out and lump together those symptoms that are familiar and salient ... namely the ones that fit the popular blueprint of neurasthenia" (p. 13). As might be expected, the patients' perceptions also influence the diagnosis. This is true in the United States as well.

As another example of this slippery area, consider anxiety. Anxiety has observable physical signs, but it can often be turned on and off by a person's mindset. So is it psychological? Medication can also calm anxiety. Does that mean it's biologically based? Obviously, influences and connections are easy to identify: causes are not.

Carving up the human psyche into an either/or situation is downright foolish (at least scientifically) and smacks of the Dark

Ages. And who would get to make the determinations? You guessed it—the psychiatrists, either directly or in consultation with the insurance companies. You have already seen how diagnoses are casually inflated for reimbursement purposes. If more money were at stake, you can imagine what would inevitably happen. Your diagnosis might be shocking.

Dividing up the psychological and the biological in mental health might also encourage insurance companies to cut all treatment benefits for emotional problems that do not show some evidence of biological involvement, whatever that may be. At present, many insurers are already trying to eliminate certain types of mental health coverage. And what about the ethical considerations behind this false division of biology and psychology? Should a sexually abused child receive a limited amount of psychological service, while a neighbor suffering from schizophrenia is receiving virtually unlimited psychiatric service? In spite of these considerations, most psychiatric associations are blindly pursuing vested interests as objective science flies out the door. The other professional groups are not above doing the same thing, yet they do not wield the same social or political powers. Traditionally, the public has perceived psychiatry as more "scientific" since it is tied to medicine.

Enough Already!

All mental health professional disciplines have made and will continue to make significant contributions to the field. The current divisiveness is a sad state of affairs and an embarrassment, not to mention a disservice to patients. Where it is heading, no one knows. Perhaps national health insurance would help unify the disparate forces.

One thing is for certain, however. If you listen carefully, you can hear the gnashing of teeth, the bowing and scraping, and the obedient droning of managed care mantras as therapists, professional organizations, and clinics reorganize and redefine themselves into the likeness of their funding sources. It's easy to see how things can get distorted and rationalized under such circumstances, including your diagnosis and your treatment.

HOW THE BUREAUCRACY MAY AFFECT YOU

Why You Should Care

- Your diagnosis may be inflated for insurance purposes.
- Your diagnosis may be in error because the therapist is lazy, hurried, inept, subject to social biases, influenced by diagnostic trends, or rejecting of the medical model.
- You may not fit any of the diagnostic categories, but rest assured you will be squeezed into something.
- You may be shuffled around at clinics as they try to find a therapist who has a contract with your particular insurance and managed care company. Managed care often contracts with individuals within the clinic, rather than the clinic as a whole.
- You may have trouble finding a private therapist who has a contract with your insurance company. Even if you find one, he or she may not have the proper insurance "certification" to treat your particular problem. However, the guy down the street with half the training and experience of the first therapist may have a certificate. Look out.
- Your therapist may have difficulty getting approval for more than two or three sessions at a time. You could be limited to very few sessions.
- In most cases, expect your therapist to be quite active, setting specific goals and solving specific problems. If you have a "personality disorder," you may be out of luck unless you're willing to pay out of your own pocket when the brief insurance coverage runs out.
- If you have a more serious mental disorder such as

schizophrenia, expect intermittent visits to see a case manager as well as medication visits. If strings are pulled, you might be approved for a day treatment program.

- If you need marital or family therapy, expect that you or a family member will be given a psychiatric diagnosis. This is also true for group therapy.

- And, last but not least, keep in mind that absolute confidentiality in psychotherapy is an ancient myth that seldom holds water. The insurance case manager is essentially sitting in the room with you and your therapist, although certain details are screened out. If you are being seen at an HMO, the therapist's session notes may be in the computer file that travels with you to the foot doctor. Or your diagnosis and medical summaries could end up in the vast holdings of a medical information bureau, which sells information to other institutions. (If you can bear any more, read *Privacy for Sale: How Computerization Has Made Everyone's Private Life an Open Secret*, by Jeffrey Rothfeder, published by Simon & Schuster in 1992.)

On those happy notes, you should know what you can do, as a mental health consumer, to guard against some of these problems—the subject of the next chapter.

8
HOLDING YOUR THERAPIST ACCOUNTABLE: ASKING THE RIGHT QUESTIONS

DEFENSIVE DIAGNOSTICS

Many of my colleagues will not be happy with this chapter. Most are already overwhelmed by rules, regulations, legal requirements, paperwork, lawyers, insufficient resources, lawyers, turf battles, lawyers, managed care, you name it—enough headaches to drive a reasonably sane person to Nova Scotia to raise bees.

To my beleaguered colleagues, I offer my sincerest apologies, but the time has come. We must be held accountable for the diagnostic system that we use and the manner in which we apply it, even if we look at it with a jaundiced eye. In medicine, every patient has a right to know what his or her diagnosis is and how it was determined;

since our diagnostic system is based on the medical model, we can't expect to play by different rules. With the lapses in confidentiality that occur with increasing regularity and the development of unregulated computer information banks, casual labels take on new meanings that can come back to haunt patients. The labels also affect treatment, even if they are uncertain or provisional or merely space fillers on forms.

Becoming an Active Participant

As a patient, you have a responsibility to become an active participant in your own diagnosis. Diagnosis should be something that is done for you and with you, not something that is done *to* you. But far too often, this is not the case. For reasons that probably have something to do with the mythical, unapproachable power of the therapist or a fear of finding out too much, patients seldom ask about their diagnosis and how it was determined. They might ask, "What's wrong with me?" or "Why do I feel this way?" but it has become an unstated rule of the game to avoid the specific question: "What diagnosis or diagnoses are you putting in my file and submitting to my insurance company?" It's a very simple question. Doesn't it deserve a straightforward answer?

Why Your Therapist May Hide under the Desk

Most therapists would agree that you deserve an answer, but they still cringe at the thought; as well they should, since there are some very good reasons for not telling you your diagnosis, at least in the beginning. In the first place, therapists are often uncertain about diagnostics, particularly if the case is complex, unique, or involves an Axis II personality disorder. You have seen how vague some of the diagnostic categories can be. Although some therapists would rather watch your diagnosis "evolve" as therapy progresses, they are nevertheless under great pressure to come up with a preliminary diagnosis. Some managed care companies require a phone call after the first session.

Second, therapists fear that the label could be self-fulfilling; in your search for explanations, you could start to organize your symptoms and complaints around the diagnosis. It is not at all unusual to "identify" with a diagnosis. This kind of thing happens all the time in medicine and obscures other factors that might be involved.

Third, since therapists want to help rather than simply provide a diagnosis, they fear that knowledge of your diagnosis might drive you away or force you into a defensive stance. Normally, when a patient comes into therapy he or she is not fully aware of certain patterns or defenses that may be contributing to the problem. These must be uncovered during the course of therapy, but only as the patient is ready and willing to consider them. For example, hitting someone over the head with a "personality disorder" or a "delusional disorder" is not very helpful. The patient might hit back with something more substantial.

Fourth, many therapists do not necessarily follow the medical model, at least theoretically. Rather than imposing artificial boundaries, they look at the various diminensions of your personality, your relative strengths and weaknesses, your coping styles, and so forth. They are very uncomfortable with strict categories but have little choice in the matter.

And finally, some therapists are great clinicians but terrible diagnosticians. They don't think in the detailed, nit-picking, linear manner required to navigate the diagnostic maze. Although they probably have trouble balancing their checkbooks, they may be extraordinarily perceptive and facilitative. These therapists can be worth their weight in gold, but they drive the bureaucrats crazy. (On the other hand, it is all too easy for some very incompetent, mentally disorganized therapists to play the "intuitive, holistic role," so be careful.)

Ask the Right Questions

Table 11 outlines some of the questions that you might wish to ask your therapist regarding your diagnosis. Even if your therapist appears competent and inspires trust, don't be afraid of offending him or her by your polite questions. On the other hand, don't be surprised or put off if your therapist balks or hesitates in answering—some of the reasons were discussed above. If this happens, find out his or her thinking behind the hesitation. Whether or not you choose to pursue the matter further is totally up to you. After discussions with your therapist, you may decide that there are indeed good reasons to forgo or at least postpone seeking this information.

TABLE 11: TEN IMPORTANT QUESTIONS TO ASK YOUR THERAPIST ABOUT YOUR DIAGNOSIS

After two or three sessions, consider asking the following questions:

1. **What "mental disorder" (Axis I) diagnosis will be sent to my insurance company and placed in my file?**

   Don't accept vague answers like "you are very depressed and anxious." Ask for the specific DSM name or names. You may have been given more than one Axis I diagnosis.

2. **Is the diagnosis temporary or is it more certain? Did you send a temporary diagnosis to my insurance company? Have you changed it since then?**

   Even if your first diagnosis was in error or modified, it will remain in your file. You have a right to know what it was.

3. **What led you to make this diagnosis?**

   Ask the therapist to explain the criteria for the diagnosis and how your signs and symptoms meet those criteria.

4. **How certain are you about this diagnosis?**

5. **Are there other diagnoses that you seriously considered? Why did you rule them out?**

6. **Do I have a "personality disorder" (Axis II) diagnosis? Did you send that to the insurance company also?**

   Some insurers do not ask for an Axis II diagnosis. Again, ask for the specific DSM diagnosis, if any. Do not accept vague answers.

7. If I have a personality disorder, what does that mean and what made you decide that I do?

If the therapist answers that the personality disorder is "atypical," "mixed," or "NOS," ask what the different features are that led to this diagnosis. For example, there might be "borderline" and "hysterical" features at the same time. If it is "NOS," ask if an unofficial name was added, such as self-defeating personality, sadistic personality, and so forth.

8. What does my diagnosis suggest about treatment?

9. Will you change my diagnosis in any way so that my insurance company will provide better coverage?

10. How do you feel about mental health diagnosis in general?

So Now What?

Once you get the information, what do you do with it? This is a very difficult question, but there are several options—some good, some okay, and some not so hot. How you perceive and interpret your "disorder" can affect your view of yourself, your ideas about personal responsibility, your attitude about therapy, and your chances of overcoming your difficulties.

Depending on the diagnosis, your first reaction could be one of relief, acceptance, curiosity, skepticism, anger, disbelief, or outright denial. But before relegating the therapist to the pits of hell, give him or her a chance to explain the rationale behind the diagnosis. If you disagree, state your reasons. And before jumping to conclusions, give yourself some time (days or weeks) to think about it carefully. Or, if you are so bold, discuss it with someone else you trust. Hearing a diagnosis can be difficult, particularly if it implies that your judgment, your reality base, or your personality style is being questioned.

Some diagnoses are easier to hear, since they simply describe symptoms without saying much about you as a person. Some patients take this to mean that the diagnosis is something they "have" rather than something they are a part of. Although this might be easier to accept, it makes treatment more difficult. If you react this way, you might run the risk of falling into a more passive role, waiting for the therapist or the medication to "fix" you. Even when biological factors are implicated, as in schizophrenia or bipolar (manic-depressive) disorder, they do not exist in a vacuum. Attitude, motivation, coping styles, and patterns of relating all influence recovery.

Using a diagnosis as an excuse or rationalization for one's actions can be particularly troublesome. Of course, there are times when feelings of severe depression, panic, anxiety, obsessions, substance abuse, and other overwhelming problems lead people to do things they wouldn't otherwise do—but for some, this becomes a way of life as they identify more and more with their disorder. It becomes a way to deal with the world rather than something to move beyond. Some people, consciously or unconsciously, even hold on to their problem, because they don't want to give up their therapist or their self-help group.

Another unfortunate reaction to a diagnosis is using it as a rallying point from which to blame others. Although this may be a healthy reaction in the beginning stages of therapy, for some it escalates into a long-term symbol of suffering and retribution. While there indeed may be extremely valid reasons to implicate or blame others, there is a danger of getting stuck in that position. Litigation attorneys may love eternal victims, but it is the patient who ultimately loses.

A more beneficial response might be to take the diagnosis with a grain of salt and use it as a general guideline for organizing and talking about some of your symptoms and complaints. In most cases, it is not an end in itself, nor is it written in stone. Use the diagnosis as a starting point for therapy. In time, you and your therapist may be able to move miles beyond the artifical boundaries imposed by the diagnosis. After all, you are far more complex, unique, and diverse than your "clinical symptoms and signs."

WHAT THE
DIAGNOSIS
MEANS

SELECTED ADULT
DIAGNOSTIC CATEGORIES
AND CASE EXAMPLES

ABOUT

THIS

SECTION

Categories and Code Numbers

Part 2 is divided into thirteen chapters, each covering a major adult psychiatric diagnostic category and many of the subcategories, as found in the *DSMIII-R* (1987) and/or *DSMIV* (1994). For example, chapter 11 describes the anxiety disorders as a whole, as well as some of the individual subcategories—generalized anxiety disorder, panic disorder, social phobia, OCD, and PTSD. **Not all categories or subcategories from the *DSMIII-R* and the *DSMIV* have been included.**

The numbers listed in parentheses after each category, e.g., MPD (300.14/F44.8), are the diagnostic codes used for administrative and billing purposes. You might find one or more on your insurance statement—without the actual diagnostic name(s). The first number (300.14) is the *DSM* code used in the United States, while the second number (F44.8) is the code found in the *International Classification of Diseases*, 10th edition. Depending upon the diagnostic category, the last decimal digit in both versions is often used to indicate the subtype, severity, or special feature of the disorder. Thus, if a patient has been given one of the diagnoses listed in this book, the code number may not match exactly.

The descriptions of the categories and the associated symptoms have been compiled from the *DSM*, as well as many other sources. Please be aware that they have been simplified for the general reader and are not meant to serve as definitive diagnostic criteria or as substitutes for the *DSM* criteria. This material is supplied for general information only. Readers wishing more in-depth technical information are strongly encouraged to purchase the *DSM*, available from the American Psychiatric Press, Inc., 1400 K Street, NW, Washington, DC 20005.

Making Sense of the Diagnoses

Each chapter describes the major features of each disorder, followed by a list of additional symptoms or factors commonly seen. Not everyone suffering from the disorder experiences all the symptoms listed. In fact, in many instances a person only needs to experience, say, four out of eight symptoms to meet the *DSM* criteria for the diagnosis. In addition, certain symptoms must persist for a certain period of time before the therapist can make the *DSM* diagnosis. Thus the kind of symptoms, the number of symptoms, and the duration of symptoms all need to be considered by the therapist in order to make a diagnosis. You saw examples of the diagnostic procedure in chapter 6.

The list of symptoms and features is followed by other information that therapists might look for in making the diagnosis. This includes relevant information from the psychosocial history and other important clues.

Also listed are other diagnoses that might be confused with the one being considered. These diagnoses may have similar but different symptom and duration criteria. It is extremely important for therapists to consider carefully each of the other diagnoses listed. In some cases, patients may meet the diagnostic criteria for more than one category. Needless to say, distinguishing between similar diagnostic categories is one of the most difficult tasks faced by therapists.

Case examples are provided to illustrate the typical symptoms and patterns found in selected diagnostic categories. Some of the cases (well disguised) have been chosen from the author's practice, while others are composites of other known cases. The cases chosen are those that clearly meet the diagnostic criteria. In actual practice, however, therapists frequently encounter more ambiguous cases.

Special Tricks

You should also be aware that therapists have an "out" if a person doesn't exactly fit a certain category or subcategory. After all the nit-picking over diagnoses, therapists can simply diagnose "mood disorder not otherwise specified (NOS)," "anxiety disorder NOS," "personality disorder NOS," and so forth, for any symptoms that don't meet the full criteria for any specific disorder. With these tricky escape routes, therapists can get you coming or going. After all, you do have a disorder—don't you?

Getting Started

As a starting point in locating a possible diagnosis, use the "Quick Guide to Selected Diagnoses and Major Symptoms" found on the following pages. Refer to the page number indicated to learn more specific diagnostic information.

TABLE 12: QUICK GUIDE TO SELECTED DIAGNOSES AND MAJOR SYMPTOMS

Axis I Psychiatric Disorders	Major Symptoms
Adjustment disorder (p. 154)	Short-term emotional reaction to a stressor. Depression, anxiety, withdrawal.
Major depressive episode (p. 158)	Depression, loss of interest, changes in sleep, appetite, energy level for at least two weeks.
Dysthymic disorder (p. 161)	Depressed mood lasting at least two years, doesn't go away for more than two months at a time.

Bipolar disorder, manic (p. 163)	Unusual elation, euphoria. Grandiose ideas, decreased need for sleep.
Cyclothymic disorder (p. 166)	Mood swings. Alternating periods of depression, elation, for at least two years. Less severe than mania.
Premenstrual dysphoric disorder (PMDD) (p. 167)	Disabling mood swings, irritability, depression, anxiety, lethargy at onset of menstrual cycles.
Generalized anxiety disorder (p. 171)	Chronic anxiety, nervousness, excessive worry for at least six months.
Panic disorder (p. 174)	Repeated panic attacks. One must occur unexpectedly. Fear of future attacks. May lead to agoraphobia.
Social phobia (p. 176)	Unreasonable fear and avoidance of certain social situations.
Obsessive-compulsive disorder (OCD) (p. 178)	Intrusive, persistent obsessions and/or compulsions.
Post traumatic stress disorder (PTSD) (p. 180)	Emotional numbing and flashbacks after a traumatic event.
Multiple personality disorder (MPD) (p. 184)	Two or more separate personalities. One predominates, but switching between them occurs.
Dissociative amnesia (p. 186)	Inability to remember past experience or identity after a traumatic event or situation.
Dissociative fugue (p. 188)	Unexpected flight from family or problems. Can't recall past.
Depersonalization disorder (p. 189)	An altered sense of reality. Self, body, or objects seem detached, unreal.
Hypoactive sexual desire disorder (p. 193)	Little if any desire for sexual activity.
Sexual arousal disorder (p. 194)	A recurrent problem in becoming physically aroused during sexual contact.

Orgasm disorder (p. 195)	Recurrent inability or delay in reaching orgasm after normal sexual excitement.
Sexual masochism (p. 198)	Being subjected to real physical pain and/or emotional abuse leads to sexual arousal.
Sexual sadism (p. 200)	Sexual arousal centers around the act of inflicting real physical pain, suffering, and humiliation.
Exhibitionism (p. 201)	Sexual arousal is achieved by showing sexual organs to unsuspecting strangers. Aroused by victim's response.
Pedophilia (p. 203)	Sexual urges are repeatedly directed toward children who have not yet reached puberty.
Frotteurism (p. 205)	Sexual arousal by furtively touching, rubbing against, or fondling a nonconsenting person.
Somatization disorder (p. 209)	A long history of many unexplained, often vague medical symptoms occurring in various parts of the body.
Hypochondriasis (p. 210)	Persistent fears of having a serious disease in spite of negative medical examinations.
Body dysmorphic disorder (BDD) (p. 212)	Strong belief that a normal body part is deformed, defective, or ugly.
Insomnia disorder (p. 216)	Problems falling or staying asleep, lasting at least one month.
Sleep-wake schedule disorder (p. 217)	Problems falling asleep or staying awake due to a mismatch between inner sleep rhythms and environmental demands.
Nightmare disorder (p. 219)	Repeated awakenings by frightening dreams, leading to intense anxiety.
Sleepwalking disorder (p. 220)	Repeated episodes of walking about while in an unresponsive state of sleep.

Anorexia nervosa (p. 224)	Refusal to eat, drastic loss of body weight, distorted body image.
Bulimia nervosa (p. 226)	Binge eating episodes, at least twice weekly for a minimum of three months. May include induced vomiting.
Intermittent explosive disorder (p. 230)	Explosions of destructive rage that are generally out of character.
Pathological gambling (p. 232)	Inability to resist impulses to gamble.
Kleptomania (p. 233)	Inability to resist impulses to steal. The act of stealing is the goal, not possession of the object.
Pyromania (p. 236)	Intense pleasure from deliberately setting fires, unrelated to financial gain, revenge, and so forth.
Substance abuse (p. 239)	Problems fulfilling personal, social, or vocational obligations because of substance use. Does not involve serious symptoms of dependence.
Substance dependence (p. 239)	Usually involves tolerance, withdrawal symptoms, inability to stop, serious problems of control.
Schizophrenia (p. 247)	May include delusions, hallucinations, impaired thinking, emotional flatness. Entire episode must last at least six months.
Schizoaffective disorder (p. 252)	Psychotic symptoms existing alone at times and with a mood disorder at other times.
Delusional disorder (p. 254)	Clinging to a false belief that defies logic, in spite of evidence to the contrary. Will not consider the possibility that belief is erroneous.
Brief psychotic disorder (p. 257)	A period of psychosis lasting less than one month. May be brought on by trauma.

Delirium (p. 261)	Brief state of fluctuating mental confusion brought on by a medical condition.
Dementia, Alzheimer's type (p. 262)	Progressive inability to learn and recall new information. Old information gradually is lost. Involves other thinking and physical impairments. An organic brain disease.
Alcohol-induced amnestic disorder (p. 265)	Severe memory impairment due to long-term, heavy alcohol use.

Axis II Personality Disorders	**Major Symptoms**
Paranoid personality disorder (p. 270)	Distrustful, suspicious, guarded, tense, rigid, critical. Misinterprets the actions of others. Expects to be exploited or harmed.
Schizoid personality disorder (p. 273)	Emotional detachment and social withdrawal. Prefers being alone. Cold, bland, flat, unresponsive.
Schizotypal personality disorder (p. 274)	Odd, eccentric, peculiar, aloof, distorted thinking and perceptions. May believe he or she has special powers.
Antisocial personality disorder (p. 276)	Violates rules, rights of others, impulsive, manipulative, seldom feels guilt or remorse.
Borderline personality disorder (BPD) (p. 278)	Intense mood swings, chronic feelings of emptiness, impulsive behavior, manipulative self-destructive acts, tumultuous interpersonal relationships.
Histrionic personality disorder (p. 281)	Very dramatic, excitable, highly emotional, but shallow, seductive. Endless need for reassurance and approval.
Narcissistic personality disorder (p. 283)	Grandiose, unrealistic view of oneself in spite of evidence to the contrary. Self-centered, demanding of special

	attention, praise. Shallow, fragile relationships.
Avoidant personality disorder (p. 286)	Avoidance of people and social activities out of fear of rejection, criticism.
Dependent personality disorder (p. 287)	Looks to other people for most decisions, clings, avoids conflict, fears loss of nurturance, fears being alone.
Obsessive-compulsive personality disorder (p. 290)	Perfectionistic, inflexible, emotionally constricted, authoritarian, engrossed in rules, regulations, lists.
Passive-aggressive personality disorder (*DSMIII-R* only) (p. 292)	Indirect expression of anger by passive resistance—forgetting, losing things, procrastinating, showing up late, and so forth.
Self-defeating personality disorder (*DSMIII-R*) only) (p. 295)	Repeatedly chooses people or enters situations that bring on hardship, suffering, and disappointment. Sabotages pleasure.
Sadistic personality disorder (*DSMIII-R* only) (p. 298)	Engages in cruel acts to control, intimidate, or humiliate others. Takes pleasure from the suffering of defenseless people and/or animals.

9

ADJUSTMENT DISORDERS

- **With Anxious Mood** (309.24/F43.2)
- **With Depressed Mood** (309.0/F43.2)
- **With Withdrawal** (309.83/F43.2)
- **With Mixed Emotional Features** (309.28/F43.2)

OVERVIEW

The adjustment disorders are probably the most overused categories diagnosed by therapists. When no other Axis I diagnoses can be found, almost anyone can qualify for an adjustment disorder, particularly if he or she is distressed enough to consider therapy. An adjustment disorder can be diagnosed if an identifiable psychosocial stressor (marriage, divorce, loss of job, change of schools, retirement, family changes, illness, and so forth) causes significant distress or interferes with normal functioning. Adjustment disorders take many different forms, ranging from depressed mood, anxiety, irritability, restlessness, withdrawal, and physical complaints to erratic behavior and conduct problems. The symptoms diminish as the stress eases or the person learns to adapt to the new situation.

ADJUSTMENT DISORDER, MIXED

Major Features—Adjustment Disorder, Mixed

- A specific life event triggers a relatively short-term emotional reaction that interferes with school, work, or relationships. Sometimes there is more than one stressor. The symptoms may last weeks or many months.
- To qualify for the *DSM* diagnosis, the emotional reaction must begin within three months after the stressful event.
- The diagnosis is not made if the symptoms are related to any other mental disorder or normal grief after the death of a loved one.

Additional Symptoms or Factors That May Be Seen

The adjustment disorders are divided into categories according to the symptoms seen:

Anxious mood: Agitation, nervousness, apprehension, worry.

Depressed mood: Frequent crying, hopelessness, and sadness.

Withdrawal: A desire to be away from people. In some individuals, social withdrawal is the most prominent symptom.

Disturbance of conduct: Fighting, disregarding the rights of others, reckless behavior, truancy, and so forth.

Physical complaints: Headaches, backaches, fatigue, and so forth.

Work or academic inhibition: A decline in the person's ability to do work and/or school tasks.

Mixed emotional features: In this type of adjustment disorder, a combination of the symptoms listed above may exist.

Other Information Helpful in Making the Diagnosis

People react to stress differently, depending on the way they perceive it, their coping abilities at that particular time in their lives, and the duration of the stressor. Something that might cause extreme distress in an adolescent may cause only minor upset in an adult, or vice versa; the severity of the life event alone does not necessarily determine the severity of the symptoms. Personal interpretation and context must always be considered.

The line between a "normal" or "expected" reaction to a stressful life event and an "adjustment disorder" has always been very hazy in spite of attempts to refine the diagnostic criteria. Nevertheless, the diagnosis does have value, since it is probably the most benign that can be given and still qualify for insurance coverage by most insurers.

Other Diagnoses and Conditions to Consider, Rule Out, or Include

All other Axis I disorders must be ruled out, including PTSD. In PTSD, the symptoms are usually more severe, last longer, and are brought on by a severe trauma that is outside the bounds of normal human experience.

Case Example—Adjustment Disorder, Mixed

Empty Spaces. Helen, a forty-eight-year-old freelance writer, wasn't certain, but she suspected that her fatigue, tearfulness, anxiety, and irritability were somehow related to the onset of menopause, although she had no other physical signs. After reading a popular book on the subject, she consulted with her physician, who assured her that she was jumping the gun. At Helen's request, he referred her to a therapist.

In therapy, Helen was able to trace the onset of her symptoms to her daughter's departure for college three months earlier. Although Helen had been extremely excited and happy for her daughter, her mood began to change several weeks after her daughter left. Helen thought about converting the empty bedroom into a den but couldn't bring herself to do it. She also sensed that her husband was becoming increasingly abrupt, aloof, and disinterested. He was generally not one to show his feelings and handled stress by burying himself in his work. There were long silences at the dinner table, silences that previously had been filled by their daughter's spirited banter. Helen suddenly felt old, alone, and empty. She missed an important writing deadline and nearly lost a lucrative contract.

Helen's symptoms were not severe enough to meet the criteria for any other mental disorders. In fact, they improved significantly after she and her husband eventually came in for couple's therapy. He was also quite upset by their daughter's departure but handled it by withdrawing from Helen. Both improved as they worked together to redefine their relationship in view of the "empty" space. They found that the space was different but certainly not empty.

10
MOOD
DISORDERS

- **Major Depressive Episode** (296.20/F32 or F33)
- **Dysthymic Disorder** (300.40/F34.1)
- **Bipolar Disorder, Manic** (296.40/F30 or F31)
- **Cyclothymic Disorder** (301.13/F34)
- **Premenstrual Dysphoric Disorder** (PMDD) (311/F32.9)
  (Included under Depressive Disorder NOS)

OVERVIEW

Anyone who has suffered from a mood disorder knows, beyond a doubt, that it bears very little relationship to the normal ups and downs of daily living. Normal moods come and go according to life circumstances or the person's ability to change focus or mind-set. People suffering from a mood disorder no longer feel in control of their mood or the way they come across to others.

Elevated mood (mania) and depressed mood are the two emotional states found in the mood disorders. They are classified according to the severity of the mania or the depression, and whether or not the mood alternates between the two.

MAJOR DEPRESSIVE EPISODE

People suffering from a depressive episode feel trapped in a depressed mood and can't seem to escape, no matter how hard they try. Most experience a variety of symptoms, including many of those listed below.

Researchers and theorists have attempted to divide major depression into various subtypes according to symptom patterns, but they have had some difficulty agreeing on the validity, usefulness, or names of the subtypes. This can be quite confusing for patients. Therapists might use words like *atypical* or *endogenous*, although these names are not used in the *DSM*. To confuse the issue further, major depression is sometimes referred to as "unipolar" depression. However, regardless of the name used, most psychiatrists prescribe a particular type of antidepressant medication according to the symptom patterns found.

No one knows what "causes" major depression, although many different contributing factors have been identified. Biology, body chemistry, genetics, stress, personality patterns, and negative attitudes all have been implicated in the disorder. Since these factors interact and influence each other, a single cause may never be determined.

Major Features—Major Depressive Episode

- Feelings of hopelessness, despondency, gloom, or sadness. Many patients feel worse in the morning, with the symptoms improving somewhat toward evening. Grooming may deteriorate. "I just don't care" is a common statement.

- An inability to enjoy or take interest in things that used to provide pleasure—hobbies, work, family, sex, food, and so forth. In mild cases, the patient can still perform tasks, although with difficulty. This may be nearly impossible in severe depression.

- Feelings of being run-down, exhausted, drained, overworked. Tasks may be left unfinished, and motivation may be decreased.

- Body functions may change, including sleep patterns, appetite, and sexual interests. Physical complaints often develop, such as indigestion, nausea, headaches, backaches, and so forth. Up to 80 percent of depressed patients experience insomnia, difficulty staying asleep, or early morning awakening. Some sleep excessively.

- Actions may be unusually slow and plodding, with little or no spontaneity. Speech is often slowed or delayed. Talking becomes an effort.

- Some patients feel agitated and have difficulty sitting still. Pacing and handwringing may be an effort to release tension.
- Anxiety often accompanies the depression, with feelings of dread and fear.
- Exaggerated feelings of low self-esteem, inadequacy, and failure. The worldview may be unusually pessimistic and hopeless.
- Problems concentrating, difficulty completing or putting thoughts together, problems making decisions. Thoughts may be full of ruminations and worries.
- Repeated thoughts of death or suicide. Most depressed patients think about suicide. One percent commit suicide during the first year of depression. The figure jumps to 10–15 percent for those experiencing recurrent depressions.

Additional Symptoms or Factors That May Be Seen

- **Delusions and hallucinations** are found in approximately 10 percent of depressed patients. Delusions usually center around ideas of serious illness, guilt, sin, persecution, and personal failure. The patient may hear voices that accuse and berate.
- **Melancholic type depression** involves a pattern of "vegetative" signs occurring together, such as slowing, early morning wakening, weight loss, and loss of pleasure.
- **Seasonal depression** comes and goes regularly according to the time of year.
- In "**masked depression**," a patient may not report feeling depressed although other depressive symptoms and signs are evident.

Other Information Helpful in Making the Diagnosis

To be considered for the *DSM* diagnosis, the individual must experience depressed mood and/or loss of interest for at least two weeks, along with four of the following symptoms: significant weight loss or gain; sleep problems; physical slowness or agitation; low energy; guilt or worthlessness; indecisiveness or problems concentrating; repeated thoughts of death or suicide.

A 1987 study by the APA estimated that 12 percent of the male population and 26 percent of the female population will experience major depressive symptoms at some point in their lives. The first episodes are likely to occur between the ages of twenty and fifty, although they can occur at any age, including childhood. According to most studies, the prevalence rate apparently does not differ according to race, culture, or socioeconomic status.

Many patients have only one episode of depression, although half experience recurrences. For some patients, the acute symptoms may disappear on their own after six months to one year. With therapy, this time averages approximately three months. Twenty percent of patients have the depression for a year or more.

Other Diagnoses and Conditions to Consider, Rule Out, or Include

At least fifteen other psychiatric disorders include depressive symptoms. Each must be considered carefully. Although most people seeking therapy do not have a contributing medical problem, a wide variety of medical problems can cause depression. Neurological and endocrine diseases, infectious diseases, cardiopulmonary disease, cancer, vitamin deficiency, exposure to toxic agents, and many other conditions may lead to depressive symptoms. You saw some of these listed in table 3 in chapter 4. However, in most of these cases, the contributing medical problems are known long before the patient ever reaches a psychotherapist. Although it sometimes happens, therapists (psychiatrists included) seldom uncover a previously undiagnosed medical disorder that may be causing the depression.

Many medications, including some antibiotics, analgesics, heart and blood pressure drugs, steroids, hormones, and even some psychiatric medications, can cause depression in certain individuals.

DYSTHYMIC DISORDER

Dysthymia used to be called "depressive neurosis" and is now considered to be a less severe form of major depression. Although it is a common diagnosis, it has also been controversial. Some clinicians argue that dysthymia doesn't belong in the same category as major depression since, in dysthymia, psychology and personality may play more predominant roles than biology and genetics. However, other clinicians have found medications useful in many cases, suggesting that dysthymia may indeed have factors in common with major depression. Some see it as a lifelong tendency to be depressed, related to personality and inborn temperament.

According to the *DSM*, the symptoms of dysthymia are very similar to but less severe than those of major depression. However, in contrast to major depression, the symptoms may persist over many years, with only mild fluctuations. In major depression, the symptoms may go away entirely for extended periods or never return.

Major Features—Dysthymic Disorder

- A depressed mood, lasting at least two years, that doesn't go away for more than two months at a time. The patient feels depressed nearly every day. Many patients report feeling depressed and unhappy, to varying degrees, most of their lives.
- Patients may be brooding, pessimistic, complaining, negative, self-critical, morose, sarcastic, and socially withdrawn.
- Depressive symptoms may include loss of energy, sleep and eating problems, irritability, hopelessness, feeling of inadequacy, inability to cope, and problems concentrating.

Additional Symptoms or Factors That May Be Seen

- Loss of interest in pleasurable activities.
- Loss of self-esteem.
- Preoccupations with health.

- **Withdrawal from emotional intimacy.**
- **Substance abuse.**
- **Decreased performance at work or school.**

Other Information Helpful in Making the Diagnosis

Women are diagnosed with dysthymia twice as often as men, although this may be because women are more likely to seek help. Most patients report that the symptoms start before age twenty-five and become a part of their lives for years. Other cases of dysthymia start after the development of another disorder, such as substance abuse, an anxiety disorder, or a medical problem. One in every five dysthymic patients eventually develops a major depression, particularly if there is a family history of depression.

Other Diagnoses and Conditions to Consider, Rule Out, or Include

Major depression, bipolar disorder, anxiety disorders, substance-related disorders, somatization disorder, personality disorders, certain medical conditions, and medication side effects.

Case Example—Dysthymic Disorder

Don Rickles. The accusation hit Jim like a searing knife to the heart, but he knew it was true. His twelve-year-old son fired out the words with angry tears in his eyes: "Dad, you don't seem to give a damn about anything. You won't go to my games; you never do anything but sit there, read your paper, and complain about other people. Something is always wrong. I'm sick of it! Sometimes I feel like I haven't had a father."

Jim, a thirty-five-year-old computer technician with a round stomach and a rapidly balding pate, related the story with great anguish to the intake therapist. The son's words hit on something Jim had known but ignored for years—he had been unhappy, depressed, and dissatisfied with himself and the world in general for as long as he could remember. Certainly, he loved his son and his wife, but he could never seem to generate much enthusiasm for anything. Left to his own devices, he would watch television or read endlessly. "The world and people are so screwed up, why bother?"

Jim had just gotten by in high school and technical college, putting in the minimum effort to pass. "I was usually down in the dumps, even then, but I tried to hide it by making fun of everything, kind of like Don Rickles. Sex was exciting for a while and kept the gray clouds away, but, you know, even that turned gray." His parents had been somewhat supportive but focused most of their attention on his older brother, who had been a star athlete. Jim felt inferior, less attractive, and fell into a pattern of "expecting nothing" to avoid disappointment. He sarcastically states, "Sometimes I think I approach life with a limp sword—ask my wife."

More recently, Jim has been having problems at work, misdiagnosing components and falling behind in repairs. "It just feels like I'm going through empty motions." However, some days are better than others and he is able to joke with his coworkers. Jim has no problems with sleep or appetite, and he denies suicidal thoughts. "But my less than diplomatic son might be happier if I stuck my nose in the pipe. This is just the way I've always been . . . a miserable creature, a malcontent, a fly in everybody's ointment. I hate it more than he does." He has frequent headaches, indigestion, and thoughts of running away to Aruba. "An oil tanker would probably disgorge itself on my beach."

BIPOLAR DISORDER, MANIC

Also known as manic-depressive disorder, bipolar disorder usually involves at least one episode of "mania" (an unusually elated, expansive, or irritable mood—described below) as well as episodes of major depression. However, some patients (approximately 15 percent) experience manic episodes without periods of depression. Others cycle back and forth between mania and depression, although there may be many months or years with no elevated or depressed symptoms. Unfortunately, most patients do experience recurrent manic symptoms, which, if untreated, may last three months or more. The depressive side of the cycle tends to last even longer without treatment. The manic-depressive cycles go beyond simple "mood swings" and significantly interfere with thinking, judgment, and insight to varying degrees according to the severity of the illness.

When maniclike symptoms last at least four days but are less severe and do not interfere as much with the person's ability to function socially or in work, the episode is referred to as *hypomania* rather than mania. Major depression with hypomanic episodes is known as bipolar II disorder.

Major Features—Bipolar Disorder, Manic

- Persistent elation or euphoria. People who know the person recognize that he or she is unusually cheerful, enthusiastic, or euphoric. Sometimes this turns to irritability and hostility as the mania progresses.
- The person may become grandiose and overconfident, with overblown ideas of importance, power, wealth, and special abilities. During the early stages, other people might find him or her witty, amusing, or even charismatic.
- A decreased need for sleep is almost always seen during a manic episode.
- Speech may be rapid and difficult to interrupt. Ideas come and go rapidly and may be only marginally related.
- As attention and concentration fade, the person may be easily distracted by insignificant details in his or her surroundings.
- The person may become very excited, hyper, and full of energy. The energy may be directed toward overly ambitious plans or high-risk behaviors such as gambling, spending sprees, impulsive traveling, promiscuity, or substance abuse.
- Insight is usually very poor. The person typically denies that there is anything wrong and often becomes increasingly belligerent and hostile as others attempt to intervene. Poor judgment is invariably present during a manic episode.

Additional Symptoms or Factors That May Be Seen

- **Delusions and/or hallucinations** (75 percent of patients). May center around grandiose or persecutory ideas.

- **Rapid mood changes**, from laughter to tearfulness, sometimes within minutes.
- **Loss of inhibitions**: imposing on other people, taking advantage, denying responsibility, lying, engaging in impulsive or bizarre acts.
- **Suicidal threats or actions.**
- **Assaultive or threatening behaviors toward others.**
- **Substance abuse.**

Other Information Helpful in Making the Diagnosis

At least one-half of those suffering from bipolar disorder have a family history of depression or mania. Manic symptoms usually begin suddenly, over several hours or days, although some may take a few weeks to develop. Most initial episodes occur in young adulthood and are often seen during or after periods of stress. Sometimes antidepressant medications trigger manic episodes in susceptible individuals. Specific personality traits do not appear to be related to bipolar disorder.

Other Diagnoses and Conditions to Consider, Rule Out, or Include

Schizophrenia, cyclothymic disorder (see next section), group B personality disorders, substance-related disorders, and certain medical conditions.

CYCLOTHYMIC DISORDER

Cyclothymia is generally considered to be a mild form of bipolar disorder: moods alternate between periods of hypomania (hypo = below, at a lower point) and moderate depression, but the symptoms do not reach the duration or severity of those found in bipolar disorder or major depression.

Major Features—Cyclothymic Disorder

- Alternating periods of depressed mood and hypomanic episodes for at least two years. Normal moods seldom last longer than a month or two.
- The symptoms during the hypomanic episodes are similar to those described for manic episodes, but they do not cause the same degree of impairment. Also, there are no delusions or hallucinations.

Additional Symptoms or Factors That May Be Seen

- **Depression is usually the reason for seeking help.**
- **Irregular and abrupt mood changes.** The cycles are shorter than those found in bipolar disorder.
- **Marked irritability.**
- **Disorganization.**
- **Conflicts with family and friends.** These are often provoked by the patient.
- **Frequent moves, job changes.**
- **Substance abuse is common.**

Other Information Helpful in Making the Diagnosis

A family history of depression and bipolar illness in first-degree relatives is found frequently. Symptoms are often seen in childhood and may become particularly troublesome by late adolescence. The unpredictable mood swings usually cause stress to the individual, family, and friends, although some people report feeling more creative and productive. Many patients with cyclothymia eventually develop a full-blown major depressive or bipolar episode.

Other Diagnoses and Conditions to Consider, Rule Out, or Include

Bipolar disorder, attention deficit hyperactivity disorder in children and adolescents, borderline personality disorder, substance-related disorders.

PREMENSTRUAL DYSPHORIC DISORDER (PMDD)

This "new" disorder is a disabling depression associated with hormonal changes that occur in women during the menstrual cycle. According to the *DSM*, it is more severe than PMS and affects less than 5 percent of the female population.

This diagnostic category has been the subject of heated controversy. Originally known as "late luteal phase dysphoric disorder," it first appeared as an unofficial diagnosis in the *DSMIII-R* (1987). Due to insufficient research data supporting the existence of the disorder, it was placed in the *DSM* appendix as a "proposed category needing further study."

However, in May 1993 the members of the APA voted to officially include PMDD in the *DSMIV* category "depressive disorder NOS" as well as in the appendix—in spite of the vocal objections of many researchers, women's groups, and therapists. Opponents of the category argue that the symptom criteria are so general and vague that they will be used to "pathologize" what for many women is a normal experience—a move that could lead to discrimination against women. Some charge that psychiatry is creating another new category simply for financial reasons. Supporters of the category contend that the diagnosis is backed by research—to ignore it would do a great disservice to the women experiencing the debilitating symptoms.

Whatever the final verdict is regarding this category, it is interesting to note an article that appeared in the APA journal *Hospital and Community Psychiatry* during the same month that PMDD was voted an official mental disorder. Coauthored by a member of the *DSMIV* work group investigating PMDD, the article briefly reviews the research findings and concludes:

> The data reanalyses showed that the prevalence of LLPDD [PMDD] varied depending on which scoring method researchers used, making it difficult to assess the validity of LLPDD [PMDD]. Results of the reanalyses in conjunction with conclusions from the literature review highlighted for the work group the true complexity of this disorder. (May 1993, 44:433)

If this is the case, the conclusions of the APA work group appear far from conclusive. One must wonder why the APA members chose to overlook these observations.

Major Features—Premenstrual Dysphoric Disorder (PMDD)

- According to the *DSM*, women with PMDD experience the symptoms listed below during the week before their period. The symptoms disappear a few days after the period actually begins.
- The symptoms have occurred during a majority of the menstrual cycles over the past year. To make the diagnosis, emotional and physical symptoms must be monitored on a daily basis for at least two months.
- Symptoms include: mood swings, anger or irritability, depressed mood, loss of interest, problems concentrating, lethargy, changes in appetite, feeling overwhelmed or out of control, and physical symptoms such as headaches, bloating, and breast tenderness. For the diagnosis, at least five of the above symptoms must be present, including at least one of the first four listed.
- The symptoms must seriously interfere with normal activities and relationships.

Additional Symptoms or Factors That May Be Seen

• **Symptoms of other mental disorders, particularly depressive disorders,** are often found in women diagnosed with PMDD.

• **Symptoms are most likely to occur in women over thirty** and often get worse with age.

• Some women develop **suicidal thoughts and feelings.**

Other Information Helpful in Making the Diagnosis

Since this diagnosis has the potential for misinterpretation and abuse, it must never be given (or accepted) in an offhand manner. A thorough evaluation is necessary to consider all factors. It must not be confused with PMS, which is not as severe or distressful.

At the present time, other than relieving some of the physical symptoms, treatment of PMDD has not been terribly successful. Hormone therapy rarely provides relief, and psychiatric medications have had only marginal results. For some women, just identifying the problem helps them to anticipate and cope with it.

Other Diagnoses and Conditions to Consider, Rule Out, or Include

PMS, other depressive disorders. When other disorders are present, unlike PMDD, they are not likely to go away several days after the menstrual period starts.

11
ANXIETY
DISORDERS

- **Generalized Anxiety Disorder** (300.02/F41.1)
- **Panic Disorder** (300.01/F41.0)
- **Social Phobia** (300.23/F40.1)
- **Obsessive-Compulsive Disorder (OCD)** (300.30/F42)
- **Post Traumatic Stress Disorder (PTSD)** (309.89/F43.1)

OVERVIEW

Since all of us experience varying degrees of anxiety, you may wonder how therapists draw the line between "normal" anxiety and an anxiety "disorder." Many questions come to mind in this regard: At what point does the *level* of anxiety become a disorder? How *often* does it have to happen? How *long* must it last? Does the *nature* of the anxious feeling make any difference? Are there different *types* of anxiety? What if it's triggered by terrible circumstances? What if it just comes out of the blue or seems to be around all the time? Don't people who have other problems such as depression also have a lot of anxiety? So why should anxiety be seen as a separate disorder?

Although they probably won't say so in public, researchers and therapists have had major problems sorting through this maze of questions. Their answers may look nice and neat and convincing on paper, but, in reality, they are far from complete at this time. Frameworks keep changing, as do the specific criteria that define the anxiety disorders. Nevertheless, researchers have had to come up with a set of guidelines for diagnostic purposes. To this end, they have tentatively identified several different types of anxiety disorders, although the boundaries between them are not hard and fast. Therapists frequently see a mix of symptoms that confuse the situation.

However, in spite of these complications, therapists and patients have found the categories useful for understanding and treating the anxiety. The nature of the anxiety will influence the focus of psychotherapy as well as the type of medication prescribed (if necessary).

GENERALIZED ANXIETY DISORDER

For most people, anxiety comes and goes according to the stresses of life. Although it can be extremely upsetting and bothersome, the anxiety usually subsides when the immediate stress is over. For other people, the anxiety experienced may be out of proportion to the stressful event and may even persist for several weeks or months after the situation is over. Either way, in both of these cases the anxiety is triggered by a real-life event and eventually goes away.

People with a generalized anxiety disorder are not so lucky. They experience chronic anxiety, worry, and physical tension nearly every day for at least six months, even when their life is going relatively well.

Major Features—Generalized Anxiety Disorder

- The person is chronically anxious, worried, and apprehensive about a variety of life circumstances. The worries are out of proportion to the circumstances and last for at least six months. One worry seems to follow another, even when things are going relatively well.
- Although the worries are unnecessary, the person has great difficulty pushing them aside and eventually becomes very

fatigued, overwrought, and unfocused. There may be problems completing daily tasks.

- The chronic tension leads to physical and emotional symptoms such as abdominal distress, headaches, shakiness, insomnia, irritability, problems concentrating, dizziness, edginess, lapses in attention, and a host of other troublesome symptoms.

- The diagnosis usually is not given to patients with another disorder such as panic disorder, social phobia, obsessive-compulsive disorder, hypochondriasis, or anorexia, since the worries in those cases are often quite specific. Sometimes, however, there is also a generalized anxiety disorder underlying those disorders.

- According to the *DSM*, anxiety brought about by substance abuse or withdrawal does not qualify for the diagnosis. In those cases, the diagnosis would be substance-induced anxiety disorder.

Additional Symptoms or Factors That May Be Seen

- **Mild depression,** which may develop into major depression.
- **Panic disorder** eventually develops in 25 percent of the people with generalized anxiety.
- **Substance abuse** may become a problem as the person attempts to self-medicate as a means of coping.

Other Information Helpful in Making the Diagnosis

The disorder most commonly begins in men and women between the ages of twenty and thirty, although it is also found in children. For some individuals, the chronic anxiety is triggered initially by a series of upsetting circumstances. The circumstances may change, but the anxiety remains. For other people, the anxiety begins after a bout with major depression. Some researchers believe that genetics plays a part in the disorder, claiming that one in every four patients has a first-degree relative with similar symptoms. Other researchers dispute these findings.

Other Diagnoses and Conditions to Consider, Rule Out, or Include

Anxiety is a part of many emotional disorders, including but not limited to depression, adjustment disorder, dysthymia, schizophrenia, depersonalization disorder, and so forth. In most of these cases, the anxiety is related to the primary disorder. A separate diagnosis of generalized anxiety is not made. Medical problems such as hyperthyroidism must also be ruled out, along with anxiety brought about by substance abuse.

Case Example—Generalized Anxiety Disorder

The Shaky Waitress. "I'm driving both of us crazy. My husband tells me I make mountains out of molehills, that I have diarrhea of the mind. He's a real turkey and no help at all. But this thing is serious! I'm ready for the fucking loony bin."

Judy, a thirty-two-year-old waitress, had just taken a leave of absence after dropping a platter of spaghetti in a customer's lap. "For the past year, I haven't been able to do a damned thing right—my mind wanders, I feel all shaky inside, I get light-headed, my heart races, and I feel totally wrung out like an old dishrag. I look and feel like shit. And if someone is stupid enough to cross me, watch out! Okay . . . so the guy with the spaghetti was getting on my nerves . . . everything gets on my screwed-up nerves, including your nosy secretary."

Judy has also been to her physician for headaches, nausea, gastrointestinal pains, and problems sleeping over the past year. "It all seemed to start after my husband lost his job. The landlord was ready to give us the boot. I couldn't shut my mind off. But we have money again and I still worry constantly—bills, my health, my job, my mother, the dog, you name it, a regular merry-go-round, and I can't get off." Judy has been a recovering alcoholic for twelve years, with no relapses. She denies any substance use. She is mildly depressed but shows no symptoms of any other psychiatric disorder.

PANIC DISORDER

People with a panic disorder (and some other anxiety disorders as well) experience repeated *panic attacks*. Panic attacks are sudden periods of intense, almost overwhelming fear and discomfort accompanied by a variety of physical symptoms such as dizziness, rapid heartbeat, trembling, hot flashes, chills, nausea, shortness of breath, chest pain, and tingling sensations. There is often a great fear of impending doom, dying, or going crazy. The attacks start abruptly and usually reach a peak within ten minutes.

Since panic attacks can occur in other anxiety disorders (e.g., certain phobias) as well as panic disorder, researchers have attempted to draw diagnostic boundaries based on the nature of the panic attacks and whether or not they are "triggered" by certain situations. As you will see, in panic disorder at least one of the attacks must come "out of the blue," without an identifiable trigger.

Major Features—Panic Disorder

- People with a panic disorder have repeated panic attacks that may fluctuate in severity and frequency. To qualify for the diagnosis, at least one of the attacks must occur unexpectedly. The attack comes out of the blue, for no good reason, or it may occur during a familiar situation that does not normally provoke so much anxiety.

- Once an attack occurs, the person may become preoccupied with fears of having another attack.

- Although at least one of the attacks is unexpected (usually in the beginning stages of the disorder), certain situations may eventually become associated with the panic attacks—crowds, driving, shopping, riding elevators, and so forth. The person fears that the situation may trigger another attack, not knowing whether it actually will or not.

- Many people with a panic disorder also develop agoraphobia. They avoid places or circumstances that might bring on an embarrassing panic attack, or places where help might not be available: closed-in spaces, bridges, shopping malls, restaurants, buses, and so forth. Some avoid these situations altogether, while others can handle them only when accompanied by another person. In severe cases, the person may refuse to leave home.

● According to the *DSM*, the diagnosis is not made if the panic attacks
  are brought on by substance use (including caffeine).

Additional Symptoms or Factors That May Be Seen

- **Depression.**
- **Suicidal feelings.**
- **Obsessive-compulsive tendencies.**
- **Relationship problems** may develop, particularly if
  agoraphobia begins to restrict activities.
- **Substance abuse** may become a problem as the person
  attempts to self-medicate as a way of coping.
- **Mitral valve prolapse**, a heart syndrome involving midsystolic
  "clicks," is found in 50 percent of panic-disorder patients.

Other Information Helpful in Making the Diagnosis

Panic disorder is very common and usually begins in the midtwen-
ties, but it can occur at any age. Agoraphobia is found in 60 to 70
percent of all panic disorder cases. Women with the disorder appear
to outnumber men 2 to 1. The disorder appears to have a strong
genetic basis, although some researchers link it with early childhood
separation and/or loss. The child's developing nervous system may
be permanently affected by the trauma.

Other Diagnoses and Conditions to Consider, Rule Out, or Include

Medical conditions such as hypoglycemia, thyroid problems, heart
conditions, neurological diseases, and pulmonary conditions must be
ruled out. Substance abuse and withdrawal must also be considered.

SOCIAL PHOBIA

Major Features—Social Phobia

- The person has recurring fears of certain social situations or activities in which he or she may be the object of public scrutiny. The fear centers around possible embarrassment, humiliation, and/or the display of anxiety symptoms.

- The person actively avoids the social situation, since it brings on intense anxiety or panic attacks. Sometimes even the thought of it can bring on great anxiety.

- The person realizes that the fear is unreasonable and finds that it is getting in the way of his or her life. The phobia can be very distressing.

- Examples include fear of public speaking, eating in public, answering the telephone, appearing foolish or saying stupid things in public, answering questions incorrectly, parties, dating, and so forth.

Additional Symptoms or Factors That May Be Seen

The *DSM* lists three different types of social phobia:

- **Performance type** involves a fear of doing something in public, even though the activity does not produce anxiety when done alone (eating, writing, speaking, playing an instrument, and so forth).

- **Limited interactional type** is a fear of one or two specific social situations involving social interactions (dating, going to parties, dealing with authorities, speaking on the telephone, and so forth).

- **Generalized type** social phobia involves fear of most social situations.

- **Depression** is often found in severe cases.

- **Substance abuse** may develop as a way of coping.

Other Information Helpful in Making the Diagnosis

People with social phobia often feel trapped in a self-fulfilling, vicious cycle—the intense anxiety they experience before or during a social situation gets in the way of their performance or activity, essentially creating the humiliating or embarrassing situation that was so feared in the first place. They are not as likely to try again.

Social phobia usually begins in adolescence and is found more often in males than females. Although the course is often chronic, it tends to decrease after middle age. Most people with the problem come to therapy because it is interfering with relationships and job advancement.

Other Diagnoses and Conditions to Consider, Rule Out, or Include

Most people have performance fears, but the symptoms are not as persistent or incapacitating as those experienced in social phobia. Also, normal performance fears do not involve the extreme avoidance behaviors found in social phobia.

Other diagnoses to consider include panic disorder and avoidant personality disorder. An additional diagnosis of panic disorder is made if the person also has had panic attacks that are unrelated to social or other specific fears.

OBSESSIVE-COMPULSIVE DISORDER (OCD)

Major Features—Obsessive-Compulsive Disorder (OCD)

- People with OCD suffer from intrusive, persistent obsessions and/or compulsions. The obsessions or compulsions are extremely upsetting, time-consuming, and interfere with daily activities.
- **Obsessions** are recurrent thoughts, feelings, ideas, images, or impulses that invade consciousness. Obsessions are intrusive,

absurd, irrational, and different from overblown worries about real-life problems. Examples are given below.

- Although the person usually realizes that the obsession is unreasonable, he or she nevertheless experiences feelings of anxious dread. To ward off these feelings or prevent a dreaded event, the person often feels compelled to carry out ritualistic behaviors or repeated mental acts. These are known as **compulsions**. Examples are given below.

- Most people with OCD try to resist the compulsions, since they realize that the compulsions are silly, ridiculously excessive, or unrelated to the event they are supposed to prevent. Nevertheless, OCD patients feel driven to perform them to relieve tension.

Additional Symptoms or Factors That May Be Seen

- **Obsessions** may include obsessive thoughts about contamination, violence, catastrophe or loss, a need for symmetry and order, or forbidden sexual thoughts.

- **Compulsions** usually fall into three categories:

    (1) **Washing**—repeated, time-consuming washing of hands, body, and other objects due to obsessions about contamination, body waste, germs, toxins, and so forth.

    (2) **Counting**—counting objects, repeating acts a certain number of times, ordering and arranging.

    (3) **Checking**—repeatedly checking locks, doors, windows, stoves, car tires, and so forth, to make certain that all is secure, even if checked minutes earlier. In spite of repeated checking, the person remains anxious, fearing that he or she has forgotten to do something, which might lead to terrible consequences.

- **Other compulsions** seen include praying, touching, wearing a certain article of clothing, repeatedly doing something in a particular manner, collecting objects, and a variety of unusual rituals. These actions go beyond simple "superstitious" behaviors.

- **Major depression** or **dysthymia** is found in nearly half of the patients with OCD.
- **Substance abuse** is common.
- **Concerning personality traits**, most patients with OCD do not have compulsive traits before the onset of the illness. OCD and obsessive-compulsive personality disorder may have little in common.

Other Information Helpful in Making the Diagnosis

Most OCD patients develop the symptoms before age thirty-five. Sometimes they come on suddenly, often after a stressful life event. For others, the symptoms develop gradually over a number of years. The course of the illness is usually chronic, although most people experience moderate to good improvement. Psychotherapy (usually behavioral therapy) coupled with medications such as Anafranil, Prozac, or Nardil, is very helpful in most cases. (See chapter 6 for an extensive case example—"Pollution Control.")

Other Diagnoses and Conditions to Consider, Rule Out, or Include

The compulsions found in OCD are not the same as the compulsivelike behaviors found in eating disorders, substance abuse, gambling, and certain sexual disorders. The *DSM* states that the latter are not true compulsions since the person gains pleasure from the activity and may not resist it. Other disorders such as major depression, schizophrenia, and delusional disorder may have obsessivelike symptoms. These must be ruled out.

POST TRAUMATIC STRESS DISORDER (PTSD)

PTSD is an emotional condition that develops after a severe trauma such as rape, combat, assault, serious accidents, natural catastrophes, and so forth. The symptoms, described below, may appear soon after the trauma or some may be delayed for many years.

Although PTSD is a very real, debilitating disorder, in recent years it has been abused as a catchall category for anyone who has gone through a traumatic experience. Litigation attorneys in civil suits have become particularly adept at stretching the diagnosis for their clients' purposes. Unfortunately, it may be all too easy to fake the symptoms for monetary gain. This state of affairs does an immense disservice to those who actually suffer from PTSD.

Major Features—Post Traumatic Stress Disorder (PTSD)

- The person with PTSD has been a part of or has witnessed a very disturbing, traumatic event. The event may have actually harmed the person physically, or it may have been very threatening. Or the person may have witnessed other people being threatened, injured, or killed.
- The person reexperiences the traumatic event in disturbing dreams, intrusive thoughts or images, flashbacks, or reenactments of the trauma. Reminders of the event (certain smells, dates, situations, and other things associated with the event) may trigger intense anxiety and physical distress.
- The person attempts to avoid situations, thoughts, feelings, or activities related to the event. Important parts of the actual trauma may not be remembered.
- A sense of detachment, estrangement, and "emotional numbing" is common. Emotions and feelings may become very restricted, particularly those involving love, intimacy, and sexuality. Pessimism about the future is the rule.
- Other anxiety-related symptoms may develop that were not present before the trauma, including problems concentrating, sleep difficulties, irritability or explosive outbursts, jumpiness, and becoming overly vigilant and on-guard.
- The symptoms must last for more than one month. Similar symptoms lasting less than one month are diagnosed as acute stress disorder (308.3).

Additional Symptoms or Factors That May Be Seen

- **Major depression.** Feelings of guilt or humiliation are common.

- Panic attacks and dissociative states.
- Illusions and hallucinations.
- Memory impairment.
- Poor impulse control.
- Self-defeating or suicidal behavior.
- Substance abuse and dependence.

Other Information Helpful in Making the Diagnosis

The likelihood that PTSD will develop, as well as the severity of the symptoms, is related to the severity of the trauma. In devastating situations such as concentration camp incarceration, up to 80 percent of the survivors develop PTSD. Although it appears that anyone can develop PTSD, certain individuals are more susceptible—the very young, older people with physical problems, people without social supports, and individuals who had a psychiatric problem or personality disorder before the trauma. These individuals may have a lower threshold for developing the disorder. In addition, the symptoms they experience are likely to be more severe or prolonged.

Other Diagnoses and Conditions to Consider, Rule Out, or Include

The symptoms of PTSD can mimic or coexist with many other disorders, resulting in a complicated diagnostic picture. Major depression, panic disorder, generalized anxiety disorder, schizophrenia, and BPD must all be considered. Substance abuse is also a common problem. Faking or exaggeration of symptoms must be ruled out in cases involving monetary gain.

Case Example—Post Traumatic Stress Disorder (PTSD)

Original Sin. Mark, a thirty-year-old physical education teacher, knew that something had happened to him in the rectory twenty years ago.

Although he couldn't remember details, fleeting images of the young priest darted in and out of Mark's consciousness, particularly when he inhaled the scent of lemon oil used on the rich mahogany woodwork at church. When Mark was a young adult, sitting in the pews became an ordeal for him, while he fought off disturbing images and waves of unbearable anxiety. When the lemon oil began to smell like semen, he fled the church and never returned.

Mark married and is now the father of two children. His marriage is satisfactory, but he has great difficulty expressing feelings of love. He tends to feel like an observer rather than a participant during lovemaking. He has concerns about his sexual orientation, although he has never felt attracted to males. He wonders if other people see him as weak and vulnerable. The nagging anxieties and feelings of shame and humiliation are worse in the morning after a night of upsetting dreams. The lengthy showers don't seem to wash away the feelings.

As Mark reads the morning paper describing other abusive sexual acts committed by the young priest, he is overwhelmed by a flood of memories. The tears flow; he curls up in a ball and shakes. His body feels separate, detached, and vulnerable. He is frightened by urges to torture, maim, and castrate the priest—to make him experience the same pains and humiliations.

12

DISSOCIATIVE

DISORDERS

- **Multiple Personality Disorder (MPD)** (300.14/F44.8)
- **Psychogenic or Dissociative Amnesia** (300.12/F44.0)
- **Psychogenic or Dissociative Fugue** (300.13/F44.1)
- **Depersonalization Disorder** (300.60/F48.1)

OVERVIEW

People suffering from any of the dissociative disorders have one major symptom in common: great difficulty putting together thoughts, feelings, and memories into one coherent stream of consciousness or sense of self. In the dissociative disorders, some of the information that a person stores about him- or herself becomes separated from other information. It's as if the information exists in different compartments, with little or no communication between the compartments. Thus a person suffering from amnesia can appear totally normal, behaving in a reasonable, coherent manner, but have no memory of who he or she is. He or she no longer seems to have access to this information.

We all dissociate or feel somewhat estranged from our usual selves to some degree, but normally we have a general sense of who we are, what our bodies look like, and what our life experiences have been. Although we sometimes forget things or feel vaguely like someone we're not, all of the information about ourselves exists within us and is accessible through our "core" personality. There is a coherent sense of self.

Concerning "causes," it is generally thought that people dissociate or alter their consciousness as a way of dealing with traumatic situations and/or severe emotional conflicts. Disturbing thoughts and impulses are blocked from consciousness and certain aspects of reality are denied.

MULTIPLE PERSONALITY DISORDER (MPD)

Commonly known as "split personality," this is the most "dramatic" of the dissociative disorders and has been the subject of extensive media and public attention. Although people sometimes confuse MPD with schizophrenia, the two do not appear to be related.

Major Features—Multiple Personality Disorder (MPD)

- Two or more separate personalities exist within the same individual.
- Each personality represents separate states of consciousness, each with its own sense of self. The different selves may have different memories, feelings, behaviors, and appearances.
- Quite remarkably, the separate personalities can have different genders, ages, IQs, blood flow rates, respiratory rates, eyesight, and handwriting, as well as their own separate mental disorders.
- One personality is dominant at any particular time, but the individual can unpredictably "switch" from one personality to another.
- Each personality state is generally not aware of the others, although some are aware to varying degrees. Sometimes a single personality is aware of all the others.
- Amnesia is an important clue seen in MPD. Questioning by a clinician often reveals large segments of unaccounted-for time and memory lapses. The person may try to hide this symptom.

Additional Symptoms or Factors That May Be Seen

- **Depression and mood swings.** Most people suffering from MPD seek help for this reason.

- **Hearing voices coming from within the head.**
- **Out-of-body experiences.**
- **Nightmares.**
- **Impulses to cut or otherwise hurt oneself.**
- **Referring to oneself as "we."**
- **Other possible symptoms:** migraine headaches, gastrointestinal problems, panic attacks.

Other Information Helpful in Making the Diagnosis

People with MPD rarely have all the symptoms listed above, although they must have at least two distinct, controlling personalities to meet the *DSM* criteria for the disorder.

MPD is more frequently found in females than males. There is an extremely high incidence of childhood sexual abuse, physical abuse, and exposure to repetitive, sadistic trauma found in MPD sufferers. As abused children, they learned to alter their state of consciousness in order to keep the trauma separate from their daily state of awareness. A series of separate identities are developed in the process.

Other Diagnoses and Conditions to Consider, Rule Out, or Include

Psychogenic or dissociative fugue, amnesia, malingering (faking), depression, schizophrenia, BPD.

Case Example—Multiple Personality Disorder (MPD)

Closets. Roberta, a redhead, was twenty-two years old when she married Jack. Jack became alarmed when, after an argument, he discovered her in their bedroom, curled up in a corner and crying like a small child. This happened more than once. At other times Roberta became aggressive, tough, crude, and demanding, most unlike the woman he thought he'd married. Jack tried to talk to Roberta about what was happening, but she said she didn't remember any of it and accused him of exaggerating. When Jack discovered unfamiliar clothing in the closet and childlike drawings of a man with a big penis, he insisted Roberta go with him to the nearby mental health clinic.

At the clinic, Roberta confided feeling depressed and having frequent mood swings. She admitted that she had certain clothes but said she had absolutely no memory of buying them. She told the therapist that she sometimes had a vague feeling that she was somehow losing time. She also said she suffered frequent nightmares and on one occasion heard a voice inside her head telling her she was a slut.

Roberta said she did not abuse drugs and drank only in moderation. The therapist found her to be logical, coherent, and in touch with reality.

At first Roberta denied that she'd experienced anything unusual while she was growing up. But when she was pressed on this by the therapist, Roberta's eyes seemed to grow cold and hard and her body twitched as she suddenly turned away. Her voice lowered an octave and became coarse. She mumbled angrily under her breath, "I'd kill the bastard if I could."

Later in the interview Roberta said that her father had sexually abused her from as early as she could remember. She said the abuse had only ended when she was fourteen and her uncle caught her father in the act. The abuse also involved painful physical restraints and confinement. She had been tied up and locked in a closet whenever she made any attempts to resist her father's advances.

PSYCHOGENIC OR DISSOCIATIVE AMNESIA

Psychogenic or dissociative amnesia is a favorite of screenwriters and playwrights—the heroine is unable to recall her past experience or identity following a traumatic life event. In fact, it is quite common and occurs most often following war trauma, natural disasters, catastrophic events, or overwhelming life situations.

Major Features—Psychogenic or Dissociative Amnesia

- Usually in response to extreme psychosocial stress, the person is not able to remember significant personal information. The extent of the inability goes beyond normal forgetfulness.
- To qualify for the *DSM* diagnosis, the inability to recall cannot be explained by an underlying organic brain disorder, MPD, or substance use or withdrawal.

Additional Symptoms or Factors That May Be Seen

- **Normal, coherent functioning, except for the amnesia.** The person usually is not confused or disorganized.
- **Awareness of the memory loss** is the rule, but the person may not be terribly upset about it.
- **Localized amnesia is the most common.** The person is unable to recall details of the traumatic event or the short period of time that immediately followed (a few hours or days).
- **Selective amnesia** is an inability to recall certain but not all the details of a trauma or the events shortly following the trauma.
- **Generalized amnesia** is rare and involves loss of recall for an entire lifetime.

Other Information Helpful in Making the Diagnosis

The amnesia usually occurs suddenly and is more likely to be found in adolescents and young adults. Sometimes the trauma is not overtly catastrophic but involves an unbearable life situation or the expression of unacceptable aggressive or sexual impulses. Depression is often a complicating factor. In most cases, the person gains emotional protection by the inability to remember. Recovery is usually complete.

Other Diagnoses and Conditions to Consider, Rule Out, or Include

Amnestic disorder due to a medical condition, epilepsy, head trauma, metabolic disorders, brain infections, strokes, substance abuse, alcohol-induced amnestic disorder, malingering.

PSYCHOGENIC OR DISSOCIATIVE FUGUE

A fugue is like amnesia, except that the person purposely runs away from family and personal problems for hours or days at a time, creates a new identity, and fails to remember most aspects of his or her past life. People with psychogenic or dissociative amnesia may also wander away from home, but their actions are not as purposeful as those seen during a fugue state.

Major Features—Psychogenic or Dissociative Fugue

- People in a fugue state unexpectedly take flight from their customary homes and jobs, often traveling far away for hours, days, or, more rarely, months.
- During the time away, they do not remember important personal information—who they are, where they came from, and so forth.
- They may be confused about their identity or take on a new identity and occupation. The new identity may be partial or complete.
- To qualify for the *DSM* diagnosis, the disorder must not be a part of MPD, a medical condition, or a substance-induced disorder.

Additional Symptoms or Factors That May Be Seen

- Normal appearance and behavior in all other respects.
- No awareness that anything has been forgotten.
- No memory of the fugue state after it has ended.

Other Information Helpful in Making the Diagnosis

Like amnesia, fugue occurs suddenly and is a response to traumatic life events. People with depression, suicide attempts, heavy alcohol abuse, and certain personality disorders are more prone to this disorder. Recovery is rapid, with little chance of recurrence. The disorder is rare.

Other Diagnoses and Conditions to Consider, Rule Out, or Include

Multiple personality disorder. In MPD, the identities are usually more complete and alternate back and forth. Unlike fugue, this happens repeatedly over extended periods of time.

Cognitive disorders. In these disorders the person has other problems functioning and does not create a new identity. Cognitive disorders involve brain dysfunctions and are not a reaction to stress.

Malingering. Faking of the symptoms is relatively easy and very difficult to detect.

DEPERSONALIZATION DISORDER

Experiencing a sense of unreality is not at all unusual. Most people, particularly as children or young adults, have passing feelings that they are in a dream or detached from their bodies. External objects suddenly may look strange and distorted. Some people can bring about a variation of this experience through meditation or substance use. However, if the feelings are persistent, severe, and cause distress, they may indicate a depersonalization disorder.

Major Features—Depersonalization Disorder

* The individual experiences an altered sense of reality involving perceptions of self, body, or external objects. He or she may feel

mechanical, detached from the physical body, or caught in a dream state. Objects may change size and seem unreal.

- The sense of time and space may seem distorted. Consciousness may feel like it exists outside the body, like an external observer. Parts of the body may seem alien.

- In spite of the distortions, the person realizes the unreality of the symptoms and remains in touch with reality in other ways. There are no hallucinations, delusions, or problems in the thinking process.

- To qualify for the *DSM* diagnosis, the symptoms must be persistent, recurrent, and cause significant distress or problems in functioning. Many people suffering from this disorder fear they are going crazy.

- The diagnosis is not made if the symptoms are part of another disorder such as schizophrenia or if they are caused by substance abuse or a medical condition.

Additional Symptoms or Factors That May Be Seen

- **Anxiety.**
- **Depression.**
- **Obsessive thoughts.**
- **Dizziness and other physical complaints.**

Other Information Helpful in Making the Diagnosis

A first episode of depersonalization disorder is rarely seen in people after age thirty. With adults over thirty, feelings of depersonalization usually are associated with some other disorder. No one knows exactly what causes the symptoms, but they often occur suddenly after a period of anxiety or depression. For some people, the symptoms come and go for many years.

Other Diagnoses and Conditions to Consider, Rule Out, or Include

Many disorders can include feelings of depersonalization, including schizophrenia, depression, OCD, anxiety disorders, organic brain disorders, personality disorders, and substance abuse. In addition, many neurological and metabolic disorders bring about the symptoms. All of these must be ruled out before the diagnosis can be made.

13
SEXUAL
DISORDERS

- **Hypoactive Sexual Desire Disorder** (302.71/F52)
- **Sexual Arousal Disorder** (302.72/F52.2)
- **Orgasm Disorder** (302.73/F52.3)
- **Sexual Masochism** (302.83/F65.5)
- **Sexual Sadism** (302.84/F65.5)
- **Exhibitionism** (302.40/F65.2)
- **Pedophilia** (302.20/F65.4)
- **Frotteurism** (302.89/F65.8)

OVERVIEW

Sexual disorders can be quite complex and may involve a whole range of factors, including biology, physiology, intrapsychic issues, interpersonal conflicts, situational stress, and other emotional distress. Whether or not a sexual disorder or practice is normal or abnormal also becomes an issue. To provide some framework for defining and evaluating sexual disorders, the *DSM* breaks them down into two major groups—the *sexual dysfunctions* and the *paraphilias* (sexual deviations).

SEXUAL DYSFUNCTIONS

The sexual dysfunctions include problems in sexual desire or problems occurring during the normal sexual response cycle. Lack of desire, aversion to sexual activity, problems becoming aroused, inability to obtain an orgasm, and painful intercourse are considered to be sexual dysfunctions—*but the diagnosis is made only if the individual experiences considerable distress or interpersonal conflict because of the difficulty.*

For some people, the problems have been lifelong, while for others, the difficulties might be related to a particular partner or situation. In all cases, the diagnosis is not made if the problem is due to a medical condition alone, if it occurs only during the course of an Axis I psychiatric disorder such as major depression, or if it is brought about by drugs or medications.

HYPOACTIVE SEXUAL DESIRE DISORDER

Major Features—Hypoactive Sexual Desire Disorder

- The person experiences little, if any, interest in sexual activity. There may be no sexual fantasies or desires for sex of any kind.
- The *DSM* does not specify criteria concerning the degree of lack of interest or how long it must last before it qualifies as a "disorder." This is left to the therapist. The age, health, life situation, and baseline level of sexual interest of the person are all taken into consideration.
- To be diagnosed, the problem must cause personal distress or relationship conflicts.

Additional Symptoms or Factors That May Be Seen

- Significant stress, anxiety, or depression.
- Relationship problems.

- **Lack of attraction to partner** or **poor sexual techniques.**
- **Fears of sexuality.**
- **Discomfort with body image.**
- **Past sexual abuse.** (This is often found when there is an aversion to sex.)

Other Information Helpful in Making the Diagnosis

As you can see, this diagnosis can be highly subjective and cannot be given lightly. Many factors need to be considered, since different people have different sexual needs at various points in their lives. The therapist and patient must determine whether or not the lack of interest is indeed a problem and whether it's related to situational factors or stems from longer-term psychological conflicts.

Other Diagnoses and Conditions to Consider, Rule Out, or Include

As indicated previously, the diagnosis is not given if the problem is directly related to another Axis I psychiatric disorder, substance abuse, a medical illness, medication, or side effects of other medical treatments.

SEXUAL AROUSAL DISORDER AND ORGASM DISORDER

Major Features—Sexual Arousal Disorder

- In females, there is a recurrent problem becoming physically aroused during the excitement phase of sexual contact. The genitals may not swell, and lubrication is absent or inadequate.
- In males, there is a recurrent problem having or maintaining an adequate erection.

Major Features—Orgasm Disorder

- In women, the disorder is defined as a recurrent delay in reaching orgasm or an inability to have orgasm after normal sexual excitement.

- To make the diagnosis, the therapist must determine whether or not the delay or inability to have orgasm is related to insufficient sexual stimulation. Since women show a great variation in the intensity and duration of the stimulation they require, this determination is extremely important.

- According to the *DSM*, the therapist must also determine whether or not the woman's capacity to have an orgasm is what might be expected for her age and experience. Ease of reaching orgasm generally increases with age and sexual experience.

- For males, an orgasmic disorder is defined as a delay in or inability to reach orgasm after normal sexual excitement.

- In generalized orgasm disorder, the person is unable to reach an orgasm in any situation.

- In situational orgasm disorder, he or she may have problems reaching an orgasm only in certain situations or with certain partners. For some people, orgasm may be reached using a vibrator, but not during intercourse.

- For both males and females, to be diagnosed the problem must cause personal distress or relationship conflicts.

Additional Symptoms or Factors That May Be Seen—Sexual Arousal and Orgasm Disorders

- **Relationship problems:** poor communication, unresolved anger, lack of love, respect, trust.

- **Acting as a detached spectator** during sex because of shame, feelings of inadequacy, fear of losing control, performance anxiety, or negative emotions about sex.

- **Poor lovemaking techniques**, either partner. Failure to communicate needs to partner.

- **Intrapsychic conflicts** related to early psychosexual development.

Other Information Helpful in Making the Diagnosis

Most men who have difficulty attaining or maintaining an erection have been able to function adequately at some point in their lives. Dysfunction is most often related to psychological factors and may change according to circumstances or partners. However, up to 50 percent of these individuals may have medical problems that are contributing to or causing the difficulty. The ability to have morning erections or spontaneous erections when sex is not anticipated suggests psychological rather than medical problems.

Problems reaching orgasm are not common in males, affecting less than 5 percent of the population. In many cases, the difficulty is related to disease, surgery, neurological disorders, or medications. On the other hand, premature ejaculation is experienced by at least 30 percent of the male population.

The *DSM* estimates that approximately 30 percent of the female population experience arousal and/or orgasm difficulties. As in males, situational and psychological factors are the usual causes if the problem isn't related to inadequate sexual techniques. Most studies have found that women become increasingly orgasmic as they age and gain sexual experience. Hormone patterns may play a role with some women, as may endocrine diseases and certain medications.

Other Diagnoses and Conditions to Consider, Rule Out, or Include

Axis I psychiatric disorders, medical disorders (e.g., neurological disorders, endocrine disorders, cardiovascular disease, liver and kidney diseases, and so forth), medications (e.g., blood pressure medications, psychiatric medications, and so forth), surgical procedures and other medical treatments such as cancer therapy, and substance abuse.

Case Example—Sexual Arousal and Orgasm Disorder

Interrupted Fantasies. Linda, a twenty-seven-year-old attorney, has been married to Frank for six months. "I thought he would never know. But one night after making love I was so frustrated and angry with myself that I just burst into tears. He was totally shocked and thought he had done something horrible. I love Frank and don't want to deceive him anymore. It's not his fault; it's me. I'm tired of acting. I knew I shouldn't have gotten married.

"He's a great guy, very attractive, and extremely patient. But the harder I try, the worse it gets. I use massage oil to hide my dryness, and try to conjure up all sorts of fantasies. This has been going on for years. The last time I had an orgasm, I was fifteen years old. This is very embarrassing. . . . One night I was talking to a boyfriend, using the phone in my mother's bedroom. As we talked, I found myself rubbing against the red velvet wing tip of a small upholstered chair . . . it was incredible . . . something I will never forget.

"The next evening, I tried to do it again. I was totally immersed in it, oblivious. To my absolute horror, my mother walked in, her eyes blazing, her mouth wrenched up in an enormous fleshy knot, a noose to squeeze my breath away. I froze, straddling the chair with my skirt raised. The humiliation was total and I felt something within me ebb away. I shot out of the room, my heart pounding, my body trembling, and eventually ended up in the bathroom vomiting until I was blue in the face.

"My mother didn't speak to me for days. To make matters worse, she told my father. I couldn't look her in the eyes. She didn't allow me to date again until I was seventeen, saying something like 'I don't want you to end up like your trampy sister. These things have a way of getting ahold of certain people. You've gotta nip it in the bud until you're mature enough to handle it.'

"To this day, I feel slightly nauseous if my body starts to react sexually. Sometimes it goes away, but I still worry that I might lose control and vomit. I love the idea of sex, but I'd really like to get my mother out of the bedroom."

THE PARAPHILIAS

The paraphilias are seen as sexual "deviations" since they involve intense, persistent sexual urges and fantasies that may require objects, nonconsenting persons, pain, humiliation, or other unusual practices. These practices are considered different from "normal" sexual behaviors or experimentation because the urges are satisfied only by very specialized fantasies and acts—sex with children, fetishes, sex with animals, exposing genitals to unsuspecting victims, inflicting or receiving pain, and so forth. In most cases, emotional intimacy, bonding, and mutual affection are not a necessary part of the process. The paraphilias are much more common in males.

For many individuals, the specialized sexual urge becomes a driving force that encroaches upon their daily life and causes great distress, both legally and emotionally. Some individuals are unable to feel sexually aroused without the special stimuli, while others may resort to them only when stressed. For diagnostic purposes, the diagnosis is made only if the individual has acted upon the urges and fantasies or is significantly distressed by them. Passing fantasies do not qualify unless they are intense, occur frequently for at least six months, and cause distress.

SEXUAL MASOCHISM

In sexual masochism, pain, humiliation, and suffering are entwined with sexual arousal. Popular notions to the contrary, sexual masochism is more commonly found in males. In the past, the term *masochist* was used to describe any individual who repeatedly sought out humiliation, martydom, or emotional suffering, but this is no longer accurate. By today's definition, the term must be associated with sexual arousal.

Major Features—Sexual Masochism

- Sexual fantasies and urges center around victimization. In fantasy or act, the person derives sexual pleasure as the subject of *real* physical pain or mutilation, rape, bondage, imposed hardships, or other forms of physical and emotional abuse. Fantasies of *simulated* abuse do not qualify.

- Urges may be acted out alone or with a partner. Self-inflicted pain while masturbating is common. Whipping, restraining, spanking, and submission to humiliating commands are frequently carried out with a sadistic partner. Many masochists also have sadistic urges.

- The same act may be repeated for years, or it may become increasingly intense and dangerous, leading to severe injury or death.

- Fantasies alone do not qualify for the *DSM* diagnosis unless they persist for at least six months and cause distress. For some people, fantasies of simulated masochistic acts add excitement to their normal sex life. Real pain and suffering may not be desired or acted upon.

Additional Symptoms or Factors That May Be Seen

- **Relationship problems:** Partners may reject the behavior. Also, the sexual masochist may repeatedly instigate fights for sexual excitement.

- **Promiscuity:** seeking out sex with abusive people or strangers.

- **A long-term personality disorder.**

- **Underlying feelings of powerlessness:** a need to prove to themselves that they can withstand punishment.

- **Depression, shame, guilt.**

- **Childhood physical and/or sexual abuse.**

- **Substance abuse.**

Other Information Helpful in Making the Diagnosis

Sexual masochism tends to be chronic. The causes are unknown, although it probably develops at some point in childhood when a physically and emotionally painful event becomes linked with sexual feelings. The link could be accidental, purposeful, or learned from others. Childhood sexual abuse is a prime example, although not all masochists have experienced this. Predisposing personality traits are also likely factors.

Other Diagnoses and Conditions to Consider, Rule Out, or Include

Other Axis I disorders may be present. Group B personality disorders (borderline, histrionic, narcissistic, antisocial) may be found. A self-defeating personality disorder is not related to masochism unless it is linked with sexual arousal.

SEXUAL SADISM

The flip side of sexual masochism, sexual sadism involves sexual arousal associated with the suffering of a willing or unwilling victim. The diagnostic criteria are similar. Most perpetrators are males. According to the *DSM*, the disorder does not necessarily go hand in hand with rape because, for the majority of rapists, the victim's suffering is not a source of *sexual* excitement. However, some sexual sadists can and do rape, mutilate, or murder their victims. Others practice only with consenting partners, usually sexual masochists.

Major Features—Sexual Sadism

- Sexual fantasies and urges center around *real* acts of inflicting physical pain, suffering, and humiliation. Fantasies of simulated abuse do not qualify.
- Sexual acts may involve confinement, beating, burning, whipping, and other forms and degrees of torture.
- Depending upon the severity of the disorder, the acts may become progressively more destructive, sometimes leading to mutilation and murder.

Additional Symptoms or Factors That May Be Seen

- **Relationship problems**; however, some individuals form relatively stable relationships with sexual masochists.
- **A long-term personality disorder.**
- **Underlying fears of sexual, physical, and emotional vulnerability.**
- **Childhood physical and/or sexual abuse.**
- **Substance abuse.**

Other Information Helpful in Making the Diagnosis

As in sexual masochism, the cause is probably related to the childhood linkage of a very strong emotional and sexual response to physical pain. The person may have witnessed intense suffering, inflicted it himself, or was the victim of physical and/or sexual assault. In addition, the disorder may involve genetics, hormonal imbalances, pathological personality traits, and other psychiatric disorders.

Other Diagnoses and Conditions to Consider, Rule Out, or Include

Dissociative disorders (chapter 12) are sometimes found in sexual sadists who actually murder their victims. All other Axis I disorders need to be considered. Antisocial personality disorder and, more rarely, sadistic personality disorder are also found. In sadistic personality disorder, the abusive pattern usually isn't linked to sexual arousal.

EXHIBITIONISM

Exhibitionism almost always involves a male exposing his genitals to an unsuspecting woman or girl. Females may engage in various degrees of exhibitionism for sexual or emotional gratification, but the acts are seldom done to frighten or shock unsuspecting victims. Although male exhibitionism is often seen as a joke or harmless nuisance, to many female victims it feels more like a "mini-rape."

Major Features—Exhibitionism

- Either in fantasy or real acts, the exhibitionist is sexually aroused by showing his penis to unsuspecting strangers, most often women or girls.
- Sexual excitement occurs in anticipation of the act and is followed by masturbation during or after the exposure.
- The victim's reaction of shock, disgust, or fear is usually an essential part of the sexual stimulation.
- There may be fear of actual physical contact. The act is often carried out in public places where contact is not possible.

Additional Symptoms or Factors That May Be Seen

- Low self-esteem.
- Feelings of sexual inadequacy.
- Social isolation.
- Emotional immaturity.

Other Information Helpful in Making the Diagnosis

As in the other paraphilias, fantasies alone do not qualify for the *DSM* diagnosis unless they persist for at least six months and are distressing to the person.

No one knows how exhibitionism develops. Psychoanalysts might relate it to fears of castration, powerlessness, and an inability to combine sexuality and intimacy. Other theorists attribute it to learning and conditioning in an individual plagued by social isolation and inadequacy. Whatever the case, it usually begins in adolescence and may dissipate to mere fantasy as the individual reaches middle age.

Other Diagnoses and Conditions to Consider, Rule Out, or Include

Other related forms of paraphilia, such as voyeurism and telephone scatologia (making obscene phone calls), must also be considered. It is not unusual for an individual to carry out or progress to several different paraphilias. If actual sexual contact does occur during or after exposure, the act primarily becomes one of rape or molestation rather than exhibitionism.

PEDOPHILIA

Of all the paraphilias, pedophilia (sexual involvement with children before they reach puberty) triggers the most public outrage. As more and more information becomes available documenting the damaging and cyclical effect of childhood sexual abuse, the identification and treatment of pedophilia has become a national concern.

The public is quickly learning that the pedophile is likely to be male, a family member, relative, teacher, clergyman, or other individual in a position of trust. They are also learning that "treatment" programs usually perform better on paper than in reality. Public trust has been thrown into turmoil as revelations of repeated abuse keep surfacing.

Major Features—Pedophilia

- For the *DSM* diagnosis, the sexual fantasies or acts must be directed toward children before they have reached puberty, generally age thirteen or younger.
- Many people with pedophilia are also attracted to adults and outwardly appear to have otherwise normal relationships and

marriages. Up to 95 percent claim to be heterosexual, although they may be attracted to children of both sexes.

- Molestation commonly involves genital fondling, oral sex, penetration with penis or objects, and picture taking (either alone or in groups).
- Emotional coercion is common, although some degree of force also may be seen. Physical violence is less likely but does occur, particularly if the perpetrator is sexually sadistic.
- Many pedophiles win over their victims with caring, kindness, and attention. In many cases, the perpetrator believes that the feelings are genuine. Whether this is true or not, the harmful effects of the acts are usually rationalized or denied.
- Pedophiles often marry women with attractive children or gravitate toward work or recreational activities involving children.

Additional Symptoms or Factors That May Be Seen

- **Alcohol and substance abuse.**
- **Childhood sexual abuse.**
- **Emotional immaturity.**
- **A need to control and dominate.**
- **Low self-esteem.**
- **Feelings of sexual inadequacy.** May be fearful of normal heterosexual or homosexual relationships.
- **Intrapsychic conflicts** related to psychosexual development.

Other Information Helpful in Making the Diagnosis

According to the *DSM*, the diagnosis is not made if the perpetrator is under sixteen years old or is less than five years older than the child involved. Clinical judgment is recommended in assessing relationships between teenagers.

The *DSM* also states that an isolated act or acts with a child may not indicate pedophilia, particularly if the event is situational and the preferred sexual partner is an adult. In addition, the acts or fantasies must persist over a period of at least six months.

Many pedophiles deny or rationalize their acts, while others are filled with immense shame and remorse as they fight seemingly irresistible urges. Some become depressed and suicidal. For reasons that are unclear, treatment generally has been more effective for individuals preferring children of the opposite sex.

Other Diagnoses and Conditions to Consider, Rule Out, or Include

Other paraphilias, such as exhibitionism, voyeurism, and sexual sadism, may also be involved. In addition, although rape and incest do not exist as specific *DSM* diagnostic categories, they may play a role in the pedophilia. Psychiatric disorders that seriously impair judgment or impulse control also must be considered.

FROTTEURISM

Anyone who has ridden a crowded subway or bus knows how easy it might be for someone to "accidentally" touch or rub against the tightly packed bodies. Such a situation is the perfect sexual habitat for a person with frotteurism.

Major Features—Frotteurism

- The sexual fantasies and/or acts involve touching, rubbing against, or fondling the body of a nonconsenting person. Males appear to be the exclusive perpetrators.
- The acts usually occur in crowded situations where the perpetrator can more easily blend in or escape.
- The person usually rubs his penis against an unsuspecting woman's buttocks or another part of her body until he reaches orgasm. Or he may use his hands to touch her breasts and genitals. The victim often doesn't know what's happening until it's too late— even then, she might not be certain it wasn't accidental.

- The sexual excitement comes from touching the victim, rather than any form of sexual aggression. The frotteurist usually fantasizes that he is having normal, loving sex with a consenting partner.

Additional Symptoms or Factors That May Be Seen

- **Shame and embarrassment.**
- **Passivity:** lack of assertiveness.
- **Social isolation:** poor social skills.
- **Fear of women and intimacy**—however, some people who practice frotteurism are married.
- **Lack of other sexual outlets.**

Other Information Helpful in Making the Diagnosis

Not much is known about frotteurism, since these individuals rarely come in for treatment unless they are caught. They usually choose scenarios carefully and plan their moves with an easy escape in mind. If that fails, they can at least claim that the contact was accidental, which might be difficult to disprove. As in the other paraphilias, fantasies alone don't qualify unless the individual is distressed by them.

Other Diagnoses and Conditions to Consider, Rule Out, or Include

Other major psychiatric disorders with impaired judgment must be ruled out, including the organic mental disorders, where uninhibited touching might occur.

Case Example—Frotteurism

Ups and Downs. Stewart always made certain that he looked like any other respectable businessman in Manhattan. He was, after all, a forty-seven-year-old insurance salesman with a knack for flawless presentations. His routine was simple yet carefully prepared and executed. Each morning, dressed in an expensive business suit and carrying a soft leather duffel bag over his shoulder, Stewart headed for his sexual playground: the high-rise elevators of New York City.

Any high rise would do, but Stewart preferred the older buildings with smaller, slower elevators. They were certain to be crowded, particularly at 8:45 in the morning. As he scanned the sleepy group of corporate workers awaiting the elevators, he invariably found *her*, early twenties, close-fitting skirt or pants, yet appearing somewhat reserved, uncertain, and deferential. It was easy to sidle up behind her as the bodies pressed into the elevator. If he was lucky, she would ride with him all the way.

The moves were almost always the same: Stewart nudged her buttocks with the protruding end of the soft duffel bag. Invariably, she would turn her head in a startled glance at the distinguished-looking gentleman carrying the bag. As he apologized profusely and won her smile, his left hand slipped toward the end of the bag and his open palm pressed against her buttocks. His right hand was busy in his pocket as he rode the rapturous fantasies to her floor. In the duffel bag, of course, there was always a change of underwear.

To his delight, Stewart found that the victims were either too shocked, afraid, unknowing, or simply too uncertain to protest. In the several instances that they reacted with strong words, Stewart gave a warm, concerned smile, apologized again, and made a quick but poised exit at the next floor.

Stewart sought therapy after his most recent victim turned and kneed him in the groin. Although he beat the legal charges, he feared further exposure. In therapy Stewart revealed that elevator sex had been his primary means of sexual gratification for the past fifteen years, even through the course of several brief relationships. "I had sex with at least two hundred different women every year. What more could I ask for?"

14
SOMATOFORM
DISORDERS

- **Somatization Disorder** (300.81/F45)
- **Hypochondriasis** (300.70/F45.2)
- **Body Dysmorphic Disorder (BDD)** (300.71/F45.2)

OVERVIEW

The somatoform disorders have two major features: (1) all involve physical symptoms of some sort that cannot be explained adequately by any known medical causes, or, if a minor medical problem is found, it is blown all out of proportion; and (2) all involve certain behavioral and emotional patterns suggesting that psychological conflicts are strongly influencing the physical symptoms.

Diagnosing the somatoform disorders can be very tricky and should never be done in an offhand manner. There are many nonspecific medical disorders and undefined syndromes that come and go and are very difficult to pin down. Chronic fatigue syndrome, lupus, and multiple sclerosis are prime examples. Diagnosing a psychiatric disorder can be all too easy. Ideally, people diagnosed with a somatoform disorder have been through extensive medical examinations many times and have psychological patterns that support the diagnosis.

SOMATIZATION DISORDER

Major Features—Somatization Disorder

- A long, complicated medical history, beginning before the age of thirty, of many different physical complaints involving **pain** in different parts of the body, **gastrointestinal problems, sexual or reproductive symptoms**, and vague **neurological symptoms**. Patients with somatoform disorder have had symptoms in each of these areas. Medical exams and lab tests cannot explain the symptoms fully.
- Diarrhea, vomiting, abdominal pain, back pain, joint pain, dizziness, palpitations, irregular menstrual periods, trouble walking, shortness of breath, and amnesia are common symptoms. The list can be extensive.
- Persistent medical help seeking is common in these patients, since they usually believe that they have been ill most of their lives. Often their life-style has been changed to accommodate the symptoms.
- The medical complaints are usually vague, inconsistent, disorganized, or exaggerated. They may be presented in a dramatic manner.
- A chronic history of emotional, interpersonal, and occupational problems is frequently seen. Anxiety and depression, including suicidal tendencies or threats, are often present.

Additional Symptoms or Factors That May Be Seen

- Manipulative, attention-seeking, dependent behavior.
- Antisocial or histrionic personality disorders.
- Substance abuse, including prescribed medications.
- **Auditory hallucinations.** (But the person remains in touch with reality.)

Other Information Helpful in Making the Diagnosis

The disorder tends to run in families and seems to involve genetic factors, learned behaviors, and cultural influences. It most often is found in the economically and educationally disadvantaged. A chaotic or unstable childhood is common. The disorder is rarely found in males.

Other Diagnoses and Conditions to Consider, Rule Out, or Include

Physical disease, depressive disorders, anxiety disorders, schizophrenia, substance abuse, personality disorders, and malingering.

HYPOCHONDRIASIS

Major Features—Hypochondriasis

- The individual is preoccupied with health concerns and fears that he or she *has* a serious disease, in spite of negative medical examinations and reassurances.
- Although the individual can consider the possibility that the fears have no basis, he or she usually insists that a disease will be found if physicians keep looking or give it more time to develop.
- The fear of serious disease often centers around cardiovascular and gastrointestinal functioning, minor body imperfections, vague pains, and numerous other minor symptoms. A fear of heart disease is seen quite frequently as the person becomes preoccupied with heartbeat and pulse.
- Sometimes symptoms of hypochondriasis develop after an actual illness or the illness or death of a loved one. However, to meet the *DSM* diagnosis, the symptoms must persist for at least six months.

Additional Symptoms or Factors That May Be Seen

- **Depression and anxiety.**
- **Obsessive-compulsive personality traits.**
- **Seeking a sick role to escape responsibilities.**

- **Dissatisfactions with physicians.**
- **Frequent childhood illness, or illness of family members.**

Other Information Helpful in Making the Diagnosis

Men and women are equally likely to be hypochondriacal, and the condition can develop at any age. Most patients usually don't seek psychotherapy and may be quick to change physicians if they recommend therapy. The medical preoccupations may come and go, returning during times of stress. Personal relationships are likely to suffer, as is job performance.

Other Diagnoses and Conditions to Consider, Rule Out, or Include

Medical conditions that are difficult to detect must be ruled out. Preoccupations with body functions and fears of disease can be a part of many psychiatric disorders that need to be considered, including delusional disorder (somatic type) and other psychotic disorders, depression, dysthymia, generalized anxiety disorder, panic disorder, OCD, phobias, and organic brain disorders. In these cases, the preoccupations are likely to diminish as the main disorder is treated.

Case Example—Hypochondriasis

False Alarms. Thirty-eight-year-old Noreen tosses and turns, stares at the ceiling, hides her head under the pillow, and finally awakens her husband. "Bob, it's real this time; please wake up. Feel my pulse!" Bob groans but complies. "My chest feels tight, and it feels like I can't breathe. . . . Bob, let's go, please!"

The emergency room nurse immediately recognized Noreen, who had been seen here approximately four times over the past eight months. It was always the same thing—chest pains, rapid pulse, and shortness of breath. Extensive testing in the past showed no abnormalities whatsoever. The nurse helped Noreen to relax and assured her that her problems were brought on by anxiety. Noreen responded but refused to take a mild tranquilizer, stating, "It might just cover up the real symptoms." She eventually spoke to a psychiatric nurse on duty.

Noreen's symptoms began eight months ago after her father died suddenly from a heart attack. "I walked around like a zombie after he died. I was in total shock. It all started one night when I couldn't sleep. Suddenly I was aware of my heartbeat, pumping away, pulsing without stop for so many years. What if it should get tired or fall out of rhythm? As I thought about it I began to panic, and my heart started to race and I could feel irregularities. I knew there was something wrong and I'm still not convinced that I'm okay. It doesn't seem to happen when I'm hooked up on the monitors."

Noreen's preoccupations brought on paniclike symptoms, but she was not suffering from a panic disorder. In addition, she had a tendency for obsessional brooding but did not meet the criteria for OCD or major depression. Psychotherapy centered around the loss of her father and dependency issues. Her preoccupations and fears diminished significantly but returned briefly during periods of stress. "I'm probably okay, but I'm not taking anything for granted."

BODY DYSMORPHIC DISORDER (BDD)

BDD is another one of those "hidden" disorders more recently discovered by the media. Since BDD involves imagined defects in appearance, predictably it has been a source of fascination for the talk shows. Self-proclaimed "experts" have come out of the woodwork to peddle their wares, while certain "wonder drugs" have been touted as treatment. Nearly everyone is insecure about some aspect of his or her body, but those who actually suffer from BDD know that the problem goes far beyond this and is anything but trivial. They also know that the new medications help some but not all.

Major Features—Body Dysmorphic Disorder (BDD)

- People with BDD strongly believe that a body part is deformed, defective, or ugly—in spite of reassurances that it is, in fact, normal. If minor imperfections do exist, they are blown out of proportion.

- Preoccupations typically center on facial features, hair, skin imperfections, breasts, genitals, hands, or feet.

- Social situations may become a source of great anguish, particularly if the imagined defect is not easily concealed. Some people with BDD go to extremes to avoid social contact and become prisoners in their own homes. Some avoid mirrors, while others constantly check the imagined defect.

- According to the *DSM*, the diagnosis is not made if the person is unable to consider the possibility that the defect is exaggerated or imagined. In those cases, the belief may have delusional, psychotic qualities. The person's grasp on reality is much more tenuous. Also, the diagnosis is not made if the person is suffering from anorexia.

Additional Symptoms or Factors That May Be Seen

- **Major depression and severe anxiety** are common.
- **Obsessive-compulsive personality traits.**
- **Social withdrawal.**
- **Shopping for doctors, unnecessary surgery.**

Other Information Helpful in Making the Diagnosis

No one knows what causes BDD. Some theorists attribute it to psychodynamic factors—e.g., the body part may hold some unconscious meaning. This explanation often infuriates those with the disorder. Others see it as a variation of OCD or delusional disorder, with a combination of psychological and underlying biological causes. The course of BDD is often chronic, although for some patients the use of Prozac reduces the intensity of the preoccupations. (See the end of chapter 5 for the case of Phil, a twenty-two-year-old male with BDD.)

Other Diagnoses and Conditions to Consider, Rule Out, or Include

The diagnosis is not made if the distorted body image is due to anorexia, a mood disorder, schizophrenia, or an organic brain disorder.

15
SLEEP
DISORDERS

- **Insomnia Disorder** (307.42/F51.0)
- **Sleep-Wake (Circadian Rhythm) Disorder** (307.45/F51.2)
- **Nightmare Disorder** (307.47/F51.5)
- **Sleepwalking Disorder** (307.45/F51.3)

OVERVIEW

Most people have had problems falling or staying asleep or awakening with nightmares at some point in their lives, particularly during periods of stress and anxiety. These episodes are usually transient and diminish as the stress- or anxiety-producing situation improves. However, if the problem is a major concern, lasts for more than a month, and causes distress or problems functioning, a sleep disorder may be diagnosed.

Sleep disorders include problems falling asleep or staying asleep, poor sleep quality, sleeping too much, or problems keeping normal sleep-wake cycles. Other sleep disorders involve unusual disturbances during sleep such as sleepwalking and nightmares. Most disorders can be traced to stress, psychological conflicts, other psychiatric disorders, unhealthy life-styles, alcohol and drug use, medications, or physical illness.

INSOMNIA DISORDER

Major Features—Insomnia Disorder

- Problems falling asleep, staying asleep, or with sleep that may be long enough but does not provide restful relief. The problems must persist for at least one month to qualify.
- During the day, the person may have problems concentrating, low energy level, and a depressed, irritable, or anxious mood.
- At bedtime, most people with insomnia ruminate about life circumstances and feel physically tense. The fear of not being able to sleep causes even more distress. Some people have a lifelong pattern of insomnia that may not be related to other emotional conflicts.
- Some types of insomnia may be symptoms of other disorders such as major depression, bipolar disorder, and the anxiety disorders. Treatment must focus on these underlying conditions.

Additional Symptoms or Factors That May Be Seen

- **Life changes, grief, loss, trauma, anticipation, apprehension, and so forth**, may trigger insomnia.
- **Alcohol and other substance abuse** is seen frequently and can lead to severe insomnia, even after the substances are discontinued. Sleeping pill abuse leads to tolerance and more insomnia.
- **Medical conditions.**
- **Aging may lead to more frequent awakenings.**

Other Information Helpful in Making the Diagnosis

Most people require six to nine hours of sleep to function adequately, although this tends to decrease with age. On the average, it normally takes half an hour or less to fall asleep. Many people with insomnia are found to have another Axis I psychiatric disorder. Depression often causes awakening during the night, early morning wakening, or excessive sleeping. Anxiety disorders and the adjustment disorders more often lead to problems falling asleep. People with the mania of bipolar disorder also have insomnia, although they may get by on very little sleep.

Other Diagnoses and Conditions to Consider, Rule Out, or Include

Axis I depressive and anxiety disorders; medical factors such as arthritis, angina, metabolic and endocrine diseases, infectious diseases; medications such as beta blockers, antidepressants, thyroid medications; withdrawal from tranquilizers; substance abuse. Sleep-wake (circadian rhythm) disorder must also be ruled out. (See next section.)

SLEEP-WAKE (CIRCADIAN RHYTHM) DISORDER

All of us have internal biological clocks that govern the cycles of certain body functions, especially sleep. Known as "circadian rhythms," these cycles generally last about twenty-four hours and persist even if a person doesn't see a clock or the sun. Problems arise when the environment demands a cycle that is out of sync with a person's internal rhythm, which may not be operating on a normal twenty-four-hour cycle. Jet lag, changes in work shifts, and frequent sleep interruptions often lead to sleep-wake disorders. The person is forced to be awake when his or her body wants to sleep, or vice versa.

Major Features—Sleep-Wake (Circadian Rhythm) Disorder

- Due to a mismatch between inner sleep rhythms and environmental demands, the person may be unable to sleep when he or she wants to sleep, may fall asleep when it is not wanted, or may have problems waking up when necessary.

● If the problem persists, the person may feel lethargic, disoriented, out of sorts, and generally sick. If the person is allowed to follow his or her normal sleep-wake cycle, the symptoms disappear.

Additional Symptoms or Factors That May Be Seen

- In **delayed sleep phase syndrome,** the person is usually a night owl whose normal sleep cycle begins late at night and extends through the morning—which may be out of whack with a job schedule.

- In **jet lag syndrome,** the person crosses time zones and is forced to follow a different sleep schedule. The symptoms may disappear in two or three days if given a chance.

- In **shift work syndrome,** the person is required to work shifts that don't match his or her natural rhythms or must switch back and forth between shifts.

Other Information Helpful in Making the Diagnosis

People tend to vary in their ability to adapt to changing schedules. Young people are generally the most adaptable, but they are more likely to fall into a delayed (late night) sleep phase disorder due to social activities or the lack of a consistent schedule. As people age, the circadian rhythm normally shortens, leading to earlier bedtimes and awakenings.

Other Diagnoses and Conditions to Consider, Rule Out, or Include

Insomnia disorder must be ruled out, since it is not the same as sleep-wake (circadian rhythm) disorder. People with a sleep schedule disorder have no problem falling asleep if allowed to do so during their normal rhythm. Treating the disorder with regular sleep medication may lead to unnecessary complications, without resolving the basic problem.

NIGHTMARE DISORDER

Major Features—Nightmare Disorder

- The person is repeatedly awakened by long, frightening, vivid dreams that provoke intense anxiety. Sometimes the dreams have similar, threatening themes.
- The person awakens very quickly and is immediately alert. He or she may even bolt from the bed. The dream usually can be remembered in detail.
- Nightmares are usually triggered by stressful events, trauma, life transitions, physical illness, or emotional problems.

Additional Symptoms or Factors That May Be Seen

- **Sensitive, creative, or fragile individuals** may be more prone to nightmares. Sometimes the problem is lifelong.
- **Mental health problems** are more likely to be found in adults with nightmares than in children, who often outgrow nightmares.
- **PTSD** may be associated with some types of nightmares.
- **Certain drugs and medications** may cause nightmares.

Other Information Helpful in Making the Diagnosis

Occasional nightmares are not necessarily indications of "deeper" problems, particularly if they occur during stressful life situations. However, apparently half the people who experience recurrent nightmares report that it's been a problem since childhood. Certain personality characteristics may set the stage for the disorder.

Other Diagnoses and Conditions to Consider, Rule Out, or Include

All current medications must be reviewed, since usage or withdrawal may lead to nightmares. Another sleep disorder, sleep terror disorder, does not involve disturbing dream sequences. The person awakens abruptly in a state of confused, disoriented panic and may scream or thrash about in great agitation. The incident is seldom remembered in the morning.

SLEEPWALKING DISORDER

Major Features—Sleepwalking Disorder

- Although in an unresponsive state of sleep, sleepwalkers can carry out complex activities such as dressing, going to the bathroom, eating, or washing. Some leave their home or even attempt to drive. Coordination is poor and clumsy.
- The person can usually see and haphazardly navigates a route, although there is always a risk of injury. The face appears blank, staring, and unresponsive. He or she is very difficult to awaken.
- The person may eventually awaken partially and return to bed or awaken elsewhere in the morning, with no memory of how he or she got there. The episode is not remembered, but the individual may recall bits and pieces of dreamlike images.

Additional Symptoms or Factors That May Be Seen

- Talking is usually mumbled or incoherent, with no dialogue.
- Aggression is seldom seen.

- Personal injury may accidentally occur.
- Normal mental functioning is seen after the person is completely awake.

Other Information Helpful in Making the Diagnosis

Sleepwalking tends to run in families and may be caused by slight neurological difficulties, although stress, fatigue, and lack of adequate sleep can set it off. The disorder usually begins in childhood and affects up to 15 percent of all children. For most, these are isolated episodes that diminish as adulthood is reached. Adults rarely have the disorder to any significant degree.

Other Diagnoses and Conditions to Consider, Rule Out, or Include

Seizure disorders, other sleep disorders, other Axis I psychiatric disorders, and, in adults, personality disorders.

Case Example—Sleepwalking Disorder

Nightmoves. Much to Barbara's chagrin, Harold went on his nightly journeys at least once a month. Over the course of their three-year marriage, she had tried everything short of harnessing him to the bed. Typically, Harold would bolt upright in bed, look around, mumble something, pick at the sheet, throw it off, and stumble over to his robe. If Barbara didn't intervene, he would head out to the kitchen and stare into the open refrigerator interminably, as if watching a movie. He never actually ate anything. More often than not, he eventually wandered into the living room and continued his sleep on the sofa. Harold never remembered the episodes, although he was no longer surprised to wake up on the sofa.

Most of the time, Harold never even reached the bedroom door, since Barbara was awake enough to steer him back to bed. One night, however, Barbara awoke to an empty bed. Assuming that Harold was watching the refrigerator or asleep on the sofa, she drowsed off again—until the phone rang. It was the police. Harold, barefoot and wearing only a robe, was in police custody after ramming the family car into a fire hydrant. The police assumed he was psychotic and wanted him committed. Barbara and the staff at the psychiatric emergency room convinced them otherwise.

Harold, for his part, was completely perplexed and embarrassed, but at least he had a good story to tell his students at the university. Barbara hid the car keys, placed double locks on the doors, and seriously considered a large harness.

16

EATING

DISORDERS

- **Anorexia Nervosa** (307.10/F50.0)
- **Bulimia Nervosa** (307.51/F50.2)

OVERVIEW

Before 1980, anorexia and bulimia were hardly mentioned in the professional literature and, in fact, did not exist as separate, official diagnostic categories. Although both disorders have been known for many years (anorexia for several centuries, bulimia for several decades), cases were relatively rare until the past twenty years. It is now estimated that up to 10 percent of young American women and adolescents have an eating disorder. Some researchers have found that 15–40 percent of college women have experienced bulimic symptoms, while 1 percent of adolescent girls are anorexic. Most theorists attribute the dramatic increase in cases to our society's obsession with thinness. Since 95 percent of the people suffering from an eating disorder are female, some theorists argue that the disorders arise from the unrealistic physical expectations of a male-dominated society.

Anorexia (refusal to eat) and bulimia (binging, often followed by purging) have many features in common, as well as many differences. Up to one-half of anorectic patients also develop bulimic symptoms, but bulimic patients are not as likely to develop anorexia.

People with bulimia alone are usually more outgoing, sexual, impulsive, and angry than those with anorexia. Either way, both disorders can lead to serious physical complications, and anorexia can lead to death.

ANOREXIA NERVOSA

Major Features—Anorexia Nervosa

- Incessant preoccupation with food and dieting, accompanied by a refusal to eat and an exaggerated fear of becoming fat. For the diagnosis, the person's body weight must be at least 15 percent below what would normally be expected according to age and height. Females with the diagnosis have also missed at least three menstrual periods in a row.
- Anorectic patients see their body in a distorted manner and insist that they feel fat, in spite of an emaciated appearance.
- Patients may obsessively count calories, exercise constantly, or take laxatives. Some give in to their hunger and go on secret eating binges, often followed by self-induced vomiting and other bulimic symptoms. Food may be hidden in odd places.
- Most anorectic patients do not acknowledge their condition and are only distressed by their fears of becoming fat. They seldom seek help on their own. Eating becomes a major battleground in relationships with others.

Additional Symptoms or Factors That May Be Seen

- **Major depression** is often present.
- **Obsessive-compulsive traits.**
- **High-achieving, perfectionistic tendencies.** Fear of being ordinary or average.
- **Problems in sexual adjustment and other normal developmental stages.**

- A sense of ineffectiveness, except around eating issues.
- Troubled family relationships.
- Medical problems related to the weight loss, e.g., heart problems, digestive disturbances, loss of menstrual periods, body temperature problems, and so forth.

Other Information Helpful in Making the Diagnosis

Anorexia usually begins between the ages of twelve and thirty, with most cases starting in adolescence. It tends to be found more often in upwardly mobile populations in the United States. Although no single family pattern has been exclusively linked to anorexia, families of anorectic patients are often described as overprotective but unable to address conflicts directly. The patient apparently diverts attention from parental conflicts and falls into an overly responsible but very insecure role. The normal stages of emotional maturation may be missed or avoided, particularly as the preoccupation with food conveniently replaces normal activities.

Since many people *without* anorexia were raised with family patterns like those described above, other important factors must be involved. Some researchers suggest that certain neurochemical processes may be triggered in vulnerable individuals, leading to a circular interaction between psychology and biology. However, at this point in time, medications have not been particularly effective.

Other Diagnoses and Conditions to Consider, Rule Out, or Include

All medical illness must be ruled out. Major depression can also lead to weight loss, but unlike anorexia, there is no preoccupation with food, fat, and body image. However, major depression and OCD are often seen with anorexia and must be considered. Bulimia is very common.

BULIMIA NERVOSA

Major Features

- People with bulimia have repeated, uncontrolled eating binges. Very large quantities of food (usually junk food) are gulped down secretly, leading to bloating and abdominal pain. For the *DSM* diagnosis, the binges must occur at least twice weekly for three months or longer.
- To prevent weight gain, the person resorts to dieting, laxatives, or diuretics. As the disorder progresses, vomiting may be induced to relieve the bloating and allow eating without fear of gaining weight.
- Binging and fasting may alternate, leading to mild weight fluctuations and further preoccupation with body image. Some people also develop anorexia.
- Depression, disgust, and anguish usually follow the eating binges. Because of this, bulimic patients are more likely to seek help than those with anorexia.

Additional Symptoms or Factors That May Be Seen

- **Impulsive behavior.**
- **Substance abuse.**
- **Depression and suicidal behavior.**
- **Shoplifting.**
- **Perfectionistic tendencies.**
- **Family difficulties—overt conflicts, lack of closeness.**
- **Medical problems from frequent vomiting,** e.g., electrolyte imbalance, dehydration, digestive problems, erosion of teeth, seizures.

Other Information Helpful in Making the Diagnosis

Bulimia usually begins in late adolescence, but some people don't develop the symptoms until their late twenties. The psychological aspects of bulimia are very similar to those found in anorexia, although personality characteristics may be somewhat different. As described earlier, people who have bulimia without anorexia tend to be more gregarious, impulsive, and angry than patients with anorexia. Families of bulimic patients are generally seen as more distant, rejecting, and overtly conflicted. For the patient, food becomes a way of coping. The parents of bulimic patients are often obese and frequently depressed.

As with anorexia, the causes are highly debatable. Some antidepressants appear to reduce binging behavior in certain individuals, although psychotherapy is the treatment of choice. Many therapists treat bulimia as a form of addictive behavior.

Other Diagnoses and Conditions to Consider, Rule Out, or Include

Anorexia, major depression, BPD, substance abuse, and certain neurological diseases.

Case Example—Bulimia

Burger Queen. For Tania, a twenty-four-year-old graduate student in fine arts, it all began after boyfriend Hans—"a golden hunk with a sculptured body"—poked his finger in her stomach and made snorting sounds like a pig. Tania was devastated, particularly since it triggered memories of childhood humiliations. Her mother was overweight, overbearing, and the subject of ridicule by Tania's friends. Tania, extremely attractive and petite, vowed to stay that way, even though she often turned to food for comfort. An overriding fear was that heredity would take its course. "I knew that if I ever became like my mother, I would kill myself." Until now, she assumed that she had been very successful in creating her own identity.

Tania is now obsessed with food and strenuous exercise. For the past eight months she has been trying to follow a strict daily routine: a diet of fruits, vegetables, chicken, fish, and "energizing" supplements from health food stores; half an hour of aerobics, half an hour of weight lifting, and, finally, one hour of jogging. Although her weight has remained nearly the same, Hans has praised her firm, well-defined body contours.

But Hans does not know that Tania is on the verge of killing herself. "I feel totally trapped and know I'm going to lose in a big way. It's like I'm living a lie. I hate it and I hate myself, how I feel, who I am." Tania reveals a secret detour during her daily jog. "Near the end of the run I am ravenous, particularly as I pass by the Burger King—the smell drives me crazy. I used to resist, but now it happens four or five times a week—I wolf down two huge burgers, a large fry, an apple pie, a chocolate shake, or even more. It's like I can't stop. I could eat until I explode. The first time I was so sick and bloated I could hardly stand it. A friend showed me what to do—it was almost too easy. A finger down the throat was all it took to bring relief and a strange feeling of well-being."

Tania's sense of relief was short-lived, as feelings of depression, disgust, and self-loathing set in. "I never knew how much I depended upon my looks and thin body, like I didn't really know the person in there. It's scary."

17
IMPULSE
CONTROL
DISORDERS

- **Intermittent Explosive Disorder** (312.34/F63.8)
- **Pathological Gambling** (312.31/F63.0)
- **Kleptomania** (312.32/F63.2)
- **Pyromania** (312.33/F63.1)

OVERVIEW

Most of us have done something impulsive at one point or another in our lives, in spite of our better judgment. If the act ended up harming us or others, it is not likely that we would make the mistake again, at least to the same degree. Somehow, we would resist the impulse or modify it in some manner, particularly if the act would lead to humiliation, social rejection, legal difficulties, and other personal turmoil.

People with an impulse control disorder repeatedly act on certain impulses that are harmful. They usually feel a tension or excitement before carrying out the act that is relieved or gratified only by the completion of the act. Afterward they often feel shame and remorse. Many people with an impulse control disorder resist it on some level but nevertheless give in to the gratification. Others plan out the act and feel very little regret after its completion.

Although substance abuse disorders and the sexual paraphilias such as pedophilia, voyeurism, exhibitionism, and so forth, also involve failures to resist impulses, the *DSM* has created a separate major category—impulse control disorders not elsewhere classified—to cover some additional impulse disorders such as intermittent explosive disorder, pathological gambling, kleptomania, pyromania, and trichotillomania. (Trichotillomania involves impulses to pull out one's hair and will not be covered here.)

INTERMITTENT EXPLOSIVE DISORDER

This category is controversial since it defines certain violent behavior as a distinct psychiatric disorder. Although not stated in the *DSM*, the diagnosis is often used when there are unconfirmed suspicions that lifelong neurological weaknesses or mild brain abnormalities are a part of the problem, as well as psychological factors from a traumatic childhood. Some theorists fear that the category is too easily abused and used as an excuse in cases of spouse battering and other wanton acts of destruction. Others argue that explosive behavior, when seen, is usually a part of other psychiatric disorders and doesn't warrant a separate category. In short, the diagnosis could disappear from the books in the future.

Major Features—Intermittent Explosive Disorder

- These individuals appear to have a "hair trigger" and may grossly overreact to stressful situations, interpersonal conflict, or perceived slights. They literally erupt in an explosion of rage—assaulting others, punching walls, destroying furniture, using their car as a weapon, and so forth.
- In some cases, there is no foresight and planning and the individual is seemingly unaware of consequences. He or she may strike out randomly. In others, the individual can delay and direct the outbursts toward a specific target.

- Some individuals claim amnesia after the outburst. Most express profound remorse or regret over their behavior.
- If a person's predominant mode of relating to the world between explosive episodes is generally impulsive and aggressive, the diagnosis usually is not given. In those cases, the violence is often part of a lifelong personality disorder.
- Many other psychiatric and medical disorders involve intermittent loss of control of aggressive impulses. According to the *DSM*, the diagnosis is not given if another disorder can better account for the behavior or if the behavior is a part of substance intoxication.

Additional Symptoms or Factors That May Be Seen

- **Depression and anxiety.** Some people become suicidal after the explosive episodes.
- **A sense of powerlessness and impotence**, an inability to otherwise control or change a threatening situation.
- **Strong, often unacknowledged dependency needs.**
- **A chaotic childhood**, often involving abusive, alcoholic parents.
- **"Soft" neurological signs** such as learning disabilities, tics, weaknesses on a particular body side, lazy eye, and so forth.
- **Head trauma and/or seizures in early childhood.**

Other Information Helpful in Making the Diagnosis

The disorder is more commonly found in males. Most patients have come from unstable family backgrounds. Emotional deprivation, parental conflict or substance abuse, and repeated displays of violence are common in the family atmosphere. Physical abuse and violence may be learned as an acceptable way to handle conflict. Learned behavior, the effects of emotional deprivation, and a highly reactive nervous system that may be "tuned" at birth have all been seen as possible factors in the disorder.

Other Diagnoses and Conditions to Consider, Rule Out, or Include

If a personality disorder is involved, such as antisocial or borderline personality, the pattern of impulsive behavior is more extensive than that seen in intermittent explosive disorder. In those cases, impulsiveness and aggression are part of the personality and do not come and go in such distinct episodes. Other disorders that may involve loss of control include psychotic disorders, substance-related disorders, and medical conditions such as epilepsy.

PATHOLOGICAL GAMBLING

Major Features—Pathological Gambling

- The person is unable to resist impulses to gamble and finds him- or herself preoccupied with behaviors and thoughts related to gambling.
- As in many addictive behaviors, the person develops a "tolerance" and needs more and more money and risk to produce the same excitement. If the person tries to control or stop the gambling, tension, irritability, and restlessness are experienced. The gambling often serves as an emotional escape.
- As problems develop as a result of the gambling (major financial loss, damage to relationships and occupational pursuits, criminal activities, and so forth) the urge to gamble usually increases, although there may be many attempts to control or stop it.
- Great efforts may be made to conceal the extent of the gambling. Lying and deceit are common, as the person increasingly structures his or her life around the gambling.
- As losses mount, the individual seeks bailouts from others and/or resorts to crimes such as embezzlement, forgery, or credit card fraud.

Additional Symptoms or Factors That May Be Seen

- **Major depression, OCD, or panic disorder.**
- **Mood swings related to winning and losing.** A high energy level and overconfidence may be followed by depression and suicidal feelings.
- **A belief that money will solve all their personal problems.**
- **Substance abuse.**
- **Antisocial personality disorder.**

Other Information Helpful in Making the Diagnosis

Many people with this problem have grown up in families or situations where gambling and alcohol abuse were present. Some researchers have found that the families of chronic gamblers valued financial success and status without teaching the planning and delay of gratification necessary to reach those goals. Others dispute these findings. Males often develop the problem in late adolescence, females much later in life. The disorder tends to progress in stages and may take up to twenty years to reach the point of desperation.

Other Diagnoses and Conditions to Consider, Rule Out, or Include

Bipolar disorder, antisocial or borderline personality disorder, alcohol or cocaine abuse, and social gambling. In social gambling, the person sets limits on losses and is able to resist activity that is too risky. The gambling is carried out with friends as a social activity.

KLEPTOMANIA

Major Features—Kleptomania

- The person is unable to resist strong and recurrent urges to steal, even if he or she has no use for the stolen objects. The act of stealing, rather than the object itself, is the goal.

- The stealing is not planned and occurs impulsively, even if the person has the money to pay for the object. Also, it is not done out of anger or revenge.
- There is a feeling of mounting tension before the act and relief or gratification after the object is stolen. This is sometimes followed by guilt and remorse.
- According to the *DSM*, the diagnosis is not made if the stealing occurs as a part of a conduct disorder or antisocial personality disorder.

Additional Symptoms or Factors That May Be Seen

- **Major depression.**
- **Anorexia and/or bulimia.**
- **Anxiety, guilt, fear of apprehension.**
- **Problems with relationships.**
- **Episodes of stealing may come and go in response to stress or loss.**
- **An underlying personality disorder.**

Other Information Helpful in Making the Diagnosis

Kleptomania is rare. According to the *DSM*, fewer than 5 percent of arrested shoplifters fit in this category. To complicate matters, some individuals fake the symptoms to avoid responsibility for their purposeful larceny. True kleptomania usually starts in childhood and persists off and on for years. No one knows what causes it, but the psychodynamic theories abound and center on feelings of neglect, low self-esteem, emptiness, vulnerability, a need for punishment, or a substitute for sexual gratification. Most people come to therapy only after they are caught.

Other Diagnoses and Conditions to Consider, Rule Out, or Include

Antisocial personality disorder, psychotic disorders, malingering, and organic disorder involving memory impairment must all be considered. Regular theft must also be ruled out. Unlike a person with kleptomania, the garden-variety thief steals for the purpose of obtaining or selling the object or as a vengeful act.

Case Example—Kleptomania

Empty Spaces. "I'm really very glad that nice young man stopped me and sent me here instead of calling the police. It couldn't go on any longer, and besides, I'm running out of room in my dresser drawers. I do try to hide the things, you know, but they're spilling out into the room. And I feel so guilty." Martha forced a smile, adjusted her glasses nervously, and primped her short gray hair. "It was terrible after my husband died in 1986, just terrible . . . all alone after fifty years together. And yes, my daughter loves me, but she has her own life, always moving from here to there."

Martha looked past the therapist in silence for several moments, then broke into sobs. "Have you ever had that empty feeling? I mean really empty, like there's nothing but pain in the pit of your stomach and a cold wind outside your door? Like warmth and love is just a bunch of dots on the TV tube? Maybe that's why I started stealing again. Now I just sit in my apartment, surrounded by all these lovely little things that I don't even need and certainly would never buy. But I do like filling the drawers, particularly the ones Fred used to use."

She blew her nose and turned in earnest toward the therapist. "I'll tell you a secret—I did it before I met Fred, but then it went away. I thought it was gone. Now the feeling starts while I'm doing the crossword puzzle, filling in the squares. I get this urge, and it builds and builds, until I know it's going to happen again. I try to fight it. But sooner or later I end up at the mall with my big shopping bags in tow. I promise myself I won't do anything, but then I pick up something smooth, round, pretty, or smelling like heaven and drop it into the bag. Such a feeling! I can almost cry with joy thinking about it! Fred's drawers are filled with such wonderful things, things that money could never buy!"

PYROMANIA

Major Features—Pyromania

- People with pyromania experience intense pleasure and gratification from deliberately setting fires. The fire setting involves impulsive feelings, but the act itself is usually planned in advance.
- Pleasure is derived from actually setting the fire, watching it burn, or helping fight it. Typically, there is a fascination with all aspects of fire, fire-fighting activities, and fire-fighting equipment. These individuals are regular fire watchers and often pull false alarms. Some become volunteer fire fighters.
- Often there is no regard for the consequences of the act. Some individuals are gratified by the destruction and deliberately leave clues to taunt fire officials.
- To make the *DSM* diagnosis, the fire setting must not be connected with financial gain, criminal activity, political activity, revenge, or psychotic behavior. The goal of the act is to satisfy the fire-setting impulse.

Additional Symptoms or Factors That May Be Seen

- **Alcohol or drug intoxication.**
- **Low intelligence.**
- **Cruelty to animals.**
- **A history of delinquency.**
- **Problems with authority figures.**
- **Sexual difficulties.** For some, fire is sexually exciting.
- **Feelings of anger, frustration, inadequacy.**

Other Information Helpful in Making the Diagnosis

Pyromania usually starts in childhood and is often associated with other childhood and adolescent difficulties such as truancy, running away, poor school performance, problems with authority, and cruelty to animals. Males are the usual perpetrators, although delinquent females are sometimes involved.

Other Diagnoses and Conditions to Consider, Rule Out, or Include

Children often experiment with fire and matches. This usually stems from natural curiosity and is not an indication of pyromania. However, recurrent fire setting is a serious problem and requires prompt treatment.

Some young people with a conduct disorder or adults with an antisocial personality disorder set fires deliberately as acts of anger and vengeance. The acts usually do not involve irresistible impulses, as in pyromania. Fire setting may also occur in psychotic or organic mental disorders.

18

SUBSTANCE-
RELATED
DISORDERS

- **Substance Abuse** (305.xx/F10–F19)
- **Substance Dependence** (303–304.xx/F10–F19)

OVERVIEW

The *DSM* lists ten classes of substances that are related to abuse and dependence: alcohol, cocaine, stimulants/amphetamines, sedatives/hypnotics, opioids, marijuana, hallucinogens, inhalants, PCP, and nicotine. Substances that don't fit into any particular category (steroids, amyl nitrite, nitrous oxide, betel nut, and so forth) are lumped together in a separate category. Although the effects of the substances and the patterns of usage may be different, the official diagnostic symptoms of abuse or dependence are the same, regardless of the substance involved. Before looking at some of the factors involved with the different substances, you need to know how therapists distinguish between abuse and dependence.

SUBSTANCE ABUSE

In actual practice, the line between substance abuse and dependence is often blurred. And the difference between abuse and "normal" use can be even more difficult to define, since this tends to vary by culture. However, in most cultures, a problem exists if the person is significantly impaired or distressed by the substance use. By *DSM* standards, the impairment seen in substance abuse is not as pervasive as that found in dependence. Of the four criteria for substance abuse listed in the *DSM*, only one needs to be seen to make the diagnosis.

Major Features—Substance Abuse

- Abuse does *not* involve extensive preoccupation with the substance, serious loss of control over the substance, unsuccessful attempts to cut down or stop, repeated use to avoid withdrawal symptoms, or the development of a significant physical tolerance. Those symptoms are more likely to be found in substance dependence.
- Substance abuse often leads to problems fulfilling personal, social, or vocational obligations. Important activities may be infringed upon by the substance use.
- Legal and personal problems may develop related to the substance abuse—driving while intoxicated, accidents, theft, physical altercations, and so forth.
- According to the *DSM*, substance abuse may also be diagnosed if the individual repeatedly uses substances when it may be physically dangerous to do so, such as when operating machinery or driving.

SUBSTANCE DEPENDENCE

Not all of the features described below need to be present to make the diagnosis of substance dependence. For example, contrary to popular definitions of drug dependence, the *DSM* diagnosis does *not* require physical dependence or withdrawal symptoms, although these symptoms are usually found in drug dependence. (Some drugs, such as marijuana, LSD, and PCP, may not lead to physical dependence.) Instead, the emphasis is placed on a pattern of compulsive use leading to impairment or distress. Of the eleven signs and symptoms listed in the *DSM*, only three are necessary to make the diagnosis. The degree of dependence varies and is rated as mild, moderate, or severe. Patterns of use and remission are also noted.

Major Features—Substance Dependence

- The development of a significant tolerance: more and more of the substance is needed to get the same effect. It would appear that all classes of substances can lead to varying degrees of tolerance.
- The person usually has withdrawal symptoms after reducing or stopping the substance use. Withdrawal means that physical dependence has developed. The person must continue taking the substance to avoid the withdrawal symptoms. However, some drugs apparently lead to psychological rather than physical dependence.
- The person often takes more of the substance than intended, e.g., one drink may lead to ten or a week-long binge. There are serious problems of control.
- There are frequent preoccupations with getting and using the substance.
- Efforts to cut down or stop are unsuccessful, although the individual may have intermittent periods of sobriety.
- There are problems fulfilling personal, social, or vocational obligations because of the substance use. Important activities may be infringed upon by the substance use.
- Legal and personal problems may develop related to the substance use—driving while intoxicated, accidents, theft, physical altercations, and so forth. The person may use substances in hazardous situations.
- The person continues to use the substance even though he or she is well aware of the negative consequences and unhealthy effects.

Additional Symptoms or Factors That May Be Seen

- **Alcohol-related:** Patterns vary and include daily drinking to maintain functioning, binges, periods of sobriety, loss of

control over frequency and amount, blackouts, denial.
Depression, anxiety, social phobia, panic attacks, and
insomnia are seen frequently.

- **Cocaine-related:** Bingeing over several days is common,
  followed by depression and exhaustion. Dependence may
  develop quickly, particularly if the cocaine is smoked as
  "crack." Strong cravings are developed. Alcohol and other
  drugs often are used to alleviate withdrawal symptoms.
  Insomnia, weight loss, irritability, depression, and
  paranoia are common.

- **Stimulant/amphetamine-related:** Binges are common,
  leading to exhaustion. A persistent craving is developed.
  An amphetamine known as "ice" is very potent and prevalent.
  Extreme nervousness, irritability, depression, paranoia,
  sexual dysfunction, and memory problems are common.

- **Sedative/hypnotic-related:** Sedatives and hypnotics include
  barbiturates, sleeping pills, and mild tranquilizers such as
  Valium. Many are prescribed medications that gradually are
  abused. All can lead to physical and psychological
  dependence. They are often taken with alcohol. This practice
  can be lethal, particularly with barbiturates.

- **Opioid-related:** Opioids include heroin, codeine, Demerol,
  morphine, Darvon, and others. High levels of tolerance
  and physical dependence are developed. Up to 90 percent of
  users have another psychiatric disorder. Depression,
  anxiety, alcoholism, and antisocial personality are common.
  For those who inject the drugs, the risk of AIDS is
  extremely high.

- **Marijuana-related:** Some tolerance may develop, along with
  mild withdrawal after very high doses, although any
  dependence is primarily psychological. Chronic use often
  leads to lethargy, lack of motivation, and memory problems.
  The use of alcohol and cocaine may complicate the problem.

- **Hallucinogen-related:** Hallucinogens include substances
  such as LSD and mescaline. Use is episodic and can lead

to increases in tolerance. Dependence is psychological rather than physical. Hallucinations, loss of touch with reality, and perceptual changes may mimic similar symptoms found in psychosis. Some people experience chronic flashbacks and visual distortions for years after heavy use.

- **Inhalant-related:** Involves inhaling the fumes from cleaning fluids, gasoline, airplane glue, lighter fluid, and so forth. Impaired judgment, aggressive behavior, and amnesia are common. Children and adolescents are more likely to use inhalants. Other substances frequently are abused as well. Family dysfunction and delinquency are the rule.

- **PCP-related:** PCP is also known as angel dust. Dependence may develop quickly in those who can tolerate the effects. Belligerence, assaultiveness, agitation, unpredictable behavior, delusions, perceptual distortions, and poor judgment are often seen. Most people use it in combination with other drugs or alcohol. Neurological problems have been reported after even brief use.

- **Nicotine-related:** Nicotine is highly toxic. Dependence develops quickly. Withdrawal symptoms include craving, tension, irritability, frustration, restlessness, insomnia, problems concentrating, increased appetite, and weight gain.

- **Other:** Steroid use can lead to depression, aggressive outbursts, and liver disease. "Poppers" (nitrite inhalants) may produce psychological dependence and lead to toxic reactions, respiratory irritations, and immune system problems.

Other Information Helpful in Making the Diagnosis

Alcohol: Alcoholism appears to have strong genetic components. Children of alcoholic parents who, as infants, were adopted into nonalcoholic families are much more likely to develop alcoholism than adopted children with nonalcoholic biological parents. Twin studies also support these conclusions. In general, children of alcoholic parents are four times more likely to become alcoholics. Psychosocial factors undoubtedly contribute to the problem, although alcoholics who don't abuse other drugs tend to have a less troublesome childhood than people who abuse a combination of many different drugs.

Researchers have been unable to identify a single "alcohol-prone" personality. Many of the traits frequently attributed to alcoholics—depression, feelings of inadequacy, low self-esteem, low stress tolerance, low impulse control, a need to please, and so forth—are probably a result rather than the cause of alcoholism. However, a history of childhood hyperactivity, conduct disorder, and antisocial personality seems to increase the risk of developing alcoholism.

Other substances: There are many factors that influence a person's "drug of choice" and the likelihood of becoming dependent—heredity, personality, childhood environment, peer culture, availability of the drug, effects of the drug and/or the relief of psychological symptoms provided by the drug, and the drug's ability to create physical dependence. Many drugs are taken as self-medication for feelings of anxiety and depression, although drug use is likely to increase these symptoms in the long run.

In contrast to single-drug users or alcoholics, people who regularly abuse several different categories of substances (except nicotine and caffeine) are much more likely to have had childhoods marked by severe emotional deprivation and instability. Serious psychological difficulties and personality problems are seen even before the onset of substance abuse.

Other Diagnoses and Conditions to Consider, Rule Out, or Include

More often than not, substance abuse and dependence exists with other psychiatric disorders—hence the popular term *dual diagnosis*. The disorders run the full spectrum, although mood and anxiety disorders are the most prevalent. Sometimes it is very difficult to separate out those symptoms that are caused by the substance abuse and those that may be due to other disorders. Several weeks or even months of sobriety may be necessary before additional diagnoses can be identified. Chronic substance abuse can also lead to a variety of organic mental syndromes, some of which are irreversible. Medical and nutritional complications must also be considered.

Case Example—Alcohol Abuse

Saturday Siestas. "She just won't get off my back about it. Every time I drink a beer, my wife goes off the deep end. Why do I have to pay for the fact that her father was an alcoholic?" Charles paced the room, throwing his hands up in exasperation. "I'm not her father," he continued, "I'm not an alcoholic, and I don't abuse the stuff! My body can hardly tolerate it. So why am I here? I'm here to get her off my back!"

At age thirty-seven, Charles is a successful advertising executive with two healthy children and an attractive wife. He and his wife have been together since they met in college. He describes the relationship as "just great except for this alcohol thing—she's been on me like an eagle ever since the keg parties in college, but those days are over. I think she has a real problem or phobia about alcohol."

As the session progressed, Charles described his history and drinking pattern, fully expecting that the therapist would vindicate him. Charles grew up with an alcoholic stepfather and a mother who occasionally abused Valium, which she easily obtained from the family doctor as treatment for "back spasms." Charles states that he was put off by drugs and alcohol. "I didn't drink until college, and then it was only beer, usually at keg parties. I drank so much I'd puke, then forget about the stuff for months. I didn't even drink between parties."

For the past several years Charles has been drinking one or two beers each weekday after work and a six-pack on each of the weekend days, usually over the course of three or four hours. "It doesn't take much for me to really feel it—I've always had a low tolerance. Too much and I get sick. I've never been able to drink like some people I know. At least I'll never be an alcoholic."

Charles has never had memory lapses for the periods when he is drinking, nor has he had any difficulty cutting back. "I was starting to get a belly, so I stopped drinking for about six months until I worked it off. No big deal." He denies thinking about alcohol. "I even drink fruit juice at lunch."

But there have been some problems; on at least six occasions over the past year he has called in late for work on Monday mornings. "Since I'm so sensitive to alcohol, sometimes I wake up with an annoying headache or slightly sick feeling. Or sometimes it keeps me awake and I feel like hell in the morning. But it goes away in a couple of hours." Charles reluctantly admits that he lost a major client at work because he failed to show up for one meeting and came in late for another. He also is in hot water with his son. "Well, I keep promising to go to his Little League games over the weekend, but usually I'm too tired and fall asleep on the couch." Further questioning revealed that the six-pack brought on the "tiredness." Social plans with his wife were also subject to cancellation for this reason.

Charles was not very receptive to the therapist's feedback, although he promised to seriously consider the fact that his drinking, even though limited in amount and frequency, was causing some recurrent problems in certain areas of his life.

19

SCHIZOPHRENIA
AND OTHER
PSYCHOTIC
DISORDERS

- **Schizophrenia** (295.9/F20)
- **Schizoaffective Disorder** (295.7/F25)
- **Delusional Disorder** (297.10/F22)
- **Brief Psychotic Disorder** (298.8/F23)

OVERVIEW

Before reading about these disorders, a word of caution is in order. Although it might not seem like it, the territory you are about to enter is highly controversial and ill-defined. To make matters worse, the only available map of the area changes radically every time it's printed—and may be only slightly more accurate than the one used by Columbus. Nevertheless, most therapists would argue that it is better than nothing.

The disorders in this category all involve at least one episode of *psychosis* that is not due to substance use, a nonpsychiatric medical illness, or a mood disorder. As you may remember from chapter 5, people who are psychotic can experience a variety of symptoms such as delusions, hallucinations, illogical thinking, disorientation, and grossly disorganized behaviors. Some, but not necessarily all, of their perceptions and thoughts are extremely inaccurate and distorted. When patients are actively psychotic, they have virtually no insight into their condition and will often insist that their version of reality is true, in spite of incontrovertible evidence to the contrary. The distortions go far beyond simple differences of opinion or cultural beliefs.

Although psychosis is a common feature of the disorders in this chapter, the other symptoms, signs, and patterns that make up each disorder are quite different. Research findings tend to show that actual differences between the disorders do exist, but no one really knows how or if the disorders are ultimately related to each other. To complicate practical matters, the diagnostic boundaries of each are significantly changed every time a new version of the *DSM* appears. For example, it is quite possible that someone diagnosed with schizoaffective disorder using *DSMII* would be rediagnosed as having major depression with psychotic features using *DSMIII-R* criteria. One study found that only thirty-five out of sixty-eight patients diagnosed as schizophrenic using *DSMII* criteria were given the same diagnosis using *DSMIII-R*. Knowing what you know by now, that shouldn't be surprising. . . .

SCHIZOPHRENIA

A Group of Disorders: The nature of "schizophrenia" is extremely difficult to understand, since it is no longer considered to be a single disorder or disease, as the name might suggest. Rather, the diagnostic category is thought to represent a large group of disorders that present with similar symptoms: hallucinations, delusions, disturbances in thought content and process, emotional blunting or flatness, lack of motivation, problems relating to the outside world, and a poor sense of self-identity. To confuse matters, not everyone with "schizophrenia" has all of these symptoms. In addition, each of the symptoms can also be seen in other psychiatric and neurological disorders.

What it boils down to is this:

- *there is no single set of symptoms that describes schizophrenia;*
- *symptoms differ from patient to patient and change over time;*
- *the course of the disorder varies widely, as does the prognosis for recovery;*
- *the various symptoms and patterns are found all over the world, in spite of cultural differences; and*
- *the effects of the illness (whatever it may actually be) are very real and, more often than not, quite devastating. Half of all mental hospital beds are occupied by patients with schizophrenia.*

Possible Causes: Since it has been very difficult to pinpoint exactly what schizophrenia is, it has been even more frustrating determining possible causes and treatments. Psychiatry has been under immense pressure from political groups, patient advocates, parent groups, and patients to isolate the "cause" of schizophrenia and develop effective treatments. In this climate, it is inevitable that inconclusive findings will be grossly overblown and oversold. In spite of all the hoopla about the "decade of the brain," the causes of schizophrenia remain unknown. Treatments suppress symptoms but do not cure the illness.

Schizophrenia is related to a wide variety of biological abnormalities involving brain structure, neurotransmitters, endocrine dysregulation, autoimmune disorders, and neurological disorders. But it has been very difficult to determine if the abnormalities are the results of the disease process itself or if they are actually causing the illness. Simply locating and identifying an abnormality, e.g., brain atrophy, does not mean it is the primary cause of the disorder. The abnormality itself may stem from a whole chain of different causes.

Some researchers speculate that schizophrenia is caused by a yet-to-be-identified prenatal virus. Strange as it may seem, most schizophrenics are born in the cold winter months between January and April. In addition, the illness is more prevalent in certain geographical areas than others. Researchers have also attempted to link certain chromosomal abnormalities with schizophrenia. One highly touted but poorly designed study claimed to have found such a link. The results have not been substantiated by further research.

From all available evidence, it would appear that schizophrenia involves genetic, biological, and psychological causes. For whatever reason, certain people may have a vulnerability to the disease that might be triggered by a variety of factors such as physical illness, drug abuse, trauma, or psychological stress. Although theories abound, researchers haven't been able to adequately determine why some people with the vulnerability develop the disorder and others do not.

Major Features—Schizophrenia

- Schizophrenia usually includes three phases: (1) a "prodromal" phase of deteriorating functioning that occurs before the onset of psychotic symptoms; (2) a phase of active psychosis; and (3) a "residual" phase following the psychosis. To qualify for the *DSM* diagnosis, all symptoms of the disorder must last at least **six months** and must include an actively psychotic phase.

- The actively psychotic phase must last at least one month (one week if using *DSMIII-R* for the diagnosis) and may include "positive" symptoms such as delusions, hallucinations, disorganized speech, catatonia, inappropriate affect, or disorganized, bizarre behaviors.

- "Negative" symptoms seen during this phase may include a dull, flat emotional state, lack of motivation, impeded thinking, and an inability to experience pleasure.

- The prodromal and residual phases occurring before and after the psychotic phase may include symptoms such as social withdrawal, strange behavior, difficulty carrying out practical tasks, blunted emotions, a decline in personal hygiene, an unusual way of speaking, odd beliefs, strange perceptual experiences, and lack of initiative. Some mild delusions or hallucinations may continue in the residual phase.

- During the course of the illness, the person's general level of functioning is significantly below the level found before the onset of the disorder.

- Other disorders such as schizoaffective disorder and a mood disorder with psychotic features must be ruled out, as well as substance-induced disorders and nonpsychiatric medical illness.

Additional Symptoms or Factors That May Be Seen

- **The prodromal phase,** which occurs before the psychosis begins, may last weeks or it may take a lengthy downhill course lasting over several years. The prognosis is better if the symptoms develop quickly.
- **Depression, anxiety, and agitation** are common.
- **Suicide is a risk,** since 50 percent of all patients attempt it at some point.
- **Full recovery is not common,** although some patients get through it with minimal impairment. Others (40 to 60 percent) remain significantly impaired. The illness usually takes a course of relapses and remissions.
- **Paranoid schizophrenia** primarily involves delusions or auditory hallucinations. They can be of any type but often include themes of persecution, grandiosity, or jealousy. Unlike other forms of schizophrenia, speech and behavior are not disorganized. The emotional state is generally appropriate.
- **Disorganized schizophrenia** involves prominent symptoms of disorganized speech and behavior, along with inappropriate emotional responses.
- **Catatonic schizophrenia** involves psychomotor problems such as extrème agitation, rigidity, posturing, mutism, resistance to instructions, or peculiar physical movements.
- **Undifferentiated schizophrenia** is a mixed bag and includes symptoms that do not fall predominantly into the other types listed above.
- **Schizophreniform disorder (295.4),** rather than schizophrenia, is diagnosed when the schizophrenic symptoms have been present for *more than one month but less than six months.*

Other Information Helpful in Making the Diagnosis

Schizophrenia most often develops in adolescence or early adulthood, although it can begin at any age. An emotional crisis can trigger the onset of symptoms in a vulnerable individual. Some people have only one episode of the illness, but most experience recurrent episodes, with a deterioration in functioning after each recurrence. The severity of the psychotic symptoms tends to diminish after the first five years of the illness, but the "negative" symptoms (lack of normal reactions, emotional flatness, withdrawal, vague or wandering speech, and so forth) are likely to persist. These symptoms can grossly interfere with the patient's ability to adjust to the usual demands of life. However, it is important to point out that, contrary to conventional wisdom, schizophrenia does not always take a progressively downhill course.

Other Diagnoses and Conditions to Consider, Rule Out, or Include

Neurological disorders, other medical illness, major depression with psychotic features, schizoaffective disorder, and delusional disorder must all be ruled out. Substance abuse is often a complicating factor. Several personality disorders, including schizoid, schizotypal, paranoid, and borderline personality disorders, have features similar to schizophrenia and must be considered.

Case Example—Schizophrenia, Disorganized

Shopping Bag Lady. Looking at Sandra now, one can hardly believe that she was once a brilliant concert pianist who toured Europe amid a blaze of flashbulbs, fanfare, and adoration. Her ragged overcoat, motley orange sneakers, and Red Sox baseball cap have long replaced her ornate gowns. A brown shopping bag stuffed full of trinkets, half-eaten crackers, and mementos from the past never leaves her side. At age fifty-two, her toothless smile is lost in an array of deep wrinkles and stray hairs. She easily could be twenty-five years older.

Sandra is at the crisis center because she ran away from her group home again and missed her Prolixin injection. She has spent the last several weeks wandering around Boston, sleeping beneath overpasses, and eating at local charities. Until the medication wore off, she successfully avoided the police. They eventually found her skipping, laughing, and jumping into the arms of startled strangers on Boston's fashionable Newbury Street. She giggled and rocked like a small child as she was gently ushered into the patrol car. The officers knew Sandra very well.

Sandra now sits across from the examiner, twiddling her hair, pointing at spots in the ceiling, and mumbling to herself. Her once graceful fingers tremble and gyrate while her tongue darts about in wormlike movements. The years of medications have taken their toll. She suddenly pushes her smiling moonbeam face inches from the examiner's nose and proclaims, "Yes, yes, yes! It is so; it is so; it is so! Ridiculous, repulsive, rockeria! Ho, ho, Horowitz!" She pulls away, delighted by her insights.

The story is tragic. Sandra was a precocious, somewhat withdrawn, shy child who filled the lonely hours with books and piano playing. She won a music scholarship and graduated with top honors. By age twenty-four, she was on a concert tour, in spite of persistent fears of leaving her mother. At age twenty-five, she began feeling slightly detached, as if walking in a fog. The slightest piano music seemed loud and overwhelming. She put cotton in her ears and continued the concerts.

Over the next year she became increasingly eccentric and unpredictable. The reflections she saw in her mirror looked vacant and distorted. She screamed, smashing furniture and hurtling it out the window. This led to the first of fifteen hospitalizations, twenty-five years of antipsychotic medications, electroconvulsive therapy, and heartbreak.

SCHIZOAFFECTIVE DISORDER

If you found the concept of schizophrenia difficult to understand, you will have major headaches with schizoaffective disorder. Take solace in the fact that you are not alone. Confusion and controversy surround this category, although therapists tend to diagnose it with reckless abandon. If pressed to explain why and how they diagnosed the disorder, most therapists are likely to avoid eye contact and lamely respond, "Well, the patient has some symptoms of both schizophrenia and major depression and I didn't know what else to call him—the diagnostic guidelines really aren't clear, but I know they won't let me give both diagnoses at the same time. So what else am I supposed to do?"

Don't be too harsh on the therapist. This slippery category was created since many patients seem to have some of the symptoms of schizophrenia along with a mood disorder such as major depression or manic-depression (bipolar disorder). This gives rise to many questions. Is schizoaffective disorder a type of schizophrenia, a type of mood disorder, or a combination of both? Or is it a completely separate, unrelated disorder?

The verdict is not yet in on any of these questions, although some researchers would claim otherwise. As it stands now, schizoaffective disorder represents a mixed group of patients, some with predominant symptoms of schizophrenia, along with a mood disorder, and others with predominant symptoms of a mood disorder, along with symptoms of schizophrenia.

Major Features—Schizoaffective Disorder

- At some point during a major depressive or manic episode, the patient also experiences symptoms found in the actively psychotic phase of schizophrenia. The psychotic symptoms must last at least one month.
- Although symptoms of the mood disorder are present during most of the psychotic episode, there must be a period of at least two weeks when delusions or hallucinations are present **without** the mood disorder symptoms.

Additional Symptoms or Factors That May Be Seen

- **Bipolar type** is diagnosed if a manic episode has been involved.
- **Depressive type** does not involve manic symptoms.
- **Symptoms of schizophrenia and the mood disorder may alternate** back and forth.

Other Information Helpful in Making the Diagnosis

The disorder is likely to begin in early adulthood. Patients with the depressed type of schizoaffective disorder may have relatives with schizophrenia, but those with the manic type are more likely to have first-degree relatives with a mood disorder. The course of the disorder varies. It may come and go, or it may become chronic. Patients tend to recover better than those with schizophrenia, but not as well as those with a mood disorder.

Other Diagnoses and Conditions to Consider, Rule Out, or Include

In major depression or mania with psychotic features, there may also be delusions or hallucinations, but unlike the symptoms of schizoaffective disorder, these symptoms are always accompanied by mood symptoms. As in schizophrenia and the mood disorders, substance use and medical conditions must also be ruled out as possible causes of the schizoaffective symptoms.

DELUSIONAL DISORDER

Except for a tenaciously held false belief that defies reason, people with a delusional disorder appear quite normal in most respects.

They usually show none of the mental impairments found in schizophrenia. The false beliefs or delusions often center around themes of persecution, jealousy, power, disease, or an imaginary love relationship.

Major Features—Delusional Disorder

- In spite of evidence to the contrary, the person clings to a "nonbizarre" delusion—a false belief or belief system about situations that could actually occur or exist in real life but are obviously not occurring in the patient's life. The belief defies logic.
- In most cases, no amount of reasoning will convince the patient that the belief is false. He or she readily dismisses this possibility.
- Aside from the thinking and behavior associated with the delusion, the person's appearance, general behavior, orientation, and thinking process appear to be unremarkable. General functioning is not impaired, although problems usually increase because of the delusions.
- If any other schizophreniclike symptoms are present (e.g., auditory hallucinations), they occur briefly and are not prominent.
- According to the *DSM*, the delusion must last at least one month and cannot be better accounted for by a mood disorder, schizophrenia, substance use, or a nonpsychiatric medical disorder.

Additional Symptoms or Factors That May Be Seen

- **Erotomanic type:** The patient falsely believes that he or she is romantically loved by another person, usually of higher status (a movie star, politician, famous personality, boss, and so forth). He or she may persistently send letters or gifts, make phone calls, or even stalk the object of the delusions.
- **Persecutory type:** These individuals are often suspicious, hostile, and quarrelsome. They are convinced that they are being plotted against, mistreated, cheated, followed, maligned, and threatened. They may file lawsuits, call the police, or directly attack the alleged perpetrators.

- **Grandiose type:** Extraordinary abilities, power, special knowledge, and wealth are themes of the delusions.
- **Somatic type:** The belief focuses on a delusional physical defect, disease, or body condition—foul odors, parasites, deformed or malfunctioning body parts, and so forth.
- **Jealous type:** The person firmly believes his or her spouse or lover is having an affair, without any basis at all. The patient is likely to look for and misinterpret benign things as "evidence" to make his or her case. He or she may resort to spying, restricting the partner, or attacking the alleged lover.

Other Information Helpful in Making the Diagnosis

Delusional disorder usually begins in middle age and is sometimes triggered by an actual event where there may have been cause for some realistic suspicions, however slight. The symptoms often come on quickly and may wax and wane for years. Sometimes they go away on their own. Some patients end up in serious legal trouble after acting on their delusions. Others are able to maintain jobs, and so forth, but are likely to have relationship problems. (See chapters 4 and 6 for an extensive case example—"Raging Jealousy.")

No one knows what causes the disorder. Relatives of patients often have certain delusional qualities about them, without evidence of schizophrenia or mood disorders. Delusional disorder does not appear to be a form of schizophrenia, although this remains to be determined. Most researchers attribute the disorder to psychological and personality factors.

Other Diagnoses and Conditions to Consider, Rule Out, or Include

Delusions can be a part of *many* nonpsychiatric medical conditions. These must be ruled out.

Schizophrenia has many more symptoms of impairment than

delusional disorder. Any delusions present in schizophrenia tend to be bizarre and impossible. However, the difference between paranoid schizophrenia and delusional disorder may be particularly difficult to determine.

Paranoid personality disorder also involves rigidity and suspiciousness, but without the fixed delusions found in delusional disorder. Sometimes, however, both diagnoses are given.

BRIEF PSYCHOTIC DISORDER

As the name implies, this category is reserved for brief psychotic episodes that don't last long enough to warrant a diagnosis of schizophreniform disorder or schizophrenia. In addition, the patient makes a full recovery from the psychotic symptoms. Most cases are triggered by a very stressful event or events. In *DSMIII-R*, this disorder is called a "brief reactive psychosis."

Major Features—Brief Psychotic Disorder

- The person experiences an episode of psychosis lasting a few hours to a maximum of **one month**. The episode may include delusions, hallucinations, disorganized speech, or disorganized behavior.
- The person eventually returns to his or her normal level of functioning after the psychotic symptoms subside.
- *DSMIII-R* states that the episode must be a reaction to an event or events that would be stressful to almost anyone. This requirement is not included in the *DSMIV*.
- Substance-induced psychosis, mood disorder with psychotic features, and psychosis related to a medical illness must be ruled out before the diagnosis can be made.

Additional Symptoms or Factors That May Be Seen

- Confusion, disorientation, memory problems.
- Emotional turmoil, rapid shifts from one emotional state to another.

- Screaming, crying, wild agitation, or refusal to speak or respond.
- Bizarre behavior or dress.
- Nonsensical, inarticulate, or silly speech.

Other Information Helpful in Making the Diagnosis

The symptoms usually appear rapidly. If a stressor is involved such as the death of a loved one, a serious accident, a move to a different culture, combat trauma, and so forth, the psychotic episode is likely to appear within a few hours. Most episodes last only a day or two. Sometimes they are followed by a period of mild depression.

The episodes are less likely to occur again if the person was relatively well adjusted before the onset of symptoms, if the symptoms appear abruptly, and if the episode was triggered by a severe stressor. However, many patients with this disorder have underlying personality problems. Paranoid, schizotypal, borderline, histrionic, and narcissistic personality disorders are commonly found in patients who experience an acute psychotic episode.

Other Diagnoses and Conditions to Consider, Rule Out, or Include

If the psychotic symptoms last more than one month, schizophreniform disorder must be considered. (A diagnosis of schizophreniform disorder is changed to schizophrenia if the symptoms last more than six months.) Other psychotic disorders, mood disorders with psychotic features, and nonpsychiatric medical conditions must be ruled out. If the patient also has a personality disorder, both diagnoses are given—acute psychotic disorder is placed on Axis I, the personality disorder on Axis II.

20
COGNITIVE
DISORDERS

- **Delirium** (293.00/F05.0, F05.8, F05.9)
- **Dementia, Alzheimer's Type** (290.00/F00)
- **Alcohol-Induced Amnestic Disorder** (291.10/F10.6)

OVERVIEW

Although there are many different varieties of cognitive mental disorders, this chapter will limit its focus to the three primary types—*delirium*, *dementia*, and organic *amnesia*. This should give you a general idea how these disorders may differ from the others you have seen. Physicians, psychiatrists, and neuropsychologists often work together to make these complex diagnoses.

The cognitive disorders have two main features in common: (1) They are all directly caused by a disease of the brain, a disease of some other body system that also affects the brain, or drugs, alcohol, or other toxic agents. (2) All involve one or more major problems in the everyday mental (*cognitive*) processes that we take for granted, such as memory, language comprehension, reasoning, recognition, judgment, orientation, and other mental processes. In these disorders, various parts of the brain seem to crash like a computer with a bad virus.

In addition, many of these disorders also involve emotional symptoms such as depression, anxiety, paranoia, mood swings, irritability, loss of impulse control, delusions, and inappropriate behaviors. The emotional symptoms may be caused directly by the brain damage, or they may arise as the patient becomes increasingly distressed by the mental and/or physical limitations.

The disorders in this category can stem from a wide variety of physical causes, including diseases of the central nervous system, endocrine disorders, cardiovascular disease, pulmonary disease, brain tumors, brain trauma, nutritional deficiency, infectious diseases such as AIDS, poisons, drugs and alcohol, and a host of other medical problems. Sometimes the exact cause is unknown, but the symptoms leave little doubt that a medical illness is involved, particularly after all other psychiatric disorders have been ruled out.

Word Games?

In *DSMIII-R*, the cognitive disorders were lumped together in a broad category called "organic mental disorders." This category included all sorts of other mental disorders caused by known medical conditions, such as depression caused by an endocrine disorder, anxiety caused by hypothyroidism, personality changes brought on by a brain tumor, and so forth. In *DSMIV*, this major category was abolished, since it implied (heaven forbid) that the other psychiatric disorders were not necessarily biological or "organic." To avoid any "misunderstanding," cognitive disorders were given a separate category and the word *organic* was carefully dropped. The other "organic" disorders were renamed as "mental disorders due to a general medical condition."

You may wonder how these disorders are different from certain other psychiatric disorders that have been associated with biological abnormalities, e.g., schizophrenia, other psychotic disorders, OCD, and manic-depressive disorder. Unfortunately, there is no clear answer at this time. For practical purposes, the cognitive disorders and other mental disorders brought on by a general medical condition are due to *identifiable* physical/organic causes, while the other psychiatric disorders, such as schizophrenia, involve a more complex interaction of biological, psychological, and social factors—the "causes" are much more difficult to determine.

Confused? You are not alone. In their efforts to define most emotional disorders as biological, psychiatrists often get lost in a semantic jungle of their own creation.

DELIRIUM

Delirium is a relatively brief state of mental confusion. It tends to come on rapidly, fluctuates widely, and disappears after the underlying medical disorder has been treated. Many people experience delirium after major surgery, although a variety of medical problems and medications can bring it on. In the elderly, infections, such as those of the urinary tract, are a common cause of delirium.

Major Features—Delirium

- Patients are not fully aware of the environment around them. Their attention span is very short and shifts rapidly. A coherent conversation may be impossible because of the wandering attention.
- Confused thinking, disorientation, rambling speech, poor reasoning, misinterpretations, illusions, hallucinations, recent memory problems, sleep disturbances, and physical agitation or stupor are common symptoms.
- The symptoms develop rapidly over several hours or days and tend to fluctuate. The person may be relatively lucid during the morning but regress at night in the dark.
- To make the *DSM* diagnosis, there must be some evidence that a medical condition is related to the onset of the delirium symptoms.

Additional Symptoms or Factors That May Be Seen

- Fear, anxiety, depression, irritability.
- Rapid changes in emotional state.

- **Racing heart, sweating, nausea, pallor.**
- **A disturbed sleep-wake cycle.**

Other Information Helpful in Making the Diagnosis

Children and the elderly appear to be the most susceptible to delirium, although it can develop at any age. Some researchers have found that it is more likely to occur in people who are particularly fearful of hospitals and medical procedures. Delirium seldom lasts longer than one week if the underlying medical problem is treated.

A *partial* list of causes includes: prescription medications (diuretics, digitalis, antihistamines, ulcer medications, and many others), street drugs, poisons, congestive heart failure, strokes (often undetected), brain tumors, head trauma, other physical injury, hypoglycemia, electrolyte imbalance, thyroid problems, vitamin deficiency, and almost any infections.

Other Diagnoses and Conditions to Consider, Rule Out, or Include

Schizophrenia and other psychotic disorders have similar symptoms and must be ruled out. Although these disorders may also involve hallucinations, delusions, and other thought disturbances, the symptoms are more organized, without the wide range of cognitive impairments seen in delirium. Dementia (the next category described) must also be ruled out.

DEMENTIA, ALZHEIMER'S TYPE

Dementia involves the significant reduction or loss of mental abilities such as memory, intellect, reasoning, and judgment. Personality changes may also occur. Depending upon the type of dementia, the disorder may get progressively worse, stay the same, or remit. The most common form of dementia is caused by Alzheimer's disease. Dementia also can be caused by stroke, heart attacks, AIDS, chronic substance abuse, and other medical disorders. Unlike some dementias, Alzheimer's type has a downhill course and is not reversible at this time.

Major Features—Dementia, Alzheimer's Type

- Memory impairment is always present. Patients have difficulty learning new information and recalling information they have learned in the past. In the early stages, certain events of the day may be forgotten, along with names, telephone numbers, and so forth. Tasks may be left unfinished. In later stages, personal information may be lost and no new learning may take place.

- There may be language difficulties, problems identifying or naming objects, problems carrying out physical movements, and major difficulties making plans. New situations may be avoided.

- The loss of functioning becomes worse over time and causes serious disruptions in all spheres of the patient's life.

- According to the *DSM*, all other possible causes of dementia must be ruled out first before the diagnosis can be made. Other psychiatric disorders must also be ruled out.

Additional Symptoms or Factors That May Be Seen

- Attempts to hide or talk around the deficits.
- Apathy, withdrawal, and poor judgment.
- Depression, anxiety, compulsive rituals, irritable outbursts, paranoia, and delusions.
- Personality changes.
- Diminishing ability for self-care.
- Death usually follows in five to eight years if the disorder begins after age sixty-five.

Other Information Helpful in Making the Diagnosis

Approximately 7–10 percent of the population over age sixty-five suffers from Alzheimer's dementia. The average age of onset is after age sixty-five, although the symptoms may slowly appear at any age. A genetic predisposition for the disease appears to be a contributing factor. In the early stages, the patient may not be aware of the mild memory lapses and personality changes, some of which are obvious to family and friends. The disease progresses and inevitably requires custodial care.

Other Diagnoses and Conditions to Consider, Rule Out, or Include

In normal aging, mental processes may slow down a bit and additional efforts may be required to learn new information. But this is not a sign of dementia. In Alzheimer's dementia, the mental difficulties get progressively worse and eventually interfere with all aspects of the patient's life. Major depression must also be ruled out, since it tends to slow intellectual processes, particularly in the elderly.

Case Example—Dementia, Alzheimer's Type

A Common Tragedy. David was forced into early retirement from his job as vice president of a multinational corporation. At age sixty-one, he was diagnosed with Alzheimer's disease. Before his death six years later, David went through the following stages:

Stage 1: David always feared that he had a less than adequate memory, but he became increasingly concerned after forgetting familiar names, losing items, and forgetting to write appointments in his schedule. Fortunately, his secretary covered the lapses. At the time, David attributed the problem to stress and took a long vacation. It didn't help.

Stage 2: David became increasingly anxious as his difficulties progressed. To keep track of things, he began to obsess about minute details and wrote constantly in a small notebook. Normally gregarious, he became irritable and extremely critical of others. He even accused his wife of cheating. At work, his problems became obvious to others as he talked around issues and failed to complete tasks.

Stage 3:   David no longer attempted to hide his illness after he found himself on an airplane with no idea where he was going. Fortunately, he was returning home from a business trip and was met at the airport by his wife. She had known for months that something was terribly wrong. After this incident, David quit his job and withdrew from all social activity. He avoided any situations that might involve problem-solving abilities. Although he could walk alone to a local store, he seldom left the house.

Stage 4:   At this stage, David could no longer remember the names of his children, although he seemed to recognize their faces. He had no memory of his phone number or address and often had no idea what year it was. He needed assistance dressing but was able to care for other personal hygiene. He became stubborn and intense, often spending hours arranging and rearranging stacks of old business papers.

Stage 5:   David's wife was devastated when he no longer remembered her name. He knew they were married but could recall little, if anything, about their shared past. Memories of his job were gone, but he did remember certain emotional events from earlier years. His wife grew weary of repeating things. Most of the time, David had no idea where he was. The doors had to be locked to keep him from wandering away. He no longer seemed to be particularly distressed, but his family was in constant torment. After dealing with enormous feelings of guilt, they moved David to a nursing facility.

Stage 6:   David no longer wandered but sat alone for hours, staring into nothing. Communication was reduced to grunts, and he didn't acknowledge family members. He was incontinent and needed constant assistance with eating and personal care. As the disease progressed, he was unable to walk. He eventually died of pneumonia.

ALCOHOL-INDUCED AMNESTIC DISORDER

Also known as Korsakoff's syndrome, this disorder involves severe memory problems brought on by years of heavy alcohol abuse.

Major Features—Alcohol-Induced Amnestic Disorder

- Because of impairments in short-term and recent memory abilities, patients are unable to learn new information. The information may be retained briefly, but it is usually forgotten after several minutes. Although surroundings are recognized, patients can't remember events that happened during the day.
- Information and events that were learned long ago (e.g., in childhood) may be remembered. Information acquired over the past decade is more likely to be obscured. This varies from patient to patient.
- Patients often make up information to fill the gaps in their memory. Most deny, rationalize, or minimize the impairment.
- To make the diagnosis, there must be evidence of long-term, heavy alcohol use.

Additional Symptoms or Factors That May Be Seen

- **Apathy, blandness, lack of initiative.**
- **Thinking and level of consciousness are usually clear,** although there may be some disorientation.
- **Other medical and neurological complications** (see below).

Other Information Helpful in Making the Diagnosis

The disorder is rarely found in people under the age of thirty-five. It is thought to be caused by a vitamin deficiency (thiamine). Heavy alcohol ingestion interferes with the absorption of food and leads to nutritional deficiencies. Thiamine deficiency is also related to Wernicke's syndrome, a neurological disease found in alcoholism that often progresses into alcohol-induced amnestic disorder if left untreated. Detoxification centers routinely administer large doses of thiamine to treat Wernicke's syndrome and prevent the amnestic disorder. However, once the symptoms of alcohol-induced amnestic disorder start, they are rarely reversible.

Other Diagnoses and Conditions to Consider, Rule Out, or Include

Alcoholics can also develop dementia. Like alcohol-induced amnestic disorder, dementia involves memory impairment. However, in dementia, other mental capabilities deteriorate as well. (See "Dementia, Alzheimer's Type.") Other forms of substance abuse can also lead to dementia or amnesia.

21
PERSONALITY
DISORDERS

Group A
- **Paranoid** (301.00/F60.0)
- **Schizoid** (301.20/F60.1)
- **Schizotypal** (301.22/F21)

Group B
- **Antisocial** (301.70/F60.2)
- **Borderline** (301.83/F60.3)
- **Histrionic** (301.50/F60.4)
- **Narcissistic** (301.81/F60.8)

Group C
- **Avoidant** (301.82/F60.6)
- **Dependent** (301.60/F60.7)
- **Obsessive-Compulsive** (301.40/F60.5)
- **Passive-Aggressive** (301.84/F60.8)

Other (*DSMIII-R* Only)
- **Self-defeating** (NOS, 301.90/F60.9)
- **Sadistic** (NOS, 301.90/F60.9)

OVERVIEW

All of us run into conflicts occasionally because we misinterpret the actions, intentions, and motivations of others or because we avoid, mishandle, or overreact to situations that trigger areas of personal vulnerability. But in spite of these temporary slips into "maladaptive behavior," people who are "well adjusted" are eventually able to see, acknowledge, and learn from their mistakes. In a word, they are "adaptable."

On the other hand, people with a "personality disorder" are shackled with certain maladaptive personality traits and behavioral patterns that persist throughout their lives. They have deeply ingrained ways of thinking and behaving that repeatedly result in a host of relationship and social problems. Although these individuals experience significant distress and unhappiness when their poor coping skills fail, most (without therapy) are unable to see their part in bringing about their difficulties. Needless to say, family members, friends, and/or coworkers bear the brunt of the person's distortions and maladjusted reactions.

As you saw in chapter 6, the diagnosis of a personality disorder is placed on Axis II of the diagnostic summary. As a general starting point in making the diagnosis, the disorders have been divided into three different groups. Each group represents individuals with certain ways of thinking, behaving, and reacting. The specific disorders that make up each group are listed at the beginning of the present chapter. (Those listed under "Other" do not fit a particular group. They are not recognized as "official" categories.)

Group A disorders: Individuals with these personality disorders often appear suspicious, odd, eccentric, aloof, or disinterested. They may be emotionally constricted, distrustful of others, difficult to get to know, or prone to peculiar behaviors.

Group B disorders: These individuals may be extremely emotional, unstable, and erratic. All have problems with emotional control and may be very impulsive, self-centered, attention-seeking, or dramatic.

Group C disorders: Individuals with these personality disorders are more likely to appear apprehensive, anxiety-ridden, phobic, or obsessive. Depending upon the type of disorder, they may be excessively shy, dependent, perfectionistic, or demanding.

In looking over the personality disorders, keep in mind that not all researchers accept them as separate, "real" categories that actually exist. Most have not been confirmed adequately by solid clinical research. Since each of us can be dependent, narcissistic, obsessive-compulsive, or histrionic at times, it is very difficult to determine at what point the behavior becomes "pathological." To complicate matters, we behave differently in different situations. Some researchers argue that there are few, if any, personality traits that remain consistent in all life situations.

Whatever the "truth" may be, these diagnostic categories are considered for every person who seeks out therapy. Needless to say, the diagnosis of a personality disorder can be very difficult. People with "personality problems" seldom fit neatly into any category. To make matters worse, therapists often have trouble agreeing on a diagnosis for a particular patient, even though they are using the same diagnostic guidelines.

GROUP A PERSONALITY DISORDERS

PARANOID PERSONALITY DISORDER

People with this disorder are extremely suspicious and distrustful of others. They seek out evidence to confirm their worst suspicions and are quick to misinterpret the actions of others as demeaning, threatening, or malevolent. Although they harbor great feelings of hostility toward other people, they typically deny these feelings and accuse others of being hostile. Other people might see these individuals as cold, rigid, humorless, secretive, devious, and self-righteous.

Major Features—Paranoid Personality Disorder

- Distrust and suspiciousness is a way of life for these people. They are extremely defensive and guarded against a world seen as hostile and threatening. They unnecessarily expect to be exploited or harmed.

- They seldom confide in others and are quick to take offense, often misinterpreting harmless actions and words as attacks on their character or reputation. They are likely to carry long-term grudges.

- They are usually very critical of others, although they have great difficulty accepting criticism themselves. Blame is shifted to other people.

- The trustworthiness of friends and the fidelity of lovers are sources of constant suspicion, even when totally unwarranted.

- These individuals are likely to be argumentative, tense, rigid, hypervigilant, and ready to counterattack with anger at the slightest provocation.

Additional Symptoms or Factors That May Be Seen

- **Difficulty making compromises.**
- **A need to control and dominate.** May be preoccupied with power and rank.
- **Fear of intimacy.**
- **Discomfort with emotional feelings.** Prefers rational "objectivity."
- **Contempt for perceived "weakness" in others.**
- **May be egocentric, self-important.**

Other Information Helpful in Making the Diagnosis

These individuals rarely seek help on their own, since they pride themselves on being objective and rational and seldom trust enough to confide in a therapist. Although they may function relatively well and even achieve status and power in certain situations, they are likely to experience great distress in close interpersonal relationships. The paranoid features usually become evident in adolescence and gradually develop into a more pervasive worldview.

Other Diagnoses and Conditions to Consider, Rule Out, or Include

Persistent psychotic symptoms such as delusions and hallucinations are not usually found in paranoid personality disorder. If these symptoms are present, delusional disorder and paranoid schizophrenia should be considered.

Case Example—Paranoid Personality Disorder

The Perfect Profession. Harrison knew he had found his perfect niche in life. As a fifty-six-year-old partner in a major law firm, he had carefully planned his rapid rise up the slippery corporate ladder. Over the years he had kept extensive notes on the activities of his coworkers and superiors, documenting their slightest faults and weaknesses. He also included any rumors about questionable behaviors.

Although wise enough to maintain a deferential attitude toward his superiors, Harrison was highly critical of coworkers, often accusing them of undermining or sabotaging his work. He saw nefarious motives where none existed. Harrison's superiors dismissed these tendencies, since his performance as an attorney was often brilliant. He earned the company millions of dollars in successful litigation suits. And clients made no complaints about him. Harrison was able to "see" every potential pitfall as cases progressed. He was ready with an answer for everything.

However, Harrison's world began to fall apart. His wife sued for divorce, stating that he was totally unavailable emotionally. She described him as cold, unyielding, and controlling. He even accused her of having an affair with her boss. Harrison's two teenage sons avoided him like the plague, since he interpreted everything they did as "spying on me to make a case for your mother." Harrison came to therapy as a legal tactic but dropped out after one session.

SCHIZOID PERSONALITY DISORDER

Major Features—Schizoid Personality Disorder

- These individuals have a lifelong pattern of social withdrawal and emotional detachment. They have very little need or desire for emotional ties. They prefer being alone.
- Emotionally, they may be very restricted and are likely to come across as cold, bland, quiet, detached, and unresponsive. They have difficulty expressing or acknowledging emotions, particularly anger and pleasure. Criticism and praise do not *appear* to affect these individuals.
- They generally don't have any close friends, although there may be casual acquaintances. Their interests and job pursuits center around solitary activities.
- Their sexual lives may exist in fantasy only. Or there may be little, if any, desire for sexual activity.
- Although these individuals often engage in fantasy and excessive daydreaming, they are in touch with reality. They do not have problems in their thinking processes. Some can be extremely creative and accomplished under the right circumstances.

Additional Symptoms or Factors That May Be Seen

- **Avoidance of spontaneous conversation and eye contact.**
- **Absentmindedness, lack of goals, poor social skills.**
- **Avid interests in philosophy, metaphysical and scientific issues,** and other interests that don't require personal involvement.
- **Fear and sensitivity** may underlie some of the indifference and aloofness.

Other Information Helpful in Making the Diagnosis

Schizoid personality disorder usually begins in early childhood and often becomes a lifelong way of relating to the world. Some theorists relate it to cold, indifferent, inadequate parenting. Although the name "schizoid" implies some connection with schizophrenia, the two do not appear to be genetically related. People with schizoid personality disorder seldom develop schizophrenia.

Other Diagnoses and Conditions to Consider, Rule Out, or Include

Unlike patients with schizophrenia, those with schizoid personality disorder do not have psychotic symptoms such as delusions, hallucinations, and disorganized thinking.

Patients with an avoidant personality disorder have a strong desire for social contact, but their fears get in the way. Schizoid personalities may also be uncomfortable and fearful around people, but they simply prefer to be alone.

SCHIZOTYPAL PERSONALITY DISORDER

Major Features—Schizotypal Personality Disorder

- People with this disorder often appear very odd and eccentric, with peculiar ways of thinking and behaving. They have major problems with close relationships and experience some distortions in their thinking as well as their perceptions.
- They often believe that they have special powers and insights such as mental telepathy and clairvoyance. Although they have difficulty knowing their own feelings, they may claim a special sense in detecting the feelings of others.
- Odd suspicions are common, along with a tendency to believe that certain incidents and events have direct personal meaning. They may erroneously believe that other people are talking about them, avoiding them, or doing something because of them.
- They may experience certain perceptual illusions such as sensing or feeling the presence of mysterious forces or spirits. At times, other people might appear unreal or not human.
- Speech may be odd, vague, or abstract, but it is not incoherent or illogical. Normal conversations may be difficult.

- They are likely to be very uncomfortable around other people and may come across as constricted, aloof, or silly. There may be odd facial expressions or gestures. Appearance may be untidy or unusual.
- Because of extreme social anxiety, paranoid fears, or a desire to be alone, these individuals rarely have close friends outside the family.

Additional Symptoms or Factors That May Be Seen

- **Psychotic symptoms may appear briefly during stress.**
- **Feelings of boredom, anxiety, and depression.**
- **Vague aches and pains.**
- Additional symptoms of **borderline personality disorder (BPD).**
- **Difficulty finding and maintaining employment.**

Other Information Helpful in Making the Diagnosis

Although upbringing and other environmental factors are thought to influence the development of the disorder, schizotypal personality disorder appears to be genetically related to schizophrenia. Because of this, some researchers feel that it should be considered a relative of schizophrenia rather than a personality disorder.

Schizotypal personality disorder can be very incapacitating, but some individuals remain relatively stable and are able to work and maintain perhaps one close relationship. Only a small percentage develop the more severe symptoms of schizophrenia.

Other Diagnoses and Conditions to Consider, Rule Out, or Include

Schizophrenia involves an extended period of psychotic symptoms. Psychotic symptoms in schizotypal personality disorder, if seen at all, are very brief and poorly defined.

Schizoid or avoidant personality disorders do not include the odd behaviors, thoughts, and perceptions found in schizotypal personality disorder.

Borderline and schizotypal personality disorders are often found together. Both diagnoses can be made in those instances.

GROUP B PERSONALITY DISORDERS

ANTISOCIAL PERSONALITY DISORDER

People with an antisocial personality disorder have no regard whatsoever for the rights of others or for social rules. They coerce, manipulate, and extort others for their own purposes and rarely feel guilt or remorse over their destructive, callous actions. They are experts at lying, cheating, and deceiving. On the surface they may appear charming, composed, and believable. Underneath, one is likely to find a caldron of rage, impulsive urges, hostility, tension, and contempt.

Major Features—Antisocial Personality Disorder

- Signs of the disorder usually begin in childhood and may include lying, stealing, vandalism, cruelty to people and animals, truancy, fighting, fire setting, aggressive sexual behaviors, and other impulsive, antisocial acts.
- The patterns continue into adulthood and may include irresponsible behavior, stealing, destroying property, harassing or abusing others, reckless behavior, engaging in illegal activities and con games, failure to plan ahead, failure to repay debts, inability to maintain relationships, and negligent parenting.
- These individuals may have a callous disregard for others and are likely to use people. They seldom feel true guilt or remorse and will blame others or rationalize their behaviors. They may be extremely glib, arrogant, and deceitful. A low tolerance for frustration is common.

- Aggression, irritability, anxiety, and depression are likely to surface if and when their antisocial activities and manipulations are thwarted.
- The diagnosis is only given to individuals eighteen years of age and older. Prior to age eighteen, the diagnosis of conduct disorder is given for similar symptoms.

Additional Symptoms or Factors That May Be Seen

- Alcohol and drug abuse.
- Spouse and child abuse.
- Frequent incarcerations.
- Suicidal threats.
- Preoccupations with physical aches and pains.
- Promiscuity, no sense of fidelity or loyalty.

Other Information Helpful in Making the Diagnosis

The disorder usually begins as a conduct disorder in childhood and progresses to more serious antisocial behaviors in adolescence and adulthood. The intensity of the disorder appears to diminish somewhat as the individual reaches middle age. More males than females are diagnosed with antisocial personality disorder.

People with the disorder are more likely to have grown up in emotionally deprived homes with inadequate parental role models and inconsistent discipline. However, there appear to be genetic and physiological predispositions for the disorder. Individuals are extremely likely to have first-degree blood relatives with the disorder as well as signs of minimal brain damage and attention deficit hyperactivity disorder. Consistent parental care and other positive influences may be able to modify or prevent the development of the disorder in susceptible children.

Other Diagnoses and Conditions to Consider, Rule Out, or Include

Criminal activity in and of itself is not necessarily an indicator of the disorder. Cultural background and socioeconomic status must always be considered. Antisocial personality disorder involves many areas of a person's life and goes beyond illegal behavior.

Substance abuse is often associated with the disorder and may complicate the diagnosis. Some individuals may blame substance use for their behavior—however, a careful history usually reveals that the antisocial behaviors started in childhood or adolescence, long before drugs became a significant factor.

BORDERLINE PERSONALITY DISORDER (BPD)

The name "borderline" implies that someone with this diagnosis teeters on the edge between "normal" behavior and a personality disorder. In fact, nothing could be further from the truth.

BPD can be a very serious, full-time disorder involving intense mood swings, impulsive behaviors, chronic feelings of emptiness, fear of being alone, overwhelming anger, manipulative self-destructive acts, and tumultuous interpersonal relationships. People with the disorder jump dramatically from one crisis to another. Some therapists refer to these individuals as "emotional hemophiliacs," since they seem to exist in a constant, unending flow of emotional pain and interpersonal turmoil.

It is no wonder that the movie industry has discovered the borderline personality. Beginning with the portrayal of a severe borderline in *Fatal Attraction*, the industry has capitalized on the dramatic, unpredictable nature of the disorder by producing an onslaught of female slasher movies. Although possible in extreme cases, this is hardly typical. Most of the film portrayals are grossly overblown, inaccurate, and bear little semblance to the varying degrees of disturbance actually found in the disorder.

Therapists have also abused the diagnosis. It has been overused during the past several years and is in danger of becoming a catchall category. Women, in particular, seem to end up in the category twice as often as men. Since many women diagnosed with the disorder have been sexually abused as children, some researchers argue that the disorder is really a form of PTSD. However, this does not account for the millions of women who have survived severe sexual abuse without developing the intense, all-encompassing symptoms of BPD.

Major Features—Borderline Personality Disorder (BPD)

- BPD involves a long-term pattern of disturbed thinking, impulsive behaviors, intense, unpredictable mood swings, an unstable self-image, and chronic interpersonal problems.

- People with BPD have chronic feelings of emptiness and cannot tolerate being alone. Sometimes they will frantically look for companionship, even from strangers and unsatisfactory partners. Promiscuity may be a method to fill the emptiness.

- They greatly fear abandonment and will go to extremes to avoid this, whether real or imagined. Although very dependent in relationships, they are likely to resent the dependency and erupt in episodes of extreme hostility. Unreasonable demands are common.

- People with BPD tend to see others as all-good or all-bad. All-good people give them security, while all-bad people fail to meet their needs. They are likely to flip-flop on these categories, suddenly hating someone they had previously elevated to saintly status. This wreaks havoc in relationships.

- To manipulate others or to express anger or pain, people with BPD often resort to suicidal threats, wrist cutting, body carving, burning, and other acts of self-mutilation.

- Other self-destructive, impulsive behaviors are common and include behaviors such as drug abuse, careless sex, gambling, binge eating, reckless driving, sabotaging their own achievements, and seeking out destructive relationships.

- People with BPD have great difficulty controlling their intense anger and may strike out with a storm of hateful words or, in some instances, physical attacks. The anger is often inappropriate and out of proportion with the alleged provocation.

- Moods are likely to shift quickly, sometimes within the course of a few hours. Anxiety, depression, optimistic exuberance, and irritability may come and go.

- People with BPD usually have a very poor, distorted, or unstable sense of self. Their sense of personal identity may feel like it's changing with the wind.

Additional Symptoms or Factors That May Be Seen

- **Short-lived psychotic symptoms**, particularly when under stress.
- **Demanding, manipulative, provocative behavior** is a primary way of relating to others—a misguided attempt to fill the seemingly bottomless emotional void.
- **Intense but emotionally shallow relationships.**
- **Denial of responsibility** for their own impulses, attributing them to someone else.
- **Major depression and substance abuse.**

Other Information Helpful in Making the Diagnosis

The family histories of patients with BPD are often filled with physical and sexual abuse, incest, alcohol and drug abuse, traumatic separations, and lack of adequate emotional support. However, this is not always true. Researchers have found that some families of borderline patients are overinvolved and do not allow the development of a separate identity and a sense of independence. Needless to say, there are many theories surrounding this complex disorder.

The signs and symptoms of BPD may begin in early adolescence; however, since normal adolescence is often chaotic and stormy, an accurate diagnosis cannot be made until the personality patterns are better established in late adolescence.

Other Diagnoses and Conditions to Consider, Rule Out, or Include

BPD seems to overlap with all the other personality disorders—so much so that some researchers do not see it as a separate, distinct disorder. Patients with the diagnosis often have signs and symptoms of at least one other personality disorder. In those cases, both diagnoses must be given.

Axis I disorders such as depression, anxiety, substance abuse, eating disorders, dissociative disorders, and somatoform disorders are commonly found in patients with BPD.

HISTRIONIC PERSONALITY DISORDER

People with this disorder attempt to gain attention and approval by being dramatic, excitable, and highly emotional. Their emotional expressions and reactions are greatly exaggerated and seem superficial and insincere. Temper tantrums and accusations are likely if these individuals are not given the praise and attention they strive for. They may be flirtatious and seductive to win over other people.

Major Features—Histrionic Personality Disorder

- These individuals have a seemingly endless need for reassurance and approval. They may become angry and distraught if they are not the center of attention.
- Emotional expressions are highly exaggerated, theatrical, and tend to come off as shallow and superficial. They can shift from anger to delight at the drop of a hat.
- These individuals are likely to be preoccupied with physical attractiveness and appearance. Inappropriate seductive, flirtatious behavior is common in both sexes, although actual promiscuity may or may not be the case. When confronted, they may deny sexual intentions.
- Their manner of thinking and speaking tends to be impressionistic, imprecise, and fanciful. Details may be overlooked or ignored.

- These individuals have great difficulty waiting for emotional or physical gratification. They strive for immediate satisfaction and may resort to temper tantrums or tears if this is not forthcoming.
- Although their relationships tend to be superficial, these individuals exaggerate the degree of closeness and intimacy that actually exists.

Additional Symptoms or Factors That May Be Seen

- **May be suggestible, impressionable, and overly trusting.** Prone to fads.
- **Acts out a "victim" role.** Looks for protectors.
- **Strong underlying feelings of dependency and helplessness.**
- **Little awareness of their true feelings and motivations.**
- **Many vague physical complaints.**
- **Unfulfilling interpersonal relationships.**

Other Information Helpful in Making the Diagnosis

Women are diagnosed with the disorder far more frequently than men. These individuals tend to seek therapy after relationships fall apart or if they are unable to handle the responsibilities of being a parent.

The most common theory explaining the disorder relates it to parental disapproval, along with a dismissal of the child's true feelings. The child blocks the feelings and resorts to dramatic, emotional behavior for attention. The behavior is likely to be directed at the parent of the opposite sex.

Other Diagnoses and Conditions to Consider, Rule Out, or Include

Many patients with this disorder also have signs of BPD. However, they are not as likely to be suicidal or to experience the overall sense of "chaos" and emptiness evident in borderline patients. Brief psychotic symptoms are seen more often in BPD. Other personality disorders, such as dependent and narcissistic, must also be considered.

NARCISSISTIC PERSONALITY DISORDER

There are times when all of us may fall into a self-centered, demanding manner of relating to others. These "regressions" are usually brought about by stress or difficult circumstances and are not our primary way of relating with the world. People with a narcissistic personality disorder, on the other hand, live in a perpetual state of self-absorption, with the persistent unrealistic belief that they are unique and special. Naturally, they expect everyone around them to treat them with great deference. Pity the person who doesn't!

Major Features—Narcissistic Personality Disorder

- These individuals harbor a grandiose, overinflated, unrealistic view of themselves, in spite of evidence to the contrary. They work very hard to dismiss, deny, or ignore anything that would challenge this unrealistic view.
- They have very little, if any, capacity to feel for, understand, and consider the needs of other people. But, to achieve selfish purposes, they can often act sympathetic and caring.
- Arrogant, extremely demanding behavior is typical, with the expectation of always getting special attention. Narcissists expect praise for even ordinary achievements. If others criticize or fail to meet their demands, narcissists react with rage, humiliation, and disdain or may simply dismiss the criticism as unimportant.
- Their relationships are generally very shallow and fragile. Narcissists use other people to support their selfish purposes and reject them when they don't—with no feelings of remorse.
- Narcissists typically see other people as either above or beneath them. They are prone to extreme envy and either work to undermine those they perceive as superior or they idealize and identify with them, taking on the envied qualities as their own. Narcissists have nothing but contempt for those perceived as subordinate.

Additional Symptoms or Factors That May Be Seen

- **Depression:** Underlying self-esteem is extremely fragile and under constant assault because of their behavior. Intense shame and depression may follow as the walls crumble.
- **Midlife crises:** As looks and physical attributes decline with age, these individuals are often thrown into crisis.
- **Chaotic interpersonal relationships:** Because of their behavior, narcissists experience frequent loss and rejection.
- **Occupational problems:** Typically very ambitious, narcissists can sometimes achieve power and fortune. More likely, however, they alienate everyone around them and fail to achieve career goals.

Other Information Helpful in Making the Diagnosis

Early history is not terribly helpful, since theorists disagree on the family patterns that may set the scene for this disorder. Some theorists feel that rejection and disapproval of the child leads to the defensive, overinflated sense of self, while others attribute it to the parents' overidealization of the child. Whatever the cause, the full-blown behavior patterns usually do not become evident until adulthood.

Other Diagnoses and Conditions to Consider, Rule Out, or Include

Histrionic personality disorder: Although dramatic and manipulative like the narcissist, the histrionic person is more aware of other people's needs and feelings.

BPD: These people usually lead more chaotic lives, with more anxiety and self-destructive behavior.

Quite frequently, however, people do not fall clearly into any one of these categories. In those cases, more than one diagnosis is given.

Case Example—Narcissistic Personality Disorder

Presumptuous Publisher. Douglas walked into the therapist's office with great aplomb. Stylishly dressed and charming in manner, he nevertheless maintained a distant, superior stance toward the therapist. "I've published many books about therapy, including some you may have used in your training," Douglas announced. "Please understand that I'm only coming here on the advice of one of my board members, who thinks that I'm far too stressed by my recalcitrant editors."

Douglas explained that he had inherited his father's medium-sized publishing business five years ago. Prior to that, he had worked in the company's sales department, doing quite well under his father's tutelage. Douglas acknowledged that he had made few friends in the department, feeling that his coworkers were merely "cogs in the wheel" and lacked the keen intelligence and marketing sense that he possessed. Their aloofness toward him was simply envy and jealousy.

After inheriting the business at age thirty-five, Douglas quickly took control, spent thousands of dollars redecorating his office, and demanded that department heads and all editors meet with him daily at 4:00 P.M. to discuss the day's events. He professed to have a "sixth sense" about publishing and frequently and angrily overruled the judgments of his best editors. After several years of this, and the predictable hiring and firing of editors, the remaining staff was on the verge of mutiny. Profits took a nosedive, but Douglas attributed this to the poor economy.

His response was to hire a "staff psychiatrist" who was paid exorbitant fees to meet with each employee and "bring about a change in their attitude." Refusal to meet with the psychiatrist resulted in immediate dismissal. Douglas expressed amazement that several more editors quit in disgust. "I simply was trying to help them."

Halfway though the evaluation interview, the therapist pointed out that Douglas seemed to be having difficulty relating to many different people. He gently asked Douglas if he felt he was contributing to the problem in some way. Douglas immediately became indignant, marched over to the door, and proclaimed, "Sir, you know nothing of the publishing business and now, I'm sorry to say, you have missed an important opportunity to learn." The door slammed behind him.

GROUP C PERSONALITY DISORDERS

AVOIDANT PERSONALITY DISORDER

In spite of a strong desire for companionship and acceptance, these individuals avoid people and social situations. They experience a great deal of social discomfort and are extremely sensitive to disapproval or rejection.

Major Features—Avoidant Personality Disorder

- These individuals avoid people and social activities because of fears of criticism, failure, disappointment, or rejection. They are forever fearful of saying or doing embarrassing, humiliating, or foolish things in front of other people.
- They are likely to avoid any social situation or intimate relationship unless there are strong guarantees that they will be liked and accepted.
- Although they may be fearful, hypersensitive, reticent, self-effacing, and lacking in confidence, they have a strong need for affection and companionship. Unfortunately, they are likely to have few friends.
- New activities involving any kind of personal risk and potential anxiety are avoided. The risks are usually exaggerated.

Additional Symptoms or Factors That May Be Seen

- Fear of speaking up, making requests, asking questions.
- Avoiding job promotions, working beneath their capacity.

- **Feelings of inferiority, ineptitude.**
- **Oversensitivity** may lead them to misinterpret the benign actions or comments of others.
- **Anxiety, depression, self-anger, and loneliness** are common, often leading to a vicious cycle of low self-esteem and avoidance.

Other Information Helpful in Making the Diagnosis

The characteristics of avoidant personality disorder usually show up in childhood. Children who are very timid, anxious, and inflexible in new situations may be more prone to developing the pattern of avoidance. Certain phobias may also be present.

People with the disorder may do very well with familiar people that they trust, particularly if they are able to fall back on a family support system. Major crises occur when relationships fail or the family support system breaks down.

Other Diagnoses and Conditions to Consider, Rule Out, or Include

Individuals with a schizoid personality also avoid people—but, unlike those with avoidant personality disorder, they have little if any desire for social contact.

People with social phobia have fears similar to those experienced by avoidant personalities, but the fears are limited to specific situations. Personal relationships are not avoided.

DEPENDENT PERSONALITY DISORDER

Dependent personalities have very low self-esteem and self-confidence and have great difficulty taking charge of their own lives. They have a strong need to be taken care of and look to other people to make most of their decisions. Fearing separation, they cling to others in a submissive manner.

Major Features—Dependent Personality Disorder

- Dependent personalities generally feel they are too incompetent to make their own decisions. They turn to family and friends for help in making the simplest decisions about everyday living.
- They totally avoid responsibility for major life decisions and encourage or allow others to assume that power.
- Preferring a submissive role, these individuals avoid positions of responsibility. They are not likely to start or persevere with projects unless they are doing them under someone else's guidance.
- Dependent personalities usually don't assert themselves or disagree with others. Instead, they will do whatever they can to avoid conflict and the potential loss of nurturance. To win approval and support, they may take on the unpleasant tasks or duties that others avoid.
- These individuals usually hate being alone because it brings on fears of helplessness. If a relationship ends, they may recklessly latch on to someone else for nurturance and support.

Additional Symptoms or Factors That May Be Seen

- **Passive toleration** of a spouse's infidelities, physical or emotional abuse, or substance abuse.
- **Limited social relationships.**
- **Occupational limitations.**
- **Passivity, self-doubt, low self-esteem, sensitivity to criticism, pessimism.**
- **Depression, anxiety, substance abuse.**

Other Information Helpful in Making the Diagnosis

People with this disorder often show up for therapy after a close relationship ends. They are likely to feel very anxious, panicky, and depressed. The diagnosis may be difficult to make, since a wide variety of emotional disorders also involve excessive dependency. However, dependent personalities have a long-term pattern of dependency that sometimes starts as a chronic childhood fear of separation from loved ones. Women are diagnosed much more frequently than men. Cultural factors and gender expectations may play a contributing role in the development of the disorder.

Other Diagnoses and Conditions to Consider, Rule Out, or Include

Although excessive dependency is also found in borderline and histrionic personality disorders, dependent personalities are not as blatantly manipulative, stormy, seductive, or emotionally volatile. Emotional control is not a central issue. Also, they are more likely to maintain long-term relationships.

Case Example—Dependent Personality Disorder

The Albatross. "I don't know why he left. He just said that I was an albatross around his neck. An albatross!" Charlene wept profusely as she described the sudden breakup of her two-year marriage. "He told me to go back to my mother's, where I belong. You've got to help me get over these awful feelings!"

Although Charlene earns enough as a telephone operator to support herself, she has indeed moved back to her mother's home. "What else could I do? Where else would I go? Do you think I did the wrong thing? I didn't really want to move back. . . . I'm twenty-eight years old and I still feel like a child around her. But she had warned me about Paul. She was right again!"

Charlene had lived with her mother until age twenty-six. After her father died when she was six years old, she and her mother were virtually inseparable. In fact, Charlene had great difficulty leaving the house to attend elementary school. Even in high school, she seldom ventured far from home and was often ridiculed by peers. Her first romantic endeavor at age seventeen ended in disaster as her boyfriend ran off with her best friend. Charlene subsequently took an overdose of pills, but her mother advised against therapy. "She was right. I wouldn't have known how to use therapy."

Charlene married Paul over her mother's objections. "I didn't care. Paul was so wonderful and loving, I'd do anything for him. And his drinking problem wasn't really that bad—my mother blew it all out of proportion. I figured he would stop when he saw it was hurting us. He usually knew what was best."

During the course of the session, Charlene repeatedly praised the therapist, responding with statements like, "You must be right! I never thought of that before. Thank you so much!" or "I just knew you would be the right person to help me!"

OBSESSIVE-COMPULSIVE PERSONALITY DISORDER

Not to be confused with OCD, obsessive-compulsive *personality* disorder involves a preoccupation with rules, regulations, orderliness, and perfection. These individuals usually come off as very stiff, formal, and constricted. Their perfectionism and lack of flexibility get in the way of the tasks they are trying to accomplish. On top of it, they alienate everyone.

Major Features—Obsessive-Compulsive Personality Disorder

- Obsessive-compulsive personalities become so engrossed in and bogged down by their adherence to lists, rules, forms, regulations, and details that they lose sight of the overall task.
- They are so perfectionistic and inflexible that they have great difficulty completing what they have started. Nothing satisfies them.
- Although they are usually eager to please people who are more powerful, they are very authoritarian with subordinates. They insist that things be done in a certain manner and can't tolerate infractions.
- Work becomes the center of their lives, at the expense of leisure

activities and relationships. They expect the same from
subordinates and coworkers.

- These individuals tend to be intolerant, stubborn,
  overconscientious, and rigid in all areas of their lives. They are
  overzealous and inflexible concerning moral and ethical issues.
- They usually lack spontaneity and have difficulty expressing warm
  emotions. Don't expect them to freely give compliments or
  gifts. Their style is miserly and stingy. They even resist throwing
  away useless objects.

Additional Symptoms or Factors That May Be Seen

- **Indecisiveness, based on a fear of making mistakes.**
- **Limited interpersonal skills.** Frequently engage in power
  struggles.
- **Inability to handle change.**
- **Serious mood.** Forced sense of humor.
- **Depression.** Their relative ineffectiveness and strained
  relationships cause considerable distress.
- **Hypochondriasis.** Fears of having serious diseases.

Other Information Helpful in Making the Diagnosis

The lives of these individuals are filled with endless concerns about
details and the need to grossly overplan every occasion. The fun and
spontaneity of life are essentially planned away. They are likely to
seek therapy because their personal lives seem hollow, along with an
inability to get things done at work.

People with this disorder often have first-degree blood relatives
with similar symptoms. Although the evidence is inconclusive, there
may be a temperamental predisposition for the disorder. Controlling,
authoritarian, harsh parenting is often found in the childhood histories of these individuals.

Other Diagnoses and Conditions to Consider, Rule Out, or Include

Many very effective, highly accomplished people have obsessive-compulsive traits. But traits alone do not make up a personality disorder. For the diagnosis, there must be a broad spectrum of impairments and difficulties related to the obsessive-compulsive pattern. People with the disorder have nearly all the major features described above.

The obsessive-compulsive disorder described in the Axis I, anxiety disorder section of this book is not a personality disorder. That disorder involves intrusive, irrational thoughts (obsessions) and ritualistic behaviors (compulsions) such as hand washing or counting. Those symptoms are not a part of obsessive-compulsive personality disorder, which is placed on Axis II in the diagnostic summary. Sometimes, however, a person has the symptoms of both disorders, in which case both diagnoses are made.

PASSIVE-AGGRESSIVE PERSONALITY DISORDER

Although this *DSMIII-R* personality disorder was demoted to the diagnostic limbo in the *DSMIV* appendix, it remains extremely popular with therapists and is likely to live on. Passive-aggressive personalities thwart the expectations of others by resorting to all sorts of passive tactics. Rather than expressing their aggression and anger directly, they "forget" to do things, lose important papers, procrastinate, make excuses, whine, show up late for appointments, and generally fail to get things done efficiently. Their aggression is expressed through passively resistant behavior.

Although this diagnosis has recently become the focus of a slew of self-help books, it stands on very shaky ground and may be eliminated from the *DSM*. It has not been adequately validated and supported by clinical studies and tends to describe a single personality trait instead of a broad disorder. Also, more than many behaviors, passive-aggressive behavior is closely tied to specific situations and may not be consistent. A person who continually resorts to passive resistance when working in a rigid, hierarchical corporation may show little evidence of the behavior in a more democratic situation.

Major Features—Passive-Aggressive Personality Disorder

- These individuals persistently obstruct the expectations of others by resorting to passive tactics, such as "forgetting," repeatedly showing up late, losing important papers, working slowly or inefficiently, and procrastinating.

- These individuals are likely to complain, whine, or sulk when asked to do something they do not wish to do. They may see even normal demands as unreasonable. On the other hand, they may smile and verbally comply with requests only to sabotage them later.

- Bosses and others in authority are the frequent targets of their unreasonable criticism. But passive-aggressive personalities seldom voice these complaints directly, since they usually lack assertiveness.

- If part of a team, these individuals rarely do their share of the work.

Additional Symptoms or Factors That May Be Seen

- **Preoccupation with resentments.** May be unable to define what they would really like or want for themselves.

- **Dependent relationships.** Although they find fault with partners or bosses, they often remain stuck in dependent relationships.

- **Manipulation.** They may get others to rally to their aid with repeated claims of unjust treatment.

- **A pessimistic, negative outlook.**

- **Depression, substance abuse.**

Other Information Helpful in Making the Diagnosis

Other people inevitably end up feeling very frustrated and angry with these individuals, although they might not even know why. People engaging in passive-aggressive behavior can be very "slippery"—their acts of sabotage are often very subtle. If confronted, they will react with shock and complete denial. Many are experts at safely walking a fine line between compliance and resistance.

Other Diagnoses and Conditions to Consider, Rule Out, or Include

Many people will resort to passive-aggressive tactics if they find themselves in situations where assertive behavior is not tolerated. The diagnosis is not used in those instances unless the behavior is part of a long-term, pervasive pattern of passive resistance.

PERSONALITY DISORDERS NEEDING FURTHER STUDY

A number of controversial personality disorders have been placed in the appendix of the *DSM*. They remain "unofficial" since there is inadequate or insufficient research to support their official existence. Nevertheless, therapists are instructed to diagnose them using the category "personality disorder NOS" (301.9). Two of the more frequently diagnosed disorders from the *DSMIII-R* appendix are presented here. Although they have been dropped from the *DSMIV* (and replaced with other dubious disorders), therapists tend to use familiar categories, regardless of their official status. Furthermore, you should know what the criteria are in case you have been diagnosed with these disorders in the past.

SELF-DEFEATING PERSONALITY DISORDER

Originally known as "masochistic personality disorder," this *DSMIII-R* category refers to a broad pattern of self-defeating behaviors. Individuals with this disorder consistently undermine their own happiness by choosing uncaring partners, placing themselves in troublesome situations, creating unnecessary conflict, provoking others to reject them, avoiding pleasure, and rejecting help. They consistently fail to act on the positive options that may be available.

Throughout its history, this category has been the source of much controversy. Although the name was changed for the *DSMIII-R*, there was always a high risk that it would be used to mislabel women caught in abusive relationships—in essence, blaming them for the abuse. This was a common practice in the past. However, the version in the *DSMIII-R* specifically states that the diagnosis is not given if the behaviors occur as a result of fear of being abused. Most battered women do not qualify for the diagnosis since their behavior is limited to a particular situation involving physical, sexual, or emotional abuse. However, if the pattern also extends to other areas of their lives, the *DSMIII-R* diagnosis can be made.

Major Features—Self-defeating Personality Disorder

- The self-defeating behavior is present in several areas of the person's life—work, school, social relationships, intimate relationships, and so forth.
- Although the person knows better, he or she repeatedly chooses people or enters into situations that are likely to bring on hurt and disappointment.
- He or she may reject, prevent, or undermine the helpful efforts of other people.
- Other people who do treat the person well may be seen as boring, unstimulating, uninteresting, or sexually unattractive. These relationships may be rejected. Most self-defeating people see themselves as undeserving of caring relationships.
- The person may intentionally provoke angry responses in others. The angry, rejecting responses bring about deep feelings of hurt

and humiliation. Other people are essentially "set up" for these purposes.

- Pleasure or the acknowledgment of pleasure is downplayed or avoided.
- Personal success is often sabotaged or avoided, in spite of obvious abilities. Positive events or achievements may be followed by feelings of depression and guilt.

Additional Symptoms or Factors That May Be Seen

- Dysthymia or major depression.
- Suicidal thoughts or behaviors.
- Unsolicited, excessive self-sacrifice.
- Unacknowledged, unexpressed anger.
- Childhood history of abuse or exposure to abuse.

Other Information Helpful in Making the Diagnosis

The diagnosis is given to women more often than men. As defined in the *DSMIII-R*, it is a fairly common disorder. Some researchers have found that these individuals either have been abused as children or have witnessed the repeated abuse of a parent. One of the parents is also likely to have self-defeating traits. Parent and child may lead a life of "stable misery."

Other Diagnoses and Conditions to Consider, Rule Out, or Include

As discussed above, the diagnosis is not given if the self-defeating pattern is limited to abusive situations. Also, the diagnosis is not given if the behavior occurs only when the person has a depressive disorder. Depression can lead to self-defeating behavior.

Quite frequently, this disorder overlaps other personality disorders such as dependent and passive-aggressive disorders. Several diagnoses may be made.

Case Example—Self-defeating Personality Disorder

Collecting Strays. Evonne is an extremely attractive, thirty-six-year-old television actress who has played minor roles in a number of situation comedies and soap operas. She is also involved in many social causes, including animal welfare rights and housing for the homeless. She is reluctantly seeking therapy on the advice of friends. "They seem to think that I bring a lot of this on myself—the stream of stormy relationships, the career that never really gets off the ground, and my endless money problems. But I warn you, I never followed through with therapy in the past."

Over the past fifteen years, Evonne has been romantically involved with at least a dozen males. "These weren't one-night stands," she quickly adds. "These were serious relationships. Some lasted a year or two. Most of them were a lot younger than me and were trying to get on their feet. I felt I could give them so much."

Evonne did, in fact, give each one financial and emotional support. At least four had serious substance abuse problems. One was physically abusive. "I didn't tolerate him long, but the others really needed me—and I needed them. All were extremely handsome, wild, unpredictable, full of contradictions, and relentlessly sexual. Most men can't give me those kinds of vibes."

She describes the inevitable hurt that follows: "Oh, it's always so devastating—the constant fighting, the betrayals, catching them cheating, listening to their lies. In nearly every case, they angrily blame me, saying that I'm critical and demanding. Maybe I am. Maybe I choose men who bring out the worst in me."

In other areas of her life, Evonne has similar difficulties. "I pick fights with directors over artistic things even though I'm just a minor player. Needless to say, they don't ask me back. It's stupid. I don't know why I do it. I even blew a really important audition that way—it was set up by a good friend. But it's weird. I think I would have been more depressed if I got the job."

Aside from helping "stray" males, Evonne gives inordinate amounts of money to her social causes—so much so that she has difficulty making ends meet. "I really want to give people and animals the things I never had, like security and unconditional love. There is so much injustice in the world."

SADISTIC PERSONALITY DISORDER

This controversial category was also eliminated in the *DSMIV*, since it apparently was not supported by clinical evidence. Nevertheless, it has been used quite often in criminal populations and is likely to persist for many years. According to the *DSMIII-R* definitions, these individuals relate to others in a cruel, aggressive, controlling, demeaning manner. They go out of their way to inflict physical and/or emotional pain.

Major Features—Sadistic Personality Disorder

- These individuals are very controlling in relationships and may use physical violence, intimidation, and terror to establish their dominance. They are likely to pick family members or subordinates for their abuse, rather than people in power.
- They have a lack of empathy and respect for people. They work to humiliate and demean others and are likely to be excessively harsh with discipline and personal comments. They may tell cruel lies to inflict pain.
- Many of these individuals take a perverse pleasure in the suffering they inflict on others. They may torture animals for amusement.
- In their efforts for control, they may virtually imprison family members or companions—restricting their activities, limiting their friendships, and so forth.
- A fascination with violence, torture, guns, knives, combat, and martial arts is common.
- According to the *DSM*, the diagnosis is not made if the sadistic behavior is aimed at only one person or if it is used only for sexual purposes.

Additional Symptoms or Factors That May Be Seen

- Physical violence is not always present.
- The person usually sees nothing wrong with his or her behavior.

- Anger is often the predominant emotion.
- A childhood history of abuse is common.
- The person may seek out companions who have been abused.
- Substance abuse is common.

Other Information Helpful in Making the Diagnosis

These individuals rarely seek out therapy on their own and are usually referred by the criminal justice system. The arrests often center around spouse or child abuse. Almost all are men and include individuals from all walks of life—executives, lawyers, teachers, and so forth. The sadistic behaviors range anywhere from demeaning emotional abuse to violent intimidation and torture.

Other Diagnoses and Conditions to Consider, Rule Out, or Include

Features of antisocial and narcissistic personality disorders are often seen along with this disorder. If the sadism occurs only for the purpose of sexual arousal, a diagnosis of sexual sadism is made. (See chapter 13, "Sexual Disorders.")

APPENDICES

A

GLOSSARY

OF TERMS

Note: For the definitions of specific psychiatric disorders, please refer to the "Quick Guide to Selected Diagnoses and Major Symptoms" on page 147 or to the more extensive definitions in part 2.

ABSTRACT THINKING The ability to grasp, relate, and use concepts and ideas.

AFFECT Refers to the outward expression of emotion observed by the therapist and covers the whole spectrum of emotions. *Constricted affect* is a reduced range of expression. *Blunted affect* refers to very little emotional expression. *Flat affect* is the absence of emotional expression.

AGORAPHOBIA Fear of being in places or circumstances that might bring on uncomfortable or embarrassing symptoms, such as panic attacks. The person may fear being trapped and/or incapacitated.

ALERTNESS Level of awareness of the environment and external stimuli, level of consciousness.

ATTENTION A person's ability to focus on specific things that are generally outside of him- or herself, like listening to directions or watching a movie.

AXIS I DISORDERS All mental disorders except personality disorders and developmental disorders. Includes mood disorders, anxiety disorders, impulse control disorders, and so forth. When diagnosed, these disorders are listed on Axis I (the first line) of a patient's diagnostic summary.

AXIS II DISORDERS Includes all personality and developmental disorders. When diagnosed, these disorders are listed on Axis II of a patient's diagnostic summary.

BLOCKING Suddenly losing a spontaneous train of thought or flow of speech. The person can't remember what he or she was thinking or meant to say.

BODY IMAGE The way a person perceives his or her body. Sometimes it is distorted, as in anorexia or body dysmorphic disorder (BDD).

CATATONIA Any unusual body activities, including purposeless excitability, stupor, or posturing. Body postures may be rigid, bizarre, or molded like wax. Seen in certain forms of schizophrenia.

CIRCADIAN RHYTHMS Naturally occurring biological rhythms within the body. Each cycle lasts about twenty-four hours.

CIRCUMSTANTIAL THINKING AND SPEECH Thought and speech are logical, but the person gets sidetracked by irrelevant details. The point is eventually reached in a roundabout manner.

CLANGING Words are connected by sounds or rhymes rather than meaning. Seen in some forms of schizophrenia.

COGNITIVE Refers to our computerlike thinking processes such as reasoning, remembering, understanding, making decisions, and so forth.

COGNITIVE THERAPY Focuses on the erroneous thinking patterns, attitudes, and perceptions that may be contributing to low self-esteem, self-defeating behavior, irrational fears, and so forth.

COMPULSIONS Repetitive, intrusive, unwanted actions that the patient feels compelled to perform. Often carried out in response to an obsession. Examples include counting, checking, and hand washing.

CONCENTRATION The ability to focus on internal tasks and thought processes, such as completing a mathematical problem or writing a poem.

CONCRETE THINKING Inability to formulate or understand symbolic, abstract meanings.

CONFABULATION Making up answers to questions in order to fill the gaps created by memory problems. Often found in patients with amnestic disorder and certain organic brain disorders such as Alzheimer's disease.

COPING MECHANISMS Conscious and unconscious psychological responses that allow one to handle and deal with stress.

COUNTERTRANSFERENCE The therapist transfers feelings about a person in his or her past onto the patient.

DEFENSE MECHANISMS Unconscious ways that a person guards against anxiety. Some defenses are very immature and create many problems for a person, while others may be more mature and helpful.

DELUSION A strongly held but false belief that a person clings to in spite of obvious evidence that the belief is not true. No amount of reasoning, logic, or incontrovertible evidence will convince the person otherwise. Delusions can be based on things that could actually happen in real life, or they can be totally impossible and bizarre. Delusions are evidence of psychosis.

DENIAL An unconscious defense mechanism. The person denies that he or she has certain intolerable thoughts and feelings, or he or she refuses to see and acknowledge something unacceptable, even though it may be obvious to others.

DEPERSONALIZATION An altered sense of reality involving perceptions of self, body, or external objects. There may be feelings of unreality and detachment.

DIAGNOSTIC AND STATISTICAL MANUAL OF MENTAL DISORDERS (DSM)
The official manual used in the United States to classify and diagnose mental disorders. It is published by the APA. The first edition was published in 1952; the latest, known as *DSMIV*, in 1994.

DISORIENTATION The person may be confused about the date, the time, where he or she is, or who he or she is.

DISTRACTIBILITY The person has great difficulty paying attention. Attention jumps from one minor distraction to another.

DYSPHORIA Any mood that is distressing, uncomfortable, or unpleasant.

EMPATHY A quality of being able to understand the experiences, feelings, emotions, and actions of another person. Empathy is an essential part of the therapy process.

EUPHORIA An unrealistic, overblown sense of well-being, elation, cheerfulness, and optimism. Often seen in substance abuse, bipolar disorder, and certain organic mental disorders.

FLIGHT OF IDEAS Jumping rapidly from one idea to another without reaching a goal. The ideas may be loosely connected.

GRANDIOSITY Exaggerated, overblown beliefs of one's great importance, unrecognized powers, talents, or discoveries. Often seen as grandiose delusions in bipolar disorder or delusional disorder.

HALLUCINATION A sensory perception that is not based on any known, real stimuli in the physical world. May involve hearing, vision, smell, or touch.

HALLUCINOGEN Chemical substance such as LSD or mescaline that produces hallucinations.

HEALTH MAINTENANCE ORGANIZATION (HMO) A large group of health care professionals who provide services to patients who enroll in their program. The patients pay a fixed yearly premium for these services.

HOLISTIC A school of thought that focuses on the entire individual rather than separate parts, such as biology or psychology.

HYPERACTIVITY Physical restlessness, excessive movement, inability to sit still.

HYPERVENTILATION Feelings such as dizziness, tingling, and faintness brought on by breathing too much or too rapidly. Usually associated with anxiety and panic attacks.

HYPOGLYCEMIA A medical condition involving low blood sugar, sometimes leading to paniclike symptoms.

HYPOMANIA Episodes of euphoric, maniclike moods that are not as severe or debilitating as the elated moods found in manic-depressive (bipolar) disorder.

IDEAS OF REFERENCE The person erroneously believes that the words and actions of others or certain events are directly referring to him or her. He or she may give these things personal meaning when none exists. Ideas of reference are not held as strongly as delusions, but sometimes they do turn into delusions—the person persists in believing them in spite of overwhelming evidence that they are not true.

IDENTITY A person's consistent sense of who he or she is, what his or her basic personality traits are, how he or she generally thinks, feels, reacts, appears, and so forth. Identity crises are a normal part of adolescence. Severe identity disturbance is found in a variety of mental disorders.

ILLOGICAL THINKING Thinking that clearly doesn't make sense, reaches faulty conclusions, or contradicts itself.

ILLUSION Misperceptions or distortions of reality based on a misinterpretation of things and experiences that actually exist, e.g., seeing shadows as monsters.

IMPULSE CONTROL The ability to control aggressive, sexual, suicidal, or any other impulses that may be harmful or seen as socially inappropriate.

INCOHERENCE Illogical, disorganized, disconnected speech that may not be understandable.

INSIGHT Intellectual insight is seen as the patient's ability to acknowledge and understand that something is wrong, that he or she may be ill. True psychological insight goes beyond this definition and involves knowledge of thoughts, feelings, motivations, and defenses that may be contributing to the distress.

INTELLIGENCE A very broad term that is used to describe the sum total of a person's capacity to learn, understand, and apply knowledge. Intelligence is made up of many different parts.

INTROVERSION Turning inward, with preoccupations centering more on personal thoughts and feelings.

JUDGMENT The patient's ability to assess social situations, understand the consequences of his or her behavior, and work toward realistic goals.

KORSAKOFF'S SYNDROME A disease involving severe memory problems, usually related to heavy alcohol abuse. (See "Alcohol-Induced Amnestic Disorder" in part 2.)

LABILE MOOD Rapidly shifting mood swings that may alternate between depression, elation, anxiety, and so forth.

LEARNING DISABILITY A problem in the development of certain skills, such as reading, writing, and arithmetic, that is not due to a lack of intelligence. One such learning disability is dyslexia, which affects word recognition and reading comprehension.

LOOSENING OF ASSOCIATIONS A problem in thinking in which the ideas expressed do not appear to be related. The patient jumps from one subject to another, unaware that there is little, if any, connection between the thoughts.

MAGICAL THINKING The person unrealistically believes that his or her thinking alone can "magically" bring about things or prevent certain events from happening.

MALINGERING Faking or exaggerating an illness or symptom for personal gain or some other ulterior motive.

MANAGED CARE Another very expensive layer of bureaucracy in the health care industry. In managed care, insurance companies hire management companies to oversee and monitor all aspects of treatment and treatment planning.

MANIPULATIVE Describes the behavior of certain individuals who indirectly attempt to get what they want from other people by using insidious, often immature tactics, words, and actions. Cutting oneself for attention, using suicidal threats to control others, playing one person off another, creating double binds, and so forth, are examples. It is found in many personality disorders, particularly antisocial and borderline personalities.

MEDICAL MODEL In traditional medicine, this refers to a method of identifying and classifying diseases according to physical symptoms as well as observable biological causes such as microorganisms, chemical imbalances, irregular electrical patterns, tissue damage, and so forth. Psychiatry has attempted to use the same model to classify all sorts of emotional difficulties, even though evidence of biological causes does not exist for the majority of the diagnoses in the *DSM*. Critics contend that the medical model used by psychiatry reduces complex mind-body interactions to simplistic, artificial categories.

MENTAL STATUS EXAMINATION (MSE) A detailed profile of a patient's appearance, speech, intellectual functioning, thinking patterns, emotional status, and any behaviors observed during a clinical interview.

MOOD The general emotional state reported by the patient, such as irritable, anxious, depressed, and so forth. It can last hours or days and may influence the way the patient sees the world.

NEOLOGISMS Seen as part of a thought disturbance, neologisms are new or distorted words created by the patient, who often gives them a special meaning.

NEUROLOGICAL DISORDERS Diseases or dysfunctions of the nervous system such as epilepsy, multiple sclerosis, Huntington's disease, brain trauma, brain lesions, central nervous system infections, and so forth.

NEUROTRANSMITTER A brain chemical involved in the transmission of nerve impulses from one cell to another. There are several different kinds of neurotransmitters, some of which may play a part in certain mental disorders. It is not known whether neurotransmitter problems cause the disorders or whether they are only one link in a long chain of factors.

OBSESSION A recurrent thought, feeling, idea, image, or impulse that invades consciousness. Obsessions are intrusive and senseless. Sometimes they center around thoughts of contamination, violence, catastrophe or loss, a need for symmetry and order, or forbidden sexual thoughts.

ORGANIC DISEASE A true medical disease in which there is evidence of a physical or biochemical abnormality directly related to the illness.

ORGANIC MENTAL DISORDER A disturbance in mental functioning directly related to a physical disease, brain damage, or toxic substances. Examples include dementia, delirium, organic amnesia, substance-induced organic disorders, and so forth.

ORIENTATION A person's ability to correctly identify the date and time of day, the place, his or her name or the names of other people.

PARANOID IDEATION A suspicious, defensive view of the world with the belief that one is being unjustly persecuted, harassed, or treated unfairly. The harmless actions of other people may be misinterpreted as threatening or demeaning; however, the person can listen to reason and is not psychotic.

PARAPHILIAS Disorders involving persistent sexual urges and fantasies that require objects, nonconsenting persons, pain, humiliation, or other unusual sexual practices. In most cases, emotional intimacy is not a necessary ingredient. See chapter 13 for specific definitions.

PERCEPTUAL DISTURBANCES Any distortions in the way the patient perceives "reality," either through sight, hearing, smell, taste, or touch. May include illusions, hallucinations, depersonalization, and derealization.

PERSEVERATION The patient seems to get stuck on a certain word, phrase, idea, or action and repeats it again and again, even in response to different questions.

PERSONALITY DISORDERS Maladaptive personality traits and behavioral patterns that persist throughout a person's life. They involve deeply ingrained ways of thinking and behaving that repeatedly result in a host of relationship and social problems. See chapter 21.

PHOBIAS Persistent, intense, irrational fears of certain things or situations. The phobic person actively attempts to avoid the dreaded stimulus, although he or she usually recognizes that the fear is unreasonable.

POVERTY OF CONTENT OF SPEECH Used to describe speech that essentially says very little—even if it is very lengthy. The speech may be redundant, vague, or full of words that fail to communicate much information.

PREOCCUPATIONS Thought patterns that tend to center on a particular idea. Physical symptoms, body defects, and other inadequacies often become the center of preoccupations. Unlike obsessions, preoccupations are not necessarily intrusive and senseless.

PRESSURED SPEECH Rapid, emphatic, accelerating speech that is very difficult to interrupt. Often seen during a manic episode in patients with bipolar disorder.

PROGNOSIS The predicted course and outcome of a disorder, with and without treatment.

PSYCHOMOTOR AGITATION Excessive physical or mental activity brought on by emotional tension.

PSYCHOMOTOR RETARDATION A slowing of movements, speech, and emotional responses. Often seen in depressive episodes.

PSYCHOPATHOLOGY Refers to any of the symptoms, signs, and impairments in functioning that are associated with mental disorders.

PSYCHOSIS A serious inability to realistically assess the external world and separate it from the fantasies of the internal world. The psychotic person creates a new version of reality based on grossly impaired, inaccurate perceptions and thoughts. Delusions and most hallucinations are examples of psychosis.

PSYCHOSOMATIC Usually refers to a physical illness brought on, at least in part, by emotional factors.

RATIONALIZATION An unconscious defense mechanism used to justify or explain away certain behaviors, thoughts, or feelings that would otherwise be unacceptable.

REALITY TESTING A person's ability to objectively and accurately evaluate the external world. People who are psychotic have impaired reality testing.

REMISSION A reduction in the signs and symptoms of a mental disorder or illness.

REPRESSION An unconscious defense mechanism that keeps unacceptable ideas or feelings from conscious awareness. According to psychoanalytic theory, the repressed material is never really forgotten and may come out in other symbolic behavior.

RESIDUAL PHASE One of the three phases usually found in schizophrenia. The residual phase follows a period of blatant psychosis and may include symptoms such as social withdrawal, blunted emotions, and lack of initiative. See chapter 19.

RESISTANCE In therapy, this refers to the patient's conscious and unconscious attempts to avoid dealing with painful or unacceptable material.

RIGIDITY A particularly strong resistance to any kind of change involving new ideas, attitudes, perspectives, beliefs, and so forth.

RITUAL In psychiatry, a ritual is a compulsive, repetitive, purposeful act usually carried out to ward off the feelings of anxiety associated with obsessive thoughts. For example, a person obsessed about germs and contamination may resort to a daily ritual of twenty-five hand washings or to praying before every bite of food. Failure to complete the ritual may bring on feelings of anxious dread.

SEPARATION ANXIETY A pattern of fear, anxiety, and apprehension associated with separation from loved ones, people that are depended upon, familiar situations, and so forth. Serious separation anxiety is more common in childhood, but it may persist in certain individuals.

SIGNS In psychiatry, these are the objective indications of a mental disorder seen by an evaluator—pressured speech, unusual mannerisms, slowed responses, illogical speech and thought, and so forth.

SOMATIC COMPLAINTS Complaints related to the physical body, such as headaches, gastrointestinal problems, pain symptoms, and so forth.

SUPPORTIVE THERAPY Focuses on building a patient's strengths, assets, and coping skills without delving into deep emotional conflicts.

SYMPTOMS Like signs, symptoms may be indicators of emotional problems. Symptoms include the patient's subjective reports of distress—anxiety, feelings of worthlessness, suicidal feelings, depression, hopelessness, and so forth. Therapists often use the terms *symptoms* and *signs* interchangeably, in spite of the official definitions.

SYNDROME This is simply a group of symptoms that allegedly have been seen together enough to warrant a name. These days, there's a syndrome for everything. Technically, syndromes aren't as clear-cut or definitive as "disorders." In reality, a syndrome becomes a disorder if it makes its way into the *DSM*. (Researchers actually lobby for their pet syndromes.)

TANGENTIAL THINKING AND SPEECH The patient gets sidetracked by irrelevant details or unrelated thoughts and never finds his or her way back to the point he or she was trying to make.

TARDIVE DYSKINESIA Involuntary, abnormal body movements caused by use of antipsychotic medications. Tardive dyskinesia can occur at any point; however, it is more frequently seen after years on these medications. Symptoms sometimes include chewing motions, lip puckering, extending the tongue, involuntary hand and finger movements, and walking in a stooped, shuffling manner. All antipsychotic medications must be monitored carefully for these side effects.

THOUGHT CONTENT The predominant themes in a person's thinking. May include delusions, obsessions, phobias, preoccupations, and so forth.

THOUGHT DISORDER Any disturbance in the content of thought, the form of thought, or how the thought is communicated. Hallucinations and delusions are disturbances in thought content, while illogical, disorganized thinking indicates a disturbance in the form of thought. Thought disorders are found in psychosis and certain medical conditions. See chapter 5.

TIC Involuntary, spasticlike movements often seen on the face. Tics can be caused by neurological or emotional problems.

TRANSFERENCE Feelings a patient may have toward a therapist, based on the patient's past experience with other significant people. All sorts of qualities, positive and negative, may be unconsciously transferred to the therapist. See chapter 3.

UNCONSCIOUS According to psychoanalytic theory, this is an area of the mind that holds certain information away from our general level of awareness. Some of the information has always been in the unconscious, never working its way into conscious awareness. Other information was known at one time but was eventually repressed or sent to the unconscious, since it was too painful or unacceptable to the conscious mind.

WORD SALAD An illogical mixture of words and phrases often found in certain forms of schizophrenia.

IF YOU NEED HELP...

A Guide to Mental Health Professional Associations, Information and Referral Sources, and Self-Help Groups

Professional Associations Providing Information and Referral

Keep in mind that these organizations represent *many* different viewpoints. Their inclusion on this list is not meant as a recommendation or endorsement. Also, don't be intimidated by the heavy-handed names. Although some professional organizations take themselves far too seriously and are drowning in their collective egos, most will be pleased by your interest.

American Association for Marriage and Family Therapy
1717 K Street, NW, Suite 407
Washington, DC 20006
(202) 452-0109

An organization of clinical therapists trained to work with couples and families. Has divisions throughout the United States. Provides information and referral.

American Association of Pastoral Counselors
9508A Lee Highway
Fairfax, VA 22031
(703) 385-6967

American Association of Professional Hypnotherapists
Box 731
McLean, VA 22101-0731
(703) 631-1810

Members are social workers, psychologists, psychiatrists, physicians, and other professionals trained in clinical hypnosis.

American Association of Sex Educators, Counselors, and Therapists
11 Dupont Circle, NW, Suite 220
Washington, DC 20036-1207
(202) 462-1171

Call or write for a membership directory. No direct referrals.

American Association of Suicidology
2459 Ash Street
Denver, CO 80222
(303) 692-0985

An organization of professional and lay people dedicated to research, education, and training. Provides up-to-date listings of suicide prevention centers, survivors' groups, and general information.

American Association on Mental Retardation
1719 Kalorama Road, NW
Washington, DC 20009
(202) 387-1968

American Family Therapy Association
2020 Pennsylvania Avenue, NW, #273
Washington, DC 20006
(202) 994-2776

Researchers, therapists, and teachers trained to work with families. Provides information and referral.

American Mental Health Counselors Association
5999 Stevenson Avenue
Alexandria, VA 22304
(703) 823-9800

Part of the American Association for Counseling and Development. Will make referrals to certified mental health counselors.

American Orthopsychiatric Association
19 West 44th Street, Suite 1616
New York, NY 10036
(212) 354-5770

Members are from many different disciplines. Purpose is to study human behavior and development.

American Psychiatric Association
1400 K Street, NW
Washington, DC 20005
(202) 682-6142

A large organization representing psychiatrists, both professionally and politically. Provides extensive information and will make referrals to psychiatrists and clinics.

American Psychoanalytic Association
309 East 49th Street
New York, NY 10017
(212) 752-0450

American Psychological Association
750 First Street, NE
Washington, DC 20002-4242
(202) 336-5500
A large professional and political organization representing psychologists. Provides extensive information and will make referrals to psychologists and clinics.

American Psychosomatic Society
6728 Old McLean Village
McLean VA 22101
(703) 556-9222
Promotes research on psychosomatic problems (physical illness that may have emotional causes).

American Psychopathological Association
Western Psychiatric Institute
Pittsburgh, PA 15213-2593
(412) 624-2999
Promotes research on mental disorders.

American Schizophrenia Association
Huxley Institute
900 North Federal Highway, Suite 330
Boca Raton, FL 33432
(407) 393-6167
Promotes biochemical research on schizophrenia, alcoholism, drug addiction, learning disabilities, memory loss, and other conditions affecting brain functioning.

American Sleep Disorders Association
604 Second Street, SW
Rochester, MN 55902
(507) 287-6006
An organization of individuals and institutions concerned with the clinical care of patients with sleep disorders.

American Society for Adolescent Psychiatry
5530 Wisconsin Avenue, NW, Suite 1149
Bethesda, MD 20815
(301) 652-0646
Promotes research and provides information.

Association for Birth Psychology
444 East 82d Street
New York, NY 10028
(212) 988-6617
Studies the relationship between birth events and later personality development.

Association for Humanistic Psychology
1772 Vallejo
San Francisco, CA 94123
(415) 626-2375
Purpose is to "advance the growth of theory and research in humanistic values."

Association for Multicultural Counseling and Development
5999 Stevenson Avenue
Alexandria, VA 22304
(703) 823-9800
Part of the American Association for Counseling and Development. Research and information.

Association for Religious and Value Issues in Counseling
5999 Stevenson Avenue
Alexandria, VA 22304
(703) 823-9800

Association for the Advancement of Behavioral Therapy
15 West 36th Street
New York, NY 10018
(212) 279-7970

Provides information about behavior therapy and a member directory.

Association for the Study of Dreams
P.O. Box 1600
Vienna, VA 22180
(703) 352-3571

Association for Women in Psychology
1006 Grassy Hill Road
Orange, CT 06477-1103

Promotes unbiased research on gender issues.

Association of Black Psychologists
P.O. Box 55999
Washington, DC 20040-5999

Association of Existential Psychology and Psychiatry
40 East 89th Street
New York, NY 10128
(212) 348-3500

Members are interested in "multidimensional dialogue between all disciplines while furthering the nontechnological aspects of human existence."

Center for Cognitive Therapy
University of Pennsylvania
133 South 36th Street, Room 602
Philadelphia, PA 19104
(215) 898-4100

Will provide referrals to therapists specializing in cognitive therapy.

International Society for the Study of Multiple Personality and Dissociation
2506 Gross Point Road
Evanston, IL 60201
(312) 475-7532

International Stress and Tension Control Association
US International University
2204 El Camino Real
San Diego, CA 92131
(619) 430-4631

Organization of people "interested in the systematic relaxation of tension in everyday life."

National Association for Rural Mental Health
301 East Armour Boulevard
Campus City, MO 64111
(607) 737-4789

Therapists from all disciplines who work in rural settings.

National Association of Alcoholism and Drug Counselors
3717 Columbia Pike, Suite 300
Arlington, VA 22204
(703) 920-4644

National Association of Black Social Workers
642 Beckwith Court, SW
Atlanta, GA 30314
(404) 584-7967

National Association of Social Workers
750 First Street, NE
Washington, DC 20002-4242
(202) 408-8600

A very large professional and political organization for social workers. Provides extensive information and makes referrals.

National Consortium for Child
Mental Health Services
3615 Wisconsin Avenue, NW
Washington, DC 20016
(202) 966-7300
Gathers and exchanges information
on child mental health servies.

National Hispanic Psychological
Association
Box 451
Brookline, MA 02146
(617) 266-6336

National Mental Health Association
1021 Prince Street
Alexandria, VA 22314-2971
(703) 684-7722
Provides information as well as
referrals to local chapters and
therapists.

Society for Traumatic Stress Studies
P.O. Box 1564
Lancaster, PA 17603-1564
(717) 396-8877
Includes professionals from all
disciplines and other people
working with PTSD.

Special Organizations and Self-Help Groups

Some of these organizations provide information and referral only,
while others offer self-help support groups. If you are interested in
finding out about other self-help organizations or groups near you,
contact one of the national self-help clearinghouses listed below.
They can also give you the most up-to-date information—group
locations and phone numbers change quite frequently.

Clearinghouse of Mutual Self-Help Groups
University of Massachusetts
113 Skinner Hall
Amherst, MA 01003
(413) 545-2313

National Mental Health Consumer Self-Help Clearinghouse
311 S. Juniper Street, Room 902
Philadelphia, PA 19107
(215) 735-6367

Self-Help Clearinghouse
St. Clare's Riverside Medical Center
Pocono Road
Denville, NJ 07834
(201) 625-9565 or 1-800-367-6274 (NJ only)

Alzheimer's Disease

The Alzheimer's Disease & Related Disorders Association
70 East Lake Street, Suite 600
Chicago, IL 60601
(312) 853-3060 or 800-621-0379
Information and assistance for caregivers and families of patients. Many chapters throughout the United States.

Anxiety Disorders

Anxiety Disorders Association of America
600 Executive Boulevard, Suite 200
Rockville, MD 20852
(301) 231-8368
Provides extensive information about anxiety disorders and phobias, makes referrals.

Child Abuse (also refer to Sexual Abuse)

National Child Abuse Hotline
1345 El Centro Avenue
Hollywood, CA 90028
1-800-422-4453

National Committee for Prevention of Child Abuse
332 S. Michigan Avenue, Suite 1600
Chicago, IL 60604
(312) 663-3520
Crisis counseling and referrals.

Parents Anonymous
6733 South Sepulveda Boulevard
Los Angeles, CA 90045
1-800-421-0353
Provides group meetings for parents who feel overwhelmed and/or fear their anger toward a child.

Depression

Depression after Delivery
P.O. Box 1282
Morrisville, PA 19067
(212) 295-3994
Self-help group providing support and information for women who are experiencing postpartum depression and psychosis. Also has a newletter.

Depressives Anonymous
329 East 62d Street
New York, NY 10021
(212) 689-2600 (answering service)
For anxious and depressed people. Has groups, newsletters. Professionals are also involved.

Lithium Information Center
Department of Psychiatry
University of Wisconsin
600 Highland Avenue
Madison, WI 53792
(608) 263-6171

Manic & Depressive Support Group, Inc.
15 Charles Street, 11H
New York, NY 10014
(212) 924-4979
Support and education for people with depression or manic depression and their families.

National Foundation for Depressive Illness
P.O. Box 2257
New York, NY 10016
1-800-248-4344
Provides information, makes referrals.

Domestic Violence

Batterers Anonymous
1269 North E Street
San Bernadino, CA 92405
(714) 884-6809
Self-help program for men who wish
to control their anger and stop
abusive behavior.

**National Coalition against Domestic
Violence**
P.O. Box 34103
Washington, DC 20043
(202) 638-6388
Provides information about domestic
violence.

National Domestic Violence Hotline
P.O. Box 7032
Huntington Woods, MI 48070
1-800-333-SAFE
Crisis intervention, information, and
referral.

Drug and Alcohol Abuse

Adult Children of Alcoholics
P.O. Box 35623
Los Angeles, CA 90035
(213) 464-4423
An international twelve-step program
for adults raised in alcoholic
families.

**Al-Anon Family Group
Headquarters**
P.O. Box 862
Midtown Station
New York, NY 10018
1-800-344-2666

An international twelve-step
fellowship organization for families
and friends of alcoholics. Includes
Alateen and referrals to Adult
Children of Alcoholic groups.

Alcoholics Anonymous, Inc.
P.O. Box 459
Grand Central Station
New York, NY 10163
1-800-637-6237
An international twelve-step
fellowship organization for
alcoholics. Nonprofessional.

Cocaine Anonymous
3740 Overland Avenue, Suite G
Los Angeles, CA 90034
1-800-347-8998
A twelve-step fellowship program for
people recovering from cocaine
addiction. Nonprofessional.

Families Anonymous
P.O. Box 528
Van Nuys, CA 91408
1-800-736-9805
Relatives and friends of children and
adults involved with drugs, alcohol,
and related behavioral problems.
Follows twelve-step model.

Narcotics Anonymous
P.O. Box 9999
Van Nuys, CA 91409
(818) 780-3951
International twelve-step program for
recovering drug addicts.

**National Drug Abuse Information
and Treatment Referral Hotline**
12280 Wilkins Avenue
Rockville, MD 20852
1-800-662-HELP or 1-800-66-
AYUDA (Spanish)

Women for Sobriety, Inc.
109 West Broad Street
P.O. Box 618
Quakertown, PA 18951
(215) 536-8026
A self-help program designed
specifically for women recovering
from alcohol addiction.

Eating Disorders

Anorexia Nervosa & Associated Disorders, Inc. (ANAD)
P.O. Box 7
Highland Park, IL 60035
(708) 831-3438

Has extensive therapy referral lists for anorexics, bulimics, and their families. Forms local self-help chapters.

National Anorexic Aid Society
5796 Karl Road
Columbus, OH 43229
(614) 846-2833

Support and education for people with anorexia and/or bulimia, as well as their families and friends.

Overeaters Anonymous
4025 Spencer Street, Suite 203
Torrance, CA 90503
(310) 618-8835

Support groups and information for compulsive eaters.

Gambling

Gam-Anon
P.O. Box 157
Whitestone, NY 11357
(718) 352-1671

Provides help for families and friends of compulsiver gamblers. Has support groups following twelve-step model.

Gamblers Anonymous
P.O. Box 17173
Los Angeles, CA 90017
(213) 386-8789

An international self-help group for compulsive gamblers. Follows a twelve-step model. Nonprofessional.

National Council on Compulsive Gambling, Inc.
445 West 59th Street
New York, NY 10019
1-800-522-4700

Grief

The Compassionate Friends, Inc.
P.O. Box 3696
900 Jorie Boulevard
Oak Brook, IL 60522
(708) 990-0010

Has local self-help support groups for parents and families who have lost a child.

SHARE
St. Elizabeth's Hospital
211 South Third Street
Belleville, IL 62222
(618) 234-2120

For parents and family members who have lost an infant in miscarriage, stillbirth, or early death. Has many local self-help chapters offering support.

Survivors
P.O. Box 134
993 "C" South Santa Fe Avenue
Vista, CA 92083
(619) 727-5682

Twelve-step program for people grieving the loss of a loved one.

Survivors of Suicide
3251 North 78th Street
Milwaukee, WI 53222
(414) 442-4638

For families and friends of suicide victims. Newsletter, phone networking, groups.

Widowed Persons Service
1909 K Street, NW
Washington, DC 20049
(202) 728-4370

One-to-one peer support,
information, and referral for
windows and widowers.

Mental Health—General

Emotions Anonymous
P.O. Box 4245
St. Paul, MN 55104
(612) 647-9712

Fellowship organization for children
and adults with short- or long-term
emotional problems. Nonprofessional.
Follows twelve-step model. Has
chapters nationwide.

National Alliance for the Mentally Ill
2101 Wilson Boulevard, Suite 302
Arlington, VA 22201
(703) 524-7600

Self-help groups for relatives of the
seriously mentally ill. Has many
local chapters. Also provides
information and advocacy.

National Alliance of Mental Patients
P.O. Box 618
Sioux Falls, SD 57101
(605) 334-4067

Goal is to develop alternatives to the
mental health system, form self-help
groups, improve quality of life for
patients.

Reclamation, Inc.
2502 Waterford
San Antonio, TX 78217
(512) 824-8618

Alliance of former mental patients
"helping to eliminate the stigma of
mental illness."

Recovery, Inc.
802 North Dearborn Street
Chicago, IL 60610
(312) 337-5661

A self-help program of weekly group
meetings focusing "on a system of
techniques for controlling behavior
and changing attitudes toward
nervous symptoms and fears." Many
local chapters.

Schizophrenics Anonymous
23013 Floral
Farmington, MI 48024
(313) 477-1983

A self-help organization offering
fellowship, support, information,
and advocacy. Has a six-step program.

**Tardive Dyskinesia National
Association**
4244 University Way, NE
P.O. Box 45732
Seattle, WA 98145

Provides information on tardive
dyskinesia, a movement disorder
that is sometimes a side effect of
antipsychotic medication.

Obsessive-Compulsive Disorder (OCD)

**Obsessive Compulsive Disorder
Foundation**
P.O. Box 9573
New Haven, CT 06535
(203) 772-0565

A voluntary organization. Provides
information, advocacy, makes
referrals, develops support groups,
and links people with OCD.

Patient Rights, Advocacy

National Association for Rights Protection and Advocacy
Mental Health Association of Minnesota
328 East Hennepin Ave.
Minneapolis, MN 55414
(612) 331-6840

Open to anyone interested in advocacy, patient rights, and psychiatric reform. Provides information, holds conferences, publishes newsletters.

National Association of Protection and Advocacy Systems
220 Eye Street, NE, Suite 150
Washington, DC 20001
(202) 546-8202

Works to protect rights of patients. Provides advocacy and refers patients or ex-patients to federally funded advocacy agencies within their state. These agencies support patients' rights and investigate violations.

National Association of Psychiatric Survivors
P.O. Box 618
Sioux Falls, SD 57101
(605) 334-4067

For former patients and their families who feel they have been mistreated by the mental health system. Other interested parties may also join. Their purpose is for "moral support, political action, and the development of client-run alternatives."

Sexual Abuse

Incest Survivors Anonymous
P.O. Box 5613
Long Beach, CA 90805-0613
(213) 428-5599

A twelve-step self-help program for incest survivors. Many local groups.

Parents United International
P.O. Box 952
San Jose, CA 95108
(408) 280-5055

A self-help organization operating under the guidance of sexual abuse professionals. Provides support and professionally run groups for parents whose children have been sexually abused, for sexually molested children, and for adults who have been molested as children. Many local chapters.

VOICES in Action, Inc.
P.O. Box 148309
Chicago, IL 60614
(312) 327-1500

For victims of incest and other childhood sexual abuse. Provides support, information, guidelines for starting groups, referrals to professionals and other groups.

Sexual Problems

Impotents Anonymous
P.O. Box 5299
Maryville, TN 37802
(615) 983-6064

International self-help groups for impotent men. Partners may join I-Anon.

Sex Addicts Anonymous
P.O. Box 3038
Minneapolis, MN 55403
(612) 339-0217

Men and women attempting to overcome compulsive sexual behavior.

Sexaholics Anonymous
P.O. Box 300
Simi Valley, CA 93062
(805) 581-3343

International self-help fellowship for men and women "who want to stop sexually self-destructive thinking and behavior." Many local chapters.

INDEX